SEDUCING
AMERICA

Roderick P. Hart

SEDUCING
AMERICA

How
Television
Charms the
Modern
Voter

Revised Edition

SAGE Publications
International Educational and Professional Publisher
Thousand Oaks   London   New Delhi

For information:

SAGE Publications, Inc.
2455 Teller Road
Thousand Oaks, California 91320
E-mail: order@sagepub.com

SAGE Publications Ltd.
6 Bonhill Street
London EC2A 4PU
United Kingdom

SAGE Publications India Pvt. Ltd.
M-32 Market
Greater Kailash I
New Delhi 110 048 India

Printed in the United States of America

Library of Congress Cataloging-in-Publication Data

Hart, Roderick P.
  Seducing America: How television charms the modern voter /
by Roderick P. Hart. — Rev. ed.
     p.   cm.
  Includes bibliographical references and index.
  ISBN 0-7619-1623-7 (cloth: acid-free paper)
  ISBN 0-7619-1624-5 (pbk.: acid-free paper)
  1. Television in politics—United States.   I. Title.
  HE8700.76.U6 H37   1998
  324.7'3'0973—ddc21   98-25381
This book is printed on acid-free paper.

99 00 01 02 03 04 05 7 6 5 4 3 2 1

Acquiring Editor:	Margaret H. Seawell
Editorial Assistant:	Renée Piernot
Production Editor:	Michèle Lingre/Astrid Virding
Editorial Assistant:	Denise Santoyo
Designer/Typesetter:	Lynn Miyata

Contents

For Peggy, A New Puritan,
with Love

Preface

Professor Robert Putnam of Harvard University has begun one of the most important discussions of our times when he asks why the American people no longer feel an abiding sense of community. Putnam notes a decline in what he calls "social capital," people's willingness to reach outside of themselves, to pitch in to community projects, to have fun with one another, to vote. Putnam's now-famous example is that bowling leagues have declined in popularity in the United States, as people spend less time in group activities and more and more time at home.

Why are people "bowling alone"? There are a number of possibilities, including changes in the workplace (women on the job, more moonlighting, teenagers working part-time), changes in demography (more heterogeneous neighborhoods, greater concentration of population in urban areas, less intergenerational contact), changes in cultural traditions (a decline in voluntary associations, less civics training in the schools, more crime on the streets). What is the result of these trends? According to Putnam, they mean that political engagement now rests

> on a constricted notion of citizenship—citizen as disgruntled claimant, not citizen as participant in collective endeavor to define the public interest. Just as much of our community service today is "drop-by," much of our politics is "surf-by" and "call-in." We are no less free with our opinions, but we are listening to each other less. We are shouting and pressuring and suing, but we are not reasoning together, not even in the attenuated sense that we once did, with people we know well and will meet again tomorrow.[1]

Ultimately, though, when pressed for a single explanation for the lack of community, Putnam seizes on television. Increasingly, he says, Americans spend so much time bathed in its strange green glow that traditional modes of socializing are forsaken. Time formerly spent in fraternal associations, in church sodalities, on the company softball team, canvassing door-to-door for the United Fund is time now spent in the virtual embrace of *Home Improvement*. Although Putnam does not believe that "the boob tube is the root of all evil," he does conclude that it "has had a profoundly negative effect on community bonds in America."[2]

Seducing America is no kinder on television, but it does take a different tack. The problem with television, I shall argue, is not that it occupies too much of our time (although it surely does that), but that it occupies too much of our emotional lives. Increasingly, television tells us what to feel, when to feel it, and how and why as well. Television is our emotional tutor, teaching us which of our feelings are proper and which passé, which sports stars are worthy of emulation and which are fools. Television teaches these lessons subtly and, like any good teacher, it never takes credit for the teaching. Indeed, the medium consistently underestimates its importance ("it's only TV, after all") and so the remote-control device in our hand provides a sense of power, perhaps even a sense of dominance. Television makes us feel smart, clever, busy. Too busy for bowling.

This book surveys the many things television makes us feel. Most books about television do not do that. Most report on who watches television and why, how the nightly news changes people's agendas for discussion, which social groups are advantaged and disadvantaged by television's portrayals. Still others trace the history of media development, how new technologies change the way we shop and vote, how developing countries are reshaped when television becomes a routine. Yet other books deal with media and politics specifically: Kathleen Hall Jamieson tells us that televised politics has gotten "dirtier" in recent years[3]; Thomas Patterson explains how the voice of the journalist now overshadows the voice of our nation's leaders[4]; Michael Schudson shows how television shapes the nation's present even as it reinterprets the nation's past[5]; James Fishkin explains why media polling undermines a nation's self-understanding instead of improving it[6]; Timothy Cook traces the influence wielded by media conglomerates[7]; and Marian Just and her colleagues explain why it is now hard to distinguish between the news, candidate behavior, and paid advertising during political campaigns.[8]

Although indebted to such studies, *Seducing America* shoves off in a different direction. It looks beyond specific behaviors to the attitudes informing them. It asks not how politicians spend their time but what emotions they produce in voters, not how the media present the news but why people react to the news as they do. The book explores the murky world of feelings half felt and traces those feelings to their source. Its main argument is deceptively simple: Unless we ask what viewers are feeling when they are thinking, we will be unable to understand contemporary politics.

The example to prove all this still sits in the White House. Try as they might in November of 1996, the Republicans could not fathom why Bill Clinton—who squeaked into the White House in 1992 and who let Congress slip away from him in 1994—still called Pennsylvania Avenue his home two years later. They understood the political impact of international peace and a robust economy, to be sure, but they still could not understand why an alleged draft-dodging, two-timing, gladhander could sail back into office. Those who knew television were less surprised. They knew that important rewards now go to emotionally confident people like President Clinton, people who seems vulnerable even as they seem powerful. Like Ronald Reagan before him, Mr. Clinton proved that television's power lies not in the *number* of people it reaches but in the *depth* with which it reaches them. When Bill Clinton felt your pain, you felt him feel it.

Because it looks at television perceptually, *Seducing America* supplements more traditional books in the area of media effects, mass communication theory, and political communication. It moves beyond the behavioral and sociological influences of the media to the more uncharted, but intriguing, area of political emotions. Although it is indebted to the wealth of social scientific work on politics and the media, it weaves those studies into a new tapestry. While it surveys much of what we know about press routines, voting behavior, polling effects, campaign advertising, election routines, and political information, it looks at those data through a psychological lens. The result is a fresh, perhaps revolutionary, way of understanding television and politics.

After an introductory chapter, the book proceeds through the five political emotions television inspires. At the end of each chapter, the reader is presented with a series of questions for consideration, questions that apply the chapter's insights to the practical world of politics and everyday life. In Chapter 7, a controversial solution to the dilemmas of political television is offered: a philosophy of New Puritanism. Finally, the reader is asked (in the

Postscript) to distinguish between private and public virtues and to recommit to the latter even while the former proudly beckon.

Surveying television's political feelings was not accomplished overnight and so I am grateful to a number of people for their assistance. Primarily—primordially—I am grateful to the woman who has made my life meaningful for the past 32 years and to whom this book is dedicated. She knows everything I do not know, a considerable amount indeed. More important, she is a woman of generous sentiment and hence a citizen truly.

I also wish to thank those who have advised me on earlier versions of this book: Professor Mark Levy of the University of Maryland, Professor Joshua Meyrowitz of the University of New Hampshire, Professor Diane Rubenstein of Purdue University, Professor Catherine Smith of Syracuse University and, especially, Professor Kathleen Hall Jamieson of the University of Pennsylvania, my friend, colleague, sailing companion, and best critic.

I also appreciate the invitations to try out some of the thoughts on the unsuspecting audiences rounded up by Professor Carole Blair of the University of California at Davis, Professor Robert Entman of Northwestern University, Professor Robert Wuthnow of Princeton University, Professor Everett Dennis of Columbia University, Professor Martin Medhurst of Texas A&M University, Professor Pippa Norris of Harvard University, and Professor Patricia Sias of Washington State University. I learned much from these campus exchanges and trust that the revision of this book contains less foolishness because of them.

Several other colleagues showed special interest in this project as it took shape. I thank them for their advice and, especially, for their friendship: Vanessa Beasley, Rick Cherwitz, John Daly, Joanne Gilbert, Linda Putnam, Marsha Siefert, Deborah Smith-Howell, and Bat Sparrow. The two finest research assistants a writer could hope for, John Pauley and Mary Triece, gave their all to this project and I shall never forget their kindnesses. Nor shall I forget the confidence that David Roll of Oxford University Press and, especially, Margaret Seawell of Sage Publications have had in my work.

Happily, I have managed to father two experts on the issues discussed in this book: my son Chris, who knows politics, and my daughter Kate, who knows television. The Puritans and I worry some about the latter.

Notes

1. "Robert Putnam Responds," *The American Prospect*, March-April, 1996, p. 27.

2. Ibid., 28.

3. K. Jamieson, *Dirty Politics: Deception, Distraction, and Democracy* (New York: Oxford University Press, 1992).

4. T. Patterson, *Out of Order* (New York: Knopf, 1993).

5. M. Schudson, *Watergate in American Memory: How We Remember, Forget, and Reconstruct the Past* (New York: Basic Books, 1992).

6. J. Fishkin, *The Voice of the People: Public Opinion and Democracy* (New Haven, CT: Yale University Press, 1995).

7. T. Cook, *Governing With the News: The News Media as a Political Institution* (Chicago: University of Chicago Press, 1998).

8. M. Just et al., *Crosstalk: Citizens, Candidates, and the Media in a Presidential Campaign* (Chicago: University of Chicago Press, 1996).

Political Feelings

ach age has its own conceit, but each age shares a common conceit: that
it is special. Historians may take the long view, but those who live in
history typically see history's most important moments as residing in them.
And so, predictably, the pundits closest to the action during the 1996
presidential campaign declared that the American people were now caught
up in a new technological reality that had changed electoral politics in
fundamental ways. With President Clinton's team sending region-targeted
political ads via satellite uplinks and with the not-yet-geriatric Bob Dole
proudly announcing his new Web site during a presidential debate, the 1996
campaign was something of a watershed election, at least as far as campaign
technologies were concerned.

Methodologists that they are, the American people have always been
intrigued by new political hardware. Four years earlier, for example, Jerry
Brown had received 280,000 phone calls on his newly configured 1-800 line;
computer hackers had sent electronic memos to the candidate of their choice
at only $1.50 per missive[1]; The People Incarnate had directly interrogated two
eager challengers and a listless incumbent for an hour and a half during a
debate in Richmond, Virginia, a performance repeated in 1996 (sans Mr.
Perot) in San Diego, California; the youngest candidate in 1992 played the

saxophone on the *Arsenio Hall* show only to be upstaged when his rival's wife worked the floor, *Donohue* style, four years later during the Republican National Convention; and by 1996, all the candidates had conspired to make *Larry King Live!* a new Washington monument.

Recent elections have produced even more news. Debate viewership was up 23% overall in 1992, with the third debate reaching some 90 million U.S. citizens.[2] Voter turnout increased 9.5% over 1988, and 77% of the American people reported that they had learned enough in the 1992 campaign to make an intelligent choice.[3] Entertainment outlets like MTV and the Nashville Network have suddenly turned political in recent elections and political advertising has suddenly turned apolitical, with the children of the Daisy commercial and Willie Horton being edited into grayness by their makers because of the omnipresent "ad watches" now being turned out by local and national reporters alike.

No doubt, our most recent elections had their distinctions, but mostly they retraced the political paths of the last half-century, paths blazed by the rise of the electronic media in the United States. This book traces those paths by asking what television has done to us as citizens. Unquestionably, it has done a good deal. It is television that has changed how politics is conducted and how it is received. It is television that has rewritten civic leaders' job descriptions as well as who runs for office in the first place. It is television that suggests what legislation governors should endorse and how far their support should extend. It is television that dictates the attitudes that citizens take into the voting booth as well as the criteria they use when exercising their franchises. It is television that explains who's up and who's down in the polls, who's in favor and who's doomed in the White House, who's faithful and who's not in the bedroom.

Facts like these are constantly being seared into the American mind by the colorful moving pictures that only television can produce. And because of television, certain places have become drenched in meaning for the American people even though they do not live there: Bosnia, the Falklands, Johannesburg, Tiananmen Square, and, yet again, Berlin. Television did not make these moments. But it did remake them.

If anecdotes were trustworthy, they alone could document television's importance in modern politics. That fact dismayed Walter Mondale when he ran for the presidency in 1984 but afterward he seemed to make peace with it: "Modern politics requires mastery of television. I think you know I've never really warmed up to television. And in fairness to television, it's never really warmed up to me."[4] Saddam Hussein, on the other hand, found only joy in television. As the *New York Times* reported early in the Gulf War, more than 200 print journalists tried desperately to get into Baghdad in September of 1990 but only Ted Koppel of ABC News had an easy go of it. As the *Times* reported, "[the Iraqis] presumably feel they can get their message across better on television."[5]

These were also the feelings of Clarence Thomas' supporter, John Doggett, who opined during the Senate Judiciary Committee's hearings on the Supreme Court Justice that "ever since this committee released that affidavit [about Anita Hill] to the press, the press has come to me saying, 'would you talk about that affidavit?' "[6] For John Doggett, "the press" was strictly electronic: "Ted Koppel's office called and said 'Would you be on *Nightline?* Tom Brokaw's office called. Garrick Utley's office called. I even got a call a couple of days ago saying 'Well, if you won't talk to us before you testify, will you . . . show up on *Good Morning [America]* or the *Today* show after you testify? "[7] Mr. Doggett's forbearance here shows him to be made of stern stuff, but he could not completely hide his wistfulness. He seemed to know, as so many of his contemporaries knew, that television is the neatest thing in town.

Reexamining Politics

Examining the electronic media raises special problems for those of us who grew up with it and who therefore see it but darkly. And yet the power of television cannot be denied, with its mixing of high and low culture, with its almost surreal blending of voices, with its always-starting-never-stopping texts that chain together endlessly. Those of us who study such complexities are surely all blind, grabbing fitfully at the televisual elephant in an attempt to understand it. In this book, I have chosen to grab hold of a tail. And the tale I shall tell is that television has changed how politics is done in the United States. In part, we already knew that: The traditional press conference has given way to the presidential town-hall; the scathing broadside has been supplanted by the 15-second spot; campaign oratory has been replaced by the emotional collage of the convention film. But this book makes a more ominous claim: Television has changed politics itself.

That claim will be too sweeping for some. The essentialist, for example, would argue that no matter how different it may look from time to time and from place to place, politics is, inevitably, politics. From such a perspective, politics is the story of how citizens deliberate when parceling out precious resources. As long as people choose to live together and as long as the world's resources remain finite, the essentialist would say, politics will do what it has always done: forge cooperation, enforce regulations. Television can hardly change these brute facts of public life. But television can, and does, mystify such facts. Television can, and does, make the public sphere seem more private.

Television's revolution is therefore a perceptual revolution or, more accurately, a phenomenological revolution. Television makes us see politics in a certain way but it also makes us see seeing in a certain way. Television tells us, a bit at a time, that politics can be reduced to pictures. Television is thus not only a messenger but also, as Marshall McLuhan would say, a message. Television certifies a special way of seeing and hence a special way of knowing. Most important, television endorses a special set of feelings. This book describes five of them.

Writing about feelings is hard. In many ways, it is easier to have feelings than to analyze them. Perhaps that is why most who write about television and politics take a safer route. Media economists like Jeffrey Abramson and his colleagues,[8] for example, discuss how centralization of media ownership, changing demographic patterns, and the economics of mass marketing have cooperatively determined which political messages will be carried by U.S. networks. Media sociologists like Daniel Hallin[9] emphasize other explanations of political television, such as how "professionalized" political staffs have become in recent times, and information scientists in the tradition of Daniel Bell and Walter Lippmann trace how the average citizen becomes inundated with conflicting political messages and what happens as a result.[10] Political scientists such as Bruce Buchanan[11] often view television as but a powerful adjunct to the structural factors that have long determined political outcomes—party identification, legislative initiatives, market performance, group affiliations, and so on.

For other authors, the problem with media politics is quantitative: how much of the news hole is devoted to Candidate X versus Candidate Y,[12] or whether an unpopular political stance is given any airtime at all.[13] Taking yet another approach are media theorists like Neil Postman[14] who decry the vacuousness of political discourse, a discourse that is propositionless, overly simplistic, sensationalistic. Finally, other observers argue that new technologies like cable programming, narrowcasting, satellite transmissions, and mixed media formats marrying television and computer services will reshape the political scene in new and dramatic ways.[15]

All this may be true. But my sense is that something larger, and more subtle, is happening to the American people because of their media habits. Television, I shall argue, now tells us how to feel about politics, producing in us a swagger whereby we tower above politics by making it seem beneath us. Television produces what critic Raymond Williams has called a *structure of feeling* about politics,[16] a structure that lies deeper than our individual attitudes about political parties or social issues or citizen referenda. During the last 50 years, this structure of feeling has made the burdens of citizenship increasingly taxing for us and it is, I believe, responsible for much of the alienation we now feel.

Why not abandon such feelings? Again the answer lies with television. For a host of reasons—some technological, some psychological, many of them rhetorical—the American people like televised politics no matter how much they may deny it. This is true for Democrats as well as Republicans; it is especially true for independents. It is true for those who watch a great deal of television as well as those who abhor it. It is true for political junkies and also for the politically marginalized. Televised politics, it would seem, is supported by an army of seductions.

Not everyone, of course, thinks that fixing television will fix politics. During the 1992 campaign, for example, a host of electoral surgeons went to work on the body politic. HumanServe of New York and the Gulf Coast Tenant Leadership Development Project of Louisiana sponsored voter registration drives among the underprivileged. Debate America, based in Washington, D.C., and the Working Group on Electoral Democracy, based in Chicago, sponsored a variety of issue-based, grassroots forums. California's Center for Media and Values critiqued mainstream coverage of the campaign; New York's Independent Production Fund sponsored political gatherings in minority communities; and the Arizona-based Center for National Independence in Politics set up an 800-number to dispense unbiased information about candidates' legislative records.

In addition, California's Center for Investigative Reporting produced campaign stories uncontaminated by mainstream reportorial routines and the Southern Rainbow Education Project of Alabama and the Washington-based National Library on Money and Politics gathered information on "dirty" (PAC-centered) campaign financing. Still other groups concerned themselves with motor-voter bills, term-limitation legislation, and the corporate bundling of campaign donations.

All these projects tried to counteract political laziness. I, too, shall be concerned with such matters but I shall look inside television, not elsewhere, for what ails the American people. But is examining political television at this late date an impertinence, if not an irrelevancy? After all, we, the Video Generation, are drowning in details about television. We took television to our bosoms almost as soon as we ourselves left the womb. As we grew up, we learned of its effects on us almost as quickly as those effects were produced within us. For 50 years, we have watched television and we have watched ourselves watching television. Surely there is nothing left to say.

But there may be a different way of saying it. There are surely new questions to ask: Does television make us feel one thing or many things about politics? Are we the captives of television, as some have claimed, or its masters—complex negotiators of the meanings and interpretations it offers— as others have claimed? Has television enlarged the public dialogue or constricted it? Do we feel alienated from the political sphere because of television or despite it? Is what we know about politics consistent with what we feel about it?

And who, pray tell, are we? Can the complex feelings television generates be discussed in the large, for people in general, without in-depth interviewing of particular individuals? Can yesterday's political emotions be lumped with today's? Can television's effects on the young be discussed alongside the experiences of the elderly? of blacks and Hispanics? Of men and women?

Questions like these leave us a bit at sea, but we can find dry land by accepting the social scientist's dictum that most human experiences become patterned after a while, that what is true for some people is often also true for a great many more. This is especially the case with politics, where individual wishes and desires regress to the mean when public issues are debated. Collective experiences, collective feelings, lie at the root of public decision making and they must lie at the root of political analysis as well. If a given people is commonly socialized, if they let television become their emotional tutor, they will surely develop common feelings. That, at least, is the emotional logic of this book.

The alternative logic is that of the positivists, thinkers who reduce perception to behavior and behavior to statistics. Because the positivists' assumptions have held sway, discussions about modern electioneering are now filled with numbers: audience shares; campaign expenditure limits, demographic trends, name I.D. ratings, the sizes of media markets, PAC contribution lists, and so on. In their studies, such scholars often separate television's "auditory and visual channels" and then measure the relative "contributions" of those channels to viewers' resulting attitudes.[17] When comparing news-papers to television, for example, such researchers have noted that "television naturally has the advantage in pictorial and graphic information," and they then summarize research that says that "print versions of the same information are more likely to provoke mental concentration and thought than video presentations."[18] Still other scholars treat "media discourse" as something that hovers over the voter, a thing distinct from the "real life" experiences the voter encounters in the workaday world.[19]

Reexamining Television

This book will not honor such ready distinctions. Rather than reduce television to its physical properties, I shall try to remember that watching television is above all else a human experience. People watch television—that is something they do. But people are also television watchers—that is some-thing they are. Because that is what they are, a truly rich understanding of modern governance must ask what politics feels like when people watch it. No measuring of information bits alone can explain, for example, why certain low-income Americans *increased* their support of Ronald Reagan after seeing him on television.[20] By the same token, no amount of reductionism can illustrate why those who watch a great deal of television substantially *overes-timate* the economic lots of African Americans today.[21]

To say that research findings like these make no sense is to miss the kind of sense that television makes. To understand it, we might follow the lead of communication researcher Mara Adelman who argues that adults cannot possibly reach teenagers with safe-sex messages until they better understand, and counteract, the logic of sexual passion itself.[22] Television also has a logic, and that logic is fully in force when it comes to governance. So, for example, scholars have noted that politics has become increasingly personal in the United States. Political scientist Theodore Lowi offers several functionalistic explanations for the phenomenon: the decline of party influence, the increas-ing power of the federal government (vs. state governments), White House staffing practices, the new importance of primaries, and so on.[23] Stephen Ansolabehere and his colleagues add to the list: changing news norms (e.g., the rise of the female reporter); fallout from the Watergate affair (i.e., "character" is now especially important), increasing competition from the tabloids, and so on.[24]

Here, I shall offer a different explanation for personality politics. Television, I will argue, fills an emotional void created by modern life itself. Television has become a delivery system for intimacy, that luxuriant product of the 1960s, and it delivers intimacy to us from dawn to dusk. If politics were suddenly obliterated from the television screen, if the United States suddenly enacted an even more restrictive version of the Israelis' restrictions on election-year broadcasting, politics would instantly become less personal. In response, however, television would simply deliver its intimacies in other, nonpolitical venues and would continue to have relationships with the people they see on daily soap operas. They would continue to mourn, sometimes quite literally, when a favorite character is unexpectedly removed from *Baywatch* because of stormy contract negotiations. They would do so because watching television is an oddly emotional business.

How could it be otherwise? Television is a people's medium, after all, and it celebrates that fact each day. It celebrates people's joys in its game shows, their strivings in its sports programs, their lusts via the Playboy Channel. But it is television's capacity to generate surprise that makes it especially attractive. Each time—each time—the set is turned on, new joys, new strivings, and new lusts await. Each of these emotional experiences is unanticipated and, yet, curiously anticipatable.

As an emotional medium, television performs both personal and cultural work for its viewers. It lets them learn about themselves, as when scenes from the Kennedy assassination and the *Challenger* explosion become moments of memory for two different generations of Americans. To remember such scenes is to be reminded of who we once were and of the people who shared those moments with us. In these ways and more, television expands time and enlarges the human family. It delivers Mother Teresa to us as well as the serial rapist. Even when watched alone, television reminds us that life need not be solitary.

Television has its detractors, of course, especially when it comes to politics. Social scientists have long noted, for example, that those who watch television a great deal know precious little about how they are governed, presumably because political programming is directed at the lowest common denominator. But being informed and feeling informed are different matters. Many Americans, far too many Americans, feel eminently knowledgeable about politics, and that is a danger of some consequence. A democracy, I shall argue here, becomes imperiled (a) when its people do not know what they think they know, and (b) when they do not care about what they do not know. Television miseducates the citizenry but, worse, it makes that miseducation functionally attractive.

This book will lay out, and reconceptualize, three other complaints about modern politics. Despite the slight uptick in voter turnout in 1992 (vs. 1996), for example, most studies find growing sullenness about citizen participation in the United States. Over the years, voter turnout has decreased even as television consumption has increased. A causal connection? Clearly not. Studio anchors, network executives, cable franchisers, public affairs documentarists, and a rainbow coalition of television reporters now deliver more political information—and more implicit denunciations of voter apathy—than ever before. Curiously enough, however, this political avalanche is part of the problem. Because it comes at us in such great waves, political information is impossible to avoid, both for those who seek it out on *Meet the Press* and for those who try to escape it by watching *Murphy Brown*. The result? For many citizens, watching governance has become equivalent to engaging governance. Because of television, even nonvoters can now feel politically exhausted.

Commentators have also shown how heavily campaign strategy is featured in television reportage, with more and more airtime being used to detail which candidate is ahead and which behind and, especially, how they got there. The new lexicon of politics—"spin doctors," "soft numbers," "high negatives"—is a language that *citizens* increasingly speak as well. According to one set of researchers, "horserace coverage" of this sort has had a number of unfortunate consequences: It penalizes "slow starters;" it over-emphasizes the Iowa and New Hampshire primaries; and it distorts financial contributions.[25] Moreover, as Joseph Capella and Kathleen Jamieson have found in a series of carefully controlled experiments, strategy-based coverage also depresses voter turnout, a dangerous effect indeed.[26]

What happens when people watch politics solely through a strategic lens? A cultural cynicism results, and it saps the body politic by making the miracle of self-governance seem a sham. But why is cynicism attractive? Because it is television's most natural language and because people derive pleasure from being in sync with popular culture. Because television feeds on artificiality, on the bootlegged image, it endlessly enchants us, from the 10 p.m. weather map that is there and not there at the same time, to the forecaster's smile, which is there only when it needs to be there. Because television manufactures everything, it believes in nothing. Those attitudes leak out and are easily picked up, especially by a people that has long been suspicious of formal government.

Attitudes about informal governance are another matter, and yet there, too, television's imprint can be found. Philosophers like Germany's Jürgen Habermas have worried of late about the decline of the "public sphere," about modern society's exclusion of alternative voices.[27] But the mass media have anticipated Habermas' complaint by transforming symbolic capital into a new kind of political currency. "Television presence," the ability to access the public sphere often and well, now makes a vast array of partisan groups feel included in the political process. By doing so, however, television confuses the real vectors of political influence in the United States. Treating television in information-based or economically based terms would be to miss these subtle forms of political misdirection.

Throughout this book, I will examine what researchers have discovered about contemporary politics and then reinterpret those data. My main suggestion will be that television has revolutionized politics not because of the quantity and speed of its information, not because of its practitioners' technological savvy, and not even because of its legion superficialities. Rather, *I will suggest that television makes us feel good about feeling bad about politics.*

Unlike many who study television, I will not look for a single villain here. The feelings people have when watching politics are complicated; the sources of those feelings are no less complicated. Whereas it is true, for example, that politicians have used television to manipulate their constituents, it is also true that politicians were a manipulative breed long before television made its debut in the 1940s. Similarly, although television has turned some journalists into opportunists, human nature, not television alone, can be blamed for that. Conservative writers look for their villains in the newsroom's socialization patterns, but their case is no more convincing than that of Marxists who trace all hegemony to the ways in which all things—including information—are made ready for sale and barter.

All television's critics marshall data impressively, but none has answered the questions I am asking here: Why do people feel knowledgeable about politics but ignorant about governance? Why do they now speak like critics instead of like citizens? Why do they feel so righteous when not voting? Questions of this sort are not easily answered. They certainly cannot be answered with the attitude scales social scientists use when taking citizens' pulses. Such scales have their uses, but they do not tap the residual feelings left in voters by televised politics.

Capturing such feelings is the job of phenomenology, that branch of study designed to investigate "the content of consciousness."[28] Because television is essentially a technology of consciousness and because politics is little more than public consciousness made manifest, a new phenomenology of politics is needed. It is needed for both theoretical and practical reasons. More traditional approaches to politics—calculating voter demographics or tracking macroeconomic trends, for example—often tell us much about the *how* of politics but not about the *why*. A good phenomenology, in contrast, tries to scratch an itch that is hard to find but that cannot be denied. It attaches words to perceptions that cannot be easily described. It examines taken-for-granted assumptions about politics and in that sense becomes an "investigation of appearances."[29]

Most important, phenomenology offers a language for the emotions. It captures what Hwa Yol Jung has called the perceiver's "natural attitude" toward the world, that "prereflective and naive point of view" that tells our intuitions what is intuitively true.[30] For Jung, "the ordinary language of politic[s] precedes the objectified language of political science, and the second must be consistent with the first."[31] Alas, that is rarely the case. Too often, political study is reduced to abstract talk of political systems, which causes politics to lose both its humanity and its politics when dissected.

Phenomenology tries to change that. It treats people as emotionally complicated and it questions differences between "fact" and "perception."[32] Television does the same thing when it artfully obscures differences between the real and the fictive. A clever president like Ronald Reagan, for example, could borrow effortlessly from a celluloid hero like Dirty Harry Callaghan by challenging his political antagonists to "make his day" and oppose him legislatively. By aping Callaghan's bravado, Mr. Reagan undermined simplistic distinctions between the world of movies and the world of politics and, simultaneously, questioned distinction-making itself.

George Bush tried the same thing but got caught. Although he, too, used Callaghan's line, the *New York Times* reported that the vast majority of Mr. Bush's supporters *actually believed* his pledge when he made it: " 'I'm disgusted with all politicians,' said Ron Purkhiser, a 50-year old welder in Akron, Ohio. 'They say one thing, then they go ahead and do the opposite. 'Read my lips: No new taxes. Yeah, right."[33] The *Times*'s writer seemed stunned that people like Mr. Purkhiser still existed in the ingenuous 1990s.

Ingenuous or not, however, televised politics reaches out and grabs us in continually surprising ways. At the moment, we do not have an efficient way of talking about such influences. To discover one, we might take the lead of culture critic Frederic Jameson who says that to appreciate postmodern architecture one must retrain the viewing habits one acquired in an earlier, modernist era.[34] So, too, with television. To appreciate what it has done to politics, we must learn to speak television's language—the language of feelings.

But learning to speak such a language is an inexact business. To understand Mr. Purkhiser's reaction to George Bush, for example, we must throw science to the winds. We must appreciate how personal political ideology becomes when it is spoken and how intensely personal it becomes when it is spoken on television. In August of 1988, that is, television brought both a Republican promise *and George Bush himself* to Akron, to Mr. Purkhiser, when the would-be president uttered his fateful promise. But it did more than that. It brought Harry Callaghan to Akron as well, his fearlessness and personal resolve in tow, and it wrapped them all in a TV-ready package.

Thus, to appreciate why Purkhiser felt what he felt, we must understand the assumptions he made about televised politics before watching it. We must inquire into the "pre-given" of television,[35] into how it causes the past and the present, the human and the mechanical, the near and the distant, the sure and the unsure, to dance before our eyes—collectively, confusedly, but pleasantly. We watch television precisely because we like such tricks, such confusions. What else could explain our appreciation of *Saturday Night Live*'s inanities?

And yet we do not watch television to *feel* confused. That is the problem televised politics presents today. It almost always makes us feel confused: hope for the economy, distrust in the economists; antipathy toward Saddam Hussein, respect for Colin Powell; depression about drug runners, pride in our astronauts. But the political feelings probed in this book transcend these specifics and deal with deeper confusions—the very model of politics television endorses.

It is this model of politics, not the details of what politicians do, that prompts our deepest dissatisfactions. Television's model of politics flatters the medium (as one might expect) and it flatters viewers, too. It makes them feel close to their leaders, at least for awhile. It makes them feel informed about public affairs, at least a bit. Television also gives certain Americans feelings of enterprise and influence, although these feelings come at a price. And this model *is* a model, a distinctive way of seeing the world. Its pieces and parts are integrated and it produces a predictable set of emotional experiences. The feelings it deposits within us are often pleasing initially but they become more disturbing later on. This contrariety of emotions is what distinguishes, and perpetuates, the model.

The strokes used to paint the picture of politics here are broad. Mine is a landscape, not an etching. And it is also self-reflexive—it is hard to paint a landscape that one already inhabits. Having been born in 1945, and thus raised on political television from the beginning, I can hardly stand apart from the picture I paint. The image of politics contained in my head is one that contains me as well. To reflect on any sort of everyday experience is to change that experience. But leaving political television unexamined seems the greater folly.

Because television's model of politics is a model, it operates in the part as well as the whole and therefore "precedes" any individual political event a citizen might witness. When watching Senator Trent Lott and Attorney General Janet Reno attack one another over campaign finance improprieties in 1997, that is, American viewers did not enter that moment newly born. They came equipped with a wealth of assumptions about politicians and newsworthiness, about political propriety and political courage. Television itself had helped to create some of those assumptions. Its model therefore binds us tightly, although it is not monolithic and it affects some people more than others.

And yet it affects all of us in part. This is a phenomenological principle philosopher Laurie Spurling calls anchorage: "If, for example, I see a stone falling through the air, this means my gaze is anchored in the garden, so that it is in terms of the garden that the stone is seen as moving."[36] In other words, because we always stand *somewhere* when watching politics, it is good to know where we stand, especially if television is helping us stand there.

In many ways, it is easy to feel superior to a book that talks this directly about feelings. That is especially true when it comes to politics, the most masculine of the human arts. When most professional commentators discuss politics, they fortify themselves by first ransacking the tool chest ("precinct modeling," "dial groups," "sampling screens") and then the gymnasium locker ("congressional arm-twisting," "primary fisticuffs," "political handlers"), trying to make empirical that which is inevitably emotional. Politics resists. The simple fact is that people feel things about politics; the complicated fact is that they feel them in often confusing ways.

And so when talking about politics we cannot let the language of the head distort the language of the heart. We must resist the comforts of empirical science, in which speech becomes "a flow of words set in motion," as well rationalism, which makes speech "solely an intellectual process."[37] The phe-

nomenological method asks us to do more: to listen between the lines of
voters' casual conversations; to interpret political activities that others have
failed to interpret; to imagine the cumulative effects of watching the news
each evening; to sense a mosaic where others sense only individual phenom-
ena. Listening, interpreting, imagining, sensing. Is phenomenology a method
of madness?

Opening oneself to the soft data of politics need not make one addle-
brained. Wherever possible, the extant literature on political behavior is
consulted here. But when all is said and done, this book is an extended
speculation, perhaps even a meditation. It examines a wide range of studies
about televised politics but treats those studies as questions rather than as
answers. Similarly, it surveys a number of theoretical writings and popular
commentaries but bends those works to its own purpose: discovering why
television makes political obligation seem irrelevant. Indeed, even a phrase
like "political obligation" smells of lilac toilet water in an age of television. It
is a phrase that can be uttered today only if one has a smirk at the ready.
Almost always, television provides the smirk.

Reexamining Remedies

Over the years, numerous commentators have suggested how televised
politics might be fixed. Collectively, they define "political television" broadly
(as I shall here), including within it the news (local, national, and international), political advertising, campaign-based communications as well as
office-holders' pronouncements, interview shows, political documentaries,
public service messages, lobbying by those in the private-sector, citizen-action
agendas, as well as a variety of popular culture formats. The solutions for
dealing with political television have been no less restricted:

1. The Debaters

Some observers, such as political scientist James Fishkin,[38] have called for
a reinvigorated public interchange to retrieve the nation from the political
doldrums. The Debaters endorse deliberative opinion polls, the televising of
House and Senate proceedings, and the regularizing of presidential press
conferences. These solutions are clearly conflict based, designed to counteract

the "soft politics" that produces excessive chumminess among the nation's elites. But can solutions like these get at the sources of unbelief that threaten the polity? Can a new dialectic counteract the forces of socialization that undergird people's attitudes? Must we look beyond changes in media formats for solutions to the alienations that confront us? Indeed we must.

2. The Entertainers

A more progressive set of observers argues that politics has fallen on hard times because it is no longer emotionally available to the citizenry. Voters are alienated, this camp holds, because politics is now gray and lifeless, drained of the human connectedness once found in the New England village. The Entertainers favor formats that draw people into the public realm by humanizing political options. They are therefore attracted to Ross Perot's electronic town halls, to Rush Limbaugh and Tom Lykas on talk radio, and to the ever-new forms of psychobiography found on television. Instead of improving things, I argue, these strategies merely usher in a distorting politics of intimacy. It seems to me that we need to become more serious, not more flighty, when imagining a politics for the future.

3. The Heralds

A third school of thought stresses the need for a more informed electorate and looks to the nation's press for solutions. The Heralds champion in-depth reporting, longer nightly news programs, less dependence on restrictive sources of information, fewer lacerating political profiles but also less toadying by the White House press corps, and elimination of Washington's employment merry-go-round between the First and Fourth Estates.[39] "Drench the people with the right kind of information," the Heralds promise, "and they will respond." Nobody can disagree with such good sense. But is it enough? Probably not. It seems to me that it is what people feel, not what they know, that must be dislodged before they will become politically involved. Finding such strategies of dislodgement will not be easy, but this book proposes a mindset, at least, for finding them.

4. The Radicals

This is a Marxian view and it features, predictably enough, money.[40] By this perspective, the mass media are corporate captives, a fact that clouds each image projected onto viewers' screens by the television networks. Political information is capitalized information, the Radicals argue, and that makes both establishment politicians and establishment reporters dance to the same tune. The solution? Break up the economic cartels, the cross-ownership patterns, the centralized news bureaus, the privately owned satellites, the news-for-profit routines. Break up, too, the cozy relationships between political contributors and political candidates, between news personnel and their corporate rolodexes, between the Corporation for "Public" Broadcasting and its non-advertising advertisers. Typically, the Radicals leave one gasping for air, so total is their critique. I think we need a more personal, less system-based, solution.

5. The Free-Marketeers

Rarely explicated in serious commentaries about televised politics, this view underlies many of them, nonetheless. The Free-marketeers acknowledge, as Alexander Hamilton might have had he lived to see television, that television dulls the senses. But they find that inevitable, not tragic. They argue that people want pleasure, not mindless wrangling, when they are relaxing before the television set in the evening, and that that is why they ignore politics. Besides, argue the Free-marketeers, television educates everyone at least a bit, including nonvoters. The result of all this is clear: an electronic republicanism that keeps the best of us active and the rest of us quiet. Surely this is a dangerous attitude. Surely a sense of citizenship cannot be allowed to pass for the real thing in an enlightened democracy. Surely a society must find a way of getting all its hands on deck.

6. The Analysts

The Analysts endorse a different kind of citizen's wisdom, a meta-wisdom, when encouraging the ongoing deconstruction of contemporary politics. The Analysts are academic pundits who make the rounds explaining politicians' advertising strategies, media critics who watch the press's political watchers, and social activists who publish monthly exposés of political journalism. Many of these Analysts are well intentioned, but an equal number preen noxiously when exposing the falseness of politics, thereby adding to an already ample supply of cultural cynicism. Although this book also promotes media awareness, it looks for a humbler, and happier, way of dealing with political television.

Each of the foregoing perspectives offers possibilities for political renewal, but each suffers from an unblinking faith that altering communication methodologies will alter political consciousness. To change politics, they suggest, one must change the political text, change how that text is formatted, or change how it is received by viewers. But will a new, less manipulative, breed of politician come of age overnight? Will media staffers caught up in complex corporate cultures suddenly become more responsible? Will new systems for delivering political information come on line and make political thinking easier? I suspect not, and I suspect, further, that any solution to political malaise must reckon, more fundamentally, with how people feel about democracy and not with what they know about it.

Conclusion

This book embraces such a solution, a solution especially needed in an age of political eclipse. Although Americans have always had a healthy skepticism about politicians, they have not always distrusted politics itself. They do now. This change has been gradual but insistent. It has also been revolutionary. And it has been unfortunate. I believe that the very concept of politics is now threatening to slip away from us as a nation, that we as citizens are vaguely aware of this slippage and, most disturbing of all, that we do not care about our loss. The reasons behind this eclipse, this deferral, of politics are many. Some of the reasons lie in the unremitting series of political debacles Americans have witnessed during the last forty years: Vietnam, Watergate, Iran-Contra, savings and loan scandals, campaign finance improprieties. Although these events have passed into history (some more quickly than others), they have left an aftertaste. Other reasons press on us: An often-sick economy opens up class divisions in the ostensibly classless United States; a growing cultural malaise envelops the citizenry; governmental leaders in the mold of Franklin Roosevelt, and even of Harry Truman, seem unavailable. These things, individually and collectively, have made Americans sad, later angry, now numb. Or so many have claimed.

My meditation runs in a different direction. I believe that it is how we talk about politics that lets us down, that turns our political will into a political won't. This book tracks this new language and argues that television presents us with an infinite set of pigments for painting politics black. Television may do so innocently, for after fifty years of programming, even media personnel may no longer be able to see beyond television's practiced routines. And so the deferral of politics may be a crime without criminals. But that is not to say it is a victimless crime. This book shows why.

Notes

1. *U.S. News & World Report,* January 4, 1993, 99.

2. Ibid., 99.

3. M. Ross, "'92 Voters Better Informed, Survey Finds," *Los Angeles Times,* November 15, 1992, A25.

4. "'Meals of Crow' Coming for Reagan," *U.S. News & World Report,* November 19, 1984, 37.

5. "Baghdad Seems to Favor U.S. Networks on Journalists' Visas," *New York Times,* September 23, 1990, A1.

6. "John Doggett's Response to Senator Joseph Biden," October 13, 1991, *Senate Judiciary Committee Hearings on the Clarence Thomas Nomination to the Supreme Court* (Washington, DC: Federal Information Systems Corporation, 1991).

7. Ibid.

8. J. Abramson, F. Arterton, and G. Orren, *The Electronic Commonwealth: The Impact of New Media Technologies on Democratic Politics* (New York: Basic Books, 1988).

9. D. Hallin, "The American News Media: A Critical Theory Perspective," in J. Forester (ed.), *Critical Theory and Public Life* (Cambridge: M.I.T. Press, 1985), 121-146.

10. See, for example, S. E. Bennett, "Trends in Americans' Political Information, 1967-1987," *American Politics Quarterly, 17* (1989), 422-435.

11. B. Buchanan, *The Citizen's Presidency* (Washington, DC: Congressional Quarterly Press, 1987).

12. S. R. Lichter, D. Amundson, and R. Noyes, *The Video Campaign: Network Coverage of the 1988 Primaries* (Washington, DC: A.E.I. Institute, 1988).

13. M. Real, "Demythologizing Media: Recent Writings in Critical and Institutional Theory," *Critical Studies in Mass Communication, 3* (1986), 458-496.

14. N. Postman, *Amusing Ourselves to Death: Public Discourse in the Age of Show Business* (New York: Penguin Books, 1985).

15. See, for example, Abramson et al. (1988).

16. R. Williams, *Marxism and Literature* (New York: Oxford University Press, 1977), 133-134.

17. See, for example, the work of Roger Masters: R. Masters et al., "Dominance and Attention: Images of Leaders in German, French, and American TV News," *Polity, 25* (1991), 373-394; and R. Masters and D. Sullivan, "Nonverbal Behavior and Leadership: Emotion and Cognition in Political Attitudes," in S. Iyengar and W. McGuire (eds.), *Explorations in Political Psychology* (Durham, NC: Duke University Press, 1993).

18. W. R. Neuman, M. Just, and A. Crigler, *Common Knowledge: News and the Construction of Political Meaning* (Chicago: University of Chicago Press, 1992), 77.

19. Although he sometimes treats "media discourse" as "not something out there but something inside our heads," sociologist William Gamson more frequently externalizes media stimuli as, for example, when he operationalizes television's influence by testing people's ability to recall specific pieces of the media text. See his nevertheless interesting book, *Talking Politics* (New York: Cambridge University Press, 1992), 122, 180-183.

20. L. Ragsdale, "Presidential Speechmaking and the Public Audience: Individual Presidents and Group Attitudes," *Journal of Politics*, 49 (1987), 704-736.

21. G.B. Armstrong and K. Neuendorf, "TV Entertainment, News, and Racial Stereotypes of College Students," *Journal of Communication*, 42 (1992), 153-176.

22. M. Adelman, "Sustaining Passion: Eroticism and Safe-Sex Talk," *Archives of Sexual Behavior*, 21 (1992), 1-14.

23. T. Lowi, *The Personal President* (Ithaca, NY: Cornell University Press, 1985).

24. S. Ansolabehere, R. Behr, and S. Iyengar, *The Media Game: American Politics in the Television Age* (New York: Macmillan, 1993), 61.

25. Ansolabehere, 59-60.

26. J. Cappella and K. H. Jamieson, *Spiral of Cynicism: The Press and the Public Good* (New York: Oxford University Press, 1997).

27. This theme can be found in almost all of Habermas's work but a useful précis of it can be found in "The Public Sphere: An Encyclopedia Article," in S. Bronner and D. Kellner (eds.), *Critical Theory and Society: A Reader* (New York: Routledge, 1989), 136-142.

28. D. Stewart and A. Mickunas, *Exploring Phenomenology: A Guide to the Field and Its Literature* (Chicago: American Library Association, 1974), 73.

29. L. Hinchman and S. Hinchman, "In Heidegger's Shadow: Hannah Arendt's Phenomenological Humanism," *The Review of Politics*, 46 (1984), 187.

30. H. Y. Jung, "Introduction," in H.Y. Jung (ed.), *Existential Phenomenology and Political Theory: A Reader* (Chicago: Henry Regnery, 1972), xxi.

31. Jung, xxx.

32. For an example of an author who doesn't question this distinction see D. Nesbit, *Videostyle in Senate Campaigns* (Knoxville: University of Tennessee Press, 1988), 21-22.

33. "Words on Bush's Lips in '88 Now Stick in Voters' Craw," *New York Times*, June 14, 1992, A1.

34. F. Jameson, "Postmodernism, or the Cultural Logic of Late Capitalism," *The New Left Review*, 146 (July/August, 1984), 80.

35. H. Reid and E. Yanarella, "Toward a Post-Modern Theory of American Political Science and Culture: Perspectives From Critical Marxism and Phenomenology," *Cultural Hermeneutics*, 2 (1974), 101.

36. L. Spurling, *Phenomenology and the Social World: The Philosophy of Merleau-Ponty and Its Relations to the Social Sciences* (London: Routledge, 1977), 38.

37. Spurling, 50.

38. J. Fishkin, *Democracy and Deliberation: New Directions for Democratic Reform* (New York: Yale University Press, 1991).

39. For a thorough presentation of the ills currently afflicting political reporting see L. Sabato, *Feeding Frenzy: How Attack Journalism Has Transformed American Politics* (New York: Free Press, 1991).

40. Because this viewpoint is so prevalent in the American academy, it has produced a corpulent bibliography. For an informed and accessible treatment see T. Luke, *Screens of Power: Ideology, Domination, and Resistance in Informational Society* (Urbana: University of Illinois Press, 1989).

Box 1.1 Inquiries and Transitions

Because politics has been televised for so many years now, do we already know everything we need to know about it? Is it somewhat silly to question how television makes us feel? After all, television is an information device, not something we cuddle up with at night. Or is it? Is television not indeed a cuddling medium and does it not often give us a sense of intimacy with all the people it brings to us, sitcom actors and political leaders alike? But if television produces strong feelings within us, how do we get in touch with those feelings? trace them to their root causes? It is one thing to say that politics is boring or trivial, but what makes us so confident when sharing those observations with others? When we do, why are our friends and neighbors so likely to agree with us? Why is it now popular to disparage politics and why do many of us feel intimidated—yes, intimidated—into rejecting civic life? Does the popularity of shows like *Politically Incorrect* tell us something important about television and politics at the turn of the century? If so, here are the hardest questions of all: If television successfully bullies us into rejecting politics, who will mind the ship of state in our absence, and will they do so wisely?

Feeling Intimate

The Rise of Personality Politics

Childhood is a fine teacher. But rarely for children. Childhood Experienced is normally too filled with bruised knees and unreasonable curfews to teach us much. But Childhood Remembered contains wisdom for all our ages. Like many, I have probably been too dull witted to learn what I should have from my youth, but I do remember almost everything that happened on October 21, 1952. That was the day that Dwight Eisenhower drove in front of my house, slowly. He passed within fifty feet of our front door, within twenty feet of me. He waved, as did I, but not as vigorously as I might have an hour earlier.

Two hours earlier, on the other hand, I would have waved madly, for it was then that I was busy making a sign in the basement of 1003 Riverside Avenue. My sign was hardly an elegant one—a piece of shirt cardboard attached to a broom handle—but it was most certainly *my* sign for it contained three of the words I could then spell without blemish: "I Like Ike." I carried my sign to the front yard of 1003 Riverside Avenue because for weeks my neighbors had told me that the General-turned-candidate would pass before us in a motorcade taking him from Fall River to Taunton.

The enthusiasm of a seven-year-old is hard to restrain, but contained it was just after I positioned myself and my sign in the front yard. Almost immediately, a tremendous shadow loomed over me, a human shadow as it

21

turned out, a motherly shadow. When wrenching the "I Like Ike" sign from
my hand and then turning on her heels, the shadow spoke in a low, almost
deathly, voice: "Not in this house."

This, I was to discover later, was the sound of genuine political emotion.
It is a sound rarely heard today but its echoes still haunt me. To a seven-year-
old, it was a simply stunning moment: What could I have done, innocent that
I was, to have summoned up such wrath? Why did this otherwise gentle
woman yank my sign away with such force, and why was there no verb in her
sentence? Why had she not prefaced her discussion with me and, oh yes, why
was there no discussion? Had she not noticed the many friends and neighbors
who had come to stand on our very own front lawn to see the great impending
sight? And I wondered, too, what that odd feeling was in her voice, why her
breathing seemed so awkward, why she spoke her vowels in such a thin-lipped
manner. What could I possibly have done to so offend Mary Claire Sullivan
Hart, granddaughter of potato Irish, member of St. Thomas More Women's
Sodality, mother of four, sister-in-law to eight?

In time, the scales were removed from my eyes. But not by my mother. We
never spoke of the matter again. It would take me many years to learn about
the politics of immigration and ethnicity in Massachusetts—what it meant in
the 1920s to be an Irish girl in a Yankee state, to be a Catholic girl in a
Protestant state, to be a Democratic girl in a Republican state. It would take
even longer to learn how political wounds suffered in Europe could bleed again
in the New World, especially when reopened by discriminatory hiring practices
and exclusionary socialization directed against the Irish, and thus how even
a kindly man with a smile in a car could make them fester anew.

This is my earliest political memory. If the assumptions of this book are
correct, such an experience is now rare. To a generation, really two generations, raised on televised politics, first political experiences are now more
orderly, less vivid, no doubt less bizarre. Seven year-olds at the turn of the
century no longer must confront a saint-turned-shrew stalking across the
stages of their minds, tearing up their artwork. Because their first political
experiences typically come to them through television, today's seven year-olds
have a cooler time of it. They experience politics inside, not outside, their
homes. They do so while seated and watching, not standing and shouting. The
scenes they witness do not fill up their eyes and there is no motorcade for them
to hear or smell.

As a result, politics cannot overpower them. The blue-suited figures who
drone on in front of their eyes are only 18 inches tall after all, precisely the

height of the average television screen. Such figures cannot possibly become magical or dominant for a seven year-old. They cannot sing or dance; they do not fire rocket launchers or do figure eights on the ice; the jokes they tell are lame. They are, at root, colossally boring, no different from the weather forecasters or used car dealers who also intrude on childhood reverie.

Perhaps that is how childhood should be—apolitical, if not anti-political. But I cannot help feeling that my first political experience shaped me in a special way, and it distresses me that politics is now so removed from people's emotional lives. There are many explanations for the increasing distance between citizens and their government and this book explores several. But the basic reason, I assert, is that politics now comes in a box. Admittedly, that box is colorful and makes joyful sounds, but it packages politics nonetheless and therefore contains it. For some, that is as it should be. Many Americans would dynamite any box lodging political commercials if they could avoid demolishing *Monday Night Football* in the bargain.

The antipathy for politics fostered by television is a complicated thing. It is not, as some conservatives suggest, simply the result of network executives getting their revenge for McCarthy-era blacklistings. The people of television—news directors, cinematographers, reporters, editors—do create problems for politics but they probably do so unconsciously. More obvious causes can be found. For one thing, television's nature as a visual, electronic medium reduces the scale of politics. To the eyes of a child in Somerset, Massachusetts, Dwight Eisenhower's pilgrimage was panoramic. On television, it would have been miniaturized and reduced in emotional scope as well. For that same child, politics meant people crowded together, excited. Television watching, in contrast, is often a lonely enterprise. Especially for the child who waited for Dwight Eisenhower, politics meant anticipation, irregularity. With television, things run on time.

Above all, though, that seven-year-old in 1952 learned that politics was an affair of the gut. It meant jobs, education, and praying where one wished. It also meant personal identity. These things are hard to show on television; they are better lived than watched. Even at its best moments, therefore, and television has had many of them, the deepest emotions of politics cannot be refracted even by a minicam behind closed doors.

So it does little good to become a naysayer when talking about television and politics. The medium is here to stay and, given its technological limitations, it may already be doing the best it can with politics. But that does not mean that *we* are doing the best we can and that is why this book was written.

It inventories five feelings television provides and then assesses their worth. This chapter, for example, asks if needs for intimacy can truly be met by television and, if so, can they be met by politics as well. To my way of thinking, it is odd to look for intimacy in politics. Families and churches seem better sites. Politics, in contrast, provides only one thing, but it is a good thing—communal power. That was one of the first lessons I learned as a child, and Dwight Eisenhower helped me learn it. Because I did not get to know Ike through television, I did not get to know him intimately. This chapter explains why that fact no longer distresses me.

Political Disclosures

Scholars have not been able to document the author of one of history's most famous political quotations: "*L'état c'est moi.*" Popularly attributed to France's Louis XIV, the phrase is probably more a representative example than an actuality. No matter. It could now serve as the motto of any U.S. politician. During the last fifty years, American politics has become personal. Research has documented, for example, that recent American presidents (Lyndon Johnson through Ronald Reagan) referred to themselves more often in their speeches than did their immediate predecessors (Harry Truman through John Kennedy) and far more often than a comparison group of business executives, social activists, congressional leaders, and preachers.[1]

At first, Presidents Johnson and Nixon were reluctant to make self-references on television, but all that has changed by now. Beginning primarily with Gerald Ford ("I will work with the Congress, and I know many, if not all, in the Congress will work with me"[2]) and continuing to Jimmy Carter, presidential politics has turned confessional. As Robert Shrum said to Carter when quitting his staff, "I am not sure what you truly believe in other than yourself."[3] Carter certainly did believe in unburdening himself, as witnessed in his "malaise" speech of July 15, 1979. During his remarks, Carter declared that a crisis of confidence had overcome the nation. He then read his negative press clippings and polling results to his audience and concluded with this: "I've worked hard to put my campaign promises into law—and I have to admit, with just mixed success."[4]

What is the source of this self-indulgence? Did it begin with Lyndon Johnson, who is alleged to have said in one state dinner receiving line, "Mr.

Prime Minister, I want you to meet a member of *my* Supreme Court" and even talked on one occasion of preparing the "State of *My* Union Address."[5] Have recent chief executives been visited by some sort of purgational plague? Is humility now in such short supply that Harry Truman's successors have forgotten his wise counsel?

> You see the thing you have to remember. When you get to be president, there are all those things, the honors, the twenty-one gun salutes, all those things, you have to remember it isn't for you. It's for the Presidency, and you've got to keep yourself separate from that in your mind. If you can't keep the two separate, yourself and the Presidency, you're in all kinds of trouble.[6]

Remarks like Truman's show he would have made a poor media president. The very superstructure of the presidency has changed since his time. It has, for example, become more insistently rhetorical, with the president now taking chief responsibility for his political circumstances. Such aggressiveness was well evidenced during the 1996 presidential campaign. The candidates sought out countless media opportunities that featured their *informal* selves. They appeared on both morning and evening talk shows, on network as well as cable programs. They took questions directly from ordinary people in town forums and one of them even fell off the stage trying to get close to the people. Some commentators praised these proletarian activities—"returning government to the people"—but what it really did was cordon off the press. Puckish though he was, Larry King was no Mike Wallace.

During the last forty years, American presidents have increasingly placed themselves on center stage whenever the occasion permitted. If the occasion did not permit it, they invented the occasion. For example, in *The Sound of Leadership*,[7] I reported the following trends in presidential speechmaking between 1945 and 1985: (a) the sheer amount of presidential oratory tripled between the Truman and Reagan administrations; (b) non-election year speaking is now almost as frequent as election-year speaking for the chief executive; rhetoric has become his way of life and also his means of life; (c) public ceremonies have risen sharply over the years, ostensibly because they allow one figure—the president—to dominate the political scene; (d) press conferences have dropped off precipitously, no doubt because they make such political domination less possible; and (e) "audience crafting" has become a standard political routine; presidents now speak almost exclusively to friendly audiences and invite the media to photograph the resulting love-ins.

Presidents, in short, try to dominate the people's emotional lives with their emotional lives.

The nation's media have helped them do so, at times unwillingly. Researchers have shown, for example, that the president is almost always the lead-off hitter on the nightly news, even if it has been a slow news day.[8] Especially, perhaps, if it has been a slow news day. Bill Clinton stopping into McDonalds; Ronald Reagan brushing his horse; George Bush playing six sports in two hours—these are now familiar images. They allow us, ostensibly, to see the person behind the person and they also dovetail with the point-and-shoot mentality of much electronic reporting. Admittedly, these scenes of domesticity are often overridden by a sonorous voice announcing the governmental things the president has done that day via fax and phone, but the pictures, always the pictures, linger in our heads, drawing the president closer and closer to us.

Alas, such intimacy comes at a price: When we become familiar with a person in these day-in and day-out ways, we develop the sorts of expectations that any intimate association promises. But intimacy with a politician is a special sort of intimacy. Because it is political it is fractious and because it is electronic it is fragile. It is intellectual intimacy, not affection based. We come to *know* politicians, not necessarily to like them. It is the sort of intimacy that once-marrieds still retain for one another, a deep knowledge that produces a knowing glance and a snarl simultaneously. And so political intimacy is almost always a case of bait-and-switch. The politician opens up his heart. We are drawn in. He or she then does something obnoxious or stupid—an inevitability in politics. We jump back, scorned, again. We declare the lot of them toxic waste. Then television brings us a new, more vulnerable soul to probe. The soap opera continues.

Presidents not only refer to themselves more often today but they also speak the language of relationships. Psychologists Nancy Miller and William Stiles, for example, tracked what they called verbal familiarity in nomination speeches and inaugural addresses over the years.[9] For Miller and Stiles, verbal familiarity emphasizes you-talk as well as I-talk, addresses experiential rather than abstract matters, avoids impersonal commands, and so on. Previous research had shown that married couples' verbal familiarity was much higher than non-marrieds and that physicians sharply increased their verbal familiarity when conducting intimate physical examinations (vs. taking medical histories). As might be expected, given the increased coverage the networks have devoted to political speechmaking over the years, verbal familiarity is now at an all-time high.

Our own experience affirms that. In 1984, for example, Democratic convention keynoter Mario Cuomo spoke of his father: "A small man with thick calluses on both hands [who worked] 15 and 16 hours a day. I saw him once literally bleed from the bottoms of his feet."[10] Four years later in a similar situation, Texas governor Ann Richards also reached inside herself: "I can remember summer nights when we'd put down what we called a Baptist pallet, and we listened to the grown-ups talk. I can still hear the sound of the dominoes clicking on the marble slab my daddy had for a tabletop."[11] During that same convention, even the fearsome Jesse Jackson became vulnerable: "At 3 o'clock on Thanksgiving Day we couldn't eat turkey because Mama was preparing someone else's turkey at 3 o'clock . . . then around 6 o'clock she would get off the Alta Vista bus; then we would bring up the leftovers and eat our turkey."[12]

Who could gainsay such powerful sentiments? Only the crassest among us. And that is the wonder of television—it brings persons of great magnitude into our own, very modest living rooms. They share themselves with us, persons whom they have never met, persons whom they will never meet. Is it any wonder, then, that they become our lovers?

Intimacy, unfortunately, is a double-edged sword. The closer we get to someone, the more pain we suffer when they hurt us. Thus, when Mario Cuomo behaved like an electoral prima donna, or when Ann Richards refused to raise taxes for education, or when Jesse Jackson became self-serving, love turned to loathing instantly. How dare such friends-of-ours act like politicians? we reason. How can persons who have bared their souls to us now behave so expediently? How can they woo us only to rape us? Phrased this baldly, such reactions seem preposterous. But television's intimacies, I argue, encourage just such overreactions. With television, politics becomes melodrama and cycles set in: Charm begets adoration begets disappointment begets cynicism. The extraordinary thing about all this is how resilient some voters are in spite of it all—the senator from Alabama is caught with his hand in the till but the new senator from California promises true goodness. This is television's morality play.

Some politicians, no doubt, are better suited to personality politics than others. George Bush, for example, was an unlikely candidate. New Englander by birth, patrician by maturation, bureaucrat by training, George Bush had three strikes against him in the intimacy department when running for the presidency. But anyone with George Bush's résumé is sure to be a quick learner, and so when asked by ABC's Ann Compton in the third debate in 1988 what he had learned thus far from Michael Dukakis, Bush replied that he had learned the intimacy thing:

> Barbara and I were sitting there before the Democratic convention, and we saw the governor and his son on television the night before, and his family and his mother who was there. And I'm saying to Barbara, "You know, we've always kept family as a bit of an oasis for us." You all know me, and we've held it back a little. But we use that as a role model, the way he took understandable pride in his heritage, what his family means to him.
>
> And we've got a strong family and we watched that and we said, "Hey, we've got to unleash the Bush kids." And so you saw 10 grandchildren there jumping all over their grandfather at the, at the [Republican] convention.[13]

Intimacy, then, transcends party lines. Communication scholar Kathleen Hall Jamieson suggests, for example, that Ronald Reagan's personalized rhetorical style represented a "feminizing" of the presidency whereby the language of relationships supplanted the language of public policy.[14] Political scientist Barbara Hinckley has shown this to be true even when presidents talk about the economy. She reports, for example, that when delivering such addresses, presidents use substantially more thinking/feeling verbs than action verbs.[15] In other words, presidents may not be able to fatten our wallets but they can be distressed by our condition.

This is not a cynical statement. It simply dramatizes the powerful option television makes available. The world politicians inhabit—the real world, that is—provides few things they can manage with confidence. Wars break out suddenly; the stock market careens out of sight; urban unrest explodes without warning. A president is therefore constantly overpedaling to keep from backpedaling. The language of intimacy gives him an edge. With it, a president can show that he knows what he feels even if he does not know what to do. The language of intimacy gives him control. Of something.

Politicians are not alone responsible for this new style of politics. Media personnel aid and abet them. Consider, for example, the near-psychiatric interview Walter Cronkite conducted with Gerald Ford during the 1980 Republican national convention. At the time, speculation was adrift that Ronald Reagan might ask Mr. Ford to join him on the ticket. Communication scholar Rebecca Cline has shown the eerie parallel between Cronkite's interviewing style and the question-answer frame of the standard therapeutic encounter. Cline suggests that Cronkite's deft probing of Ford's psyche caused Ford to think seriously about a Reagan-Ford ticket for the first time. There, on national television, with Ronald Reagan watching mouth-agape, Mr. Cronkite asked his most tantalizing question:

> Mister President, the—there are a lot of governors and senators here who are talking about a draft-Ford movement, and there's even been some suggestion that Governor Reagan would support such a movement from the floor just to convince you, if you need any convincing—I don't think you do after the demonstration for you the other night here, but if you need any convincing—that the party wants you, needs you, feels that it is your duty to answer a call. What would happen if they got out there on that floor tonight or tomorrow and said, "It's got to be Gerald Ford"?[16]

What followed was much waxing and waning on Mr. Ford's part, much double-thinking and question-begging, but also some soul-searching. The best evidence suggests that the interview threw a substantial wrench into Reagan's convention machinery, as Ford explored Ford's feelings live and in color. Mr. Reagan, of course, ultimately took a different tack, but later vice presidential candidate Jack Kemp was surely correct when he complained that "television literally affected Reagan's decision. I got the feeling that Walter Cronkite was in the middle of history."[17]

"Couch questions" like Cronkite's are now standard fare in media reporting. They are asked of political candidates from the local to the national level. Sometimes they are asked belligerently and sometimes subtly but almost always they are asked:

> *Of Gary Hart*: "Some people say you remind them more of John Kennedy in both appearance and speaking style. Is that accidental or intentional?"[18]
>
> *To Walter Mondale*: "Are you concerned that Bert Lance, your newly appointed general campaign chairman, will remind too many voters about your association with former President Carter?"[19]
>
> *To Jesse Jackson*: "If the presidential race is hopeless in practical terms, will you feel personally bitter?"[20]

For the purposes of the argument being made here, it makes little difference how these questions were answered. Suffice it to say that all of them *were* answered and, almost always, they were answered in the same exploratory spirit in which they were asked.

Most of today's politicians were raised on this language of intimacy and can now speak it without media prompting. Senator Joe Biden, for example, provided his own autotherapy when withdrawing from the 1988 presidential race: "You [in the press] warned me what it was going to be like. I thought I knew. It's a tough arena. But I'm a big boy. . . . It's time for me to remind myself why I got involved in politics in the first place."[21] When he briefly stepped back into the presidential race he had stepped out of, Gary Hart was more brusque than Biden but even he could not resist self-examination during a *60 Minutes* interview: "I mean, I'm taking certain risks. The voters can say no. But even if they say no, I'll feel better about myself than if I'd just sat up there on that mountain, wondering."[22]

In an era of intimate politics, feeling good about oneself is everything. It is as if the "therapeutic '60s" were collectively thumbing their noses at the "entrepreneurial '90s" and declaring interiority king. At times, one has to pinch oneself to be reminded that all this is going on *in public.* Even alone, on a couch, in his office, Texan Jim Wright would have been pitiable when resigning his Congressional post under fire. But standing in the well of the House with the C-SPAN cameras rolling, he was infinitely sadder:

> Have I contributed unwittingly to this manic idea of frenzy, of feeding on other people's reputations? Have I caused a lot of this? So maybe I have. God, I hope I haven't. But maybe I have. Have I been too partisan? Too insistent? Abrasive? Too determined to have my way? Perhaps. If I've offended anybody in the other party, I'm sorry. I never meant to. I would not have done so intentionally.[23]

Viewers at home, needless to say, take in such stuff in great gulps. They are, by now, addicts. They did not blink, for example, when Ross Perot declared in 1992 that George Bush had started the Gulf War to prove his masculinity. That claim made psychological sense to them even if it was ludicrous politically, militarily, and economically. Teddy Kennedy, on the other hand, found only bunk in such psychologizing. In the fabled interview he granted Roger Mudd in November of 1979, for example, Kennedy lost virtually any chance he had of becoming the Democratic nominee. It was bad enough that he could not satisfactorily deal with the accident at Chappaquiddick that cost a young woman her life many years earlier, but even more damaging was the following meta-conversation:

Mudd: What is it about a—a so-called couch question that makes you feel uncomfortable? Is it—do—do you not like to talk about yourself in public? Is—does it—is it unmanly or what? I—I'm asking you for a serious answer.

Kennedy: Well, I don't—I mean, I think it's really left to—to others. I don't—I suppose I just don't like to talk about myself just generally. I'd rather talk about why I'm in public life, is because of my care and concern about—about using the—whatever influence or—that I have to—to move the—the process towards meeting the—goals which I care very deeply about. And I think that's what—what's important. . . .

Mudd: But I—I could go to 98 senators with a camera and set up an interview, and 97 of them would start every sentence 'I—I—I.' It is a characteristic of politicians that they like to talk about themselves. And my question is why aren't you that way?

Kennedy: (laughing) Why don't you ask them about why they like to talk about themselves.[24]

In an age of intimacy, there is no sin greater than Kennedy's. Not only was he rhetorically incompetent but he gave cultural offense as well. Electronic culture is indeed a kind of culture, after all, and it is rapidly becoming a bedrock of American culture also. So when Jimmy Carter confessed to feeling lust in his heart, when Ronald Reagan displayed graphics of his colon operation, and when Michael Dukakis responded almost pleasantly when asked (by CNN's Bernard Shaw) how he would feel if his wife were raped, they showed themselves to be patriots indeed. Unlike Teddy Kennedy, they knew that intimacy was something to be used, not felt. It is little wonder, then, that the harumph issued by the *Philadelphia Inquirer* about Gary Hart's candidacy in 1988 could be heard all across the land: "Here was a man who wanted to be the leader of the Free World, who wanted Americans to trust him with their lives by placing his finger on the nuclear button. But he would not trust them with his own private life."[25] In an age of intimacy, here is an epitaph truly.

Some might be tempted to dismiss the politics of disclosure as mere rhetorical fashion—we speak emotions today, computer chips tomorrow. But the language of intimacy is both wider and deeper than politicians. They speak it but it also speaks them. It speaks the media too and it speaks much of the U.S. citizenry. It also speaks a new model of politics and that is its most troubling feature. But one cannot dismiss its effects on politicians themselves. When the Self is transformed into political barter, what remains to be traded?

Media Conspiracies

Politicians are increasingly willing to risk their private selves because they have been goaded into it by television, although, as sociologist Michael Schudson reports, this tendency had been growing in the print press prior to the 1940s.[26] When it took to the airwaves, television made this tendency an act of faith. As a result, says communication researcher Joshua Meyrowitz, the "electronic media of communication have been eroding barriers between the politician's traditional back and front regions," thereby upsetting "the traditional balance between rehearsal and performance."[27] Meyrowitz supplies a fitting example: "In her post-election interview with Mr. and Mrs. Carter in 1976, Barbara Walters asked intimate questions concerning marriage, love letters, babies, mother-in-law problems, annoying habits, and single versus double beds in the White House. The Carters answered them all."[28]

Is all this mere vanity? In part it may be, although, given changing journalistic norms, politicians have had little choice but to traffic in intimacy. Perhaps as an indirect influence of television, for example, schoolchildren's textbooks now emphasize politicians' lives much more than they did before. One researcher found, for example, that eighth grade and high school government textbooks (the sorts of textbooks that used to explain the Constitution), now refer to individual chief executives three times as often as they did forty years ago.[29] Newspapers behave similarly, giving almost 90% more coverage to "robust, outgoing presidents" than to "quiet, reserved presidents."[30]

Time magazine is little different. Between 1945 and 1985, for example, presidents' emotional qualities were given far greater attention than their physical, social or intellectual attributes. In addition, "psychological" verbs ("felt," "hoped," "worried") dominated all other predicate structures in *Time*'s coverage, and interpersonal challenges to the president were given significantly more coverage than things such as stock market fluctuations, dwindling natural resources, congressional recalcitrance, or Third World tensions.[31]

As one of television's most obvious forerunners, *Time* magazine is a good place to examine elementary forms of personality politics, forms that television later caused to flower. Consider, for example, how *Time* reported the quite ordinary day of September 17, 1951, a day on which Harry Truman gave a routine speech and then toured flooded farmland. The article began (as *Time* so often does) by reading the President's thoughts: "Travel without politicking is more unthinkable to Harry Truman than a morning without a brisk walk."[32]

The beginning of the next sentence was also telling: "As if to prove it, he cancelled his regular walk . . . to try to make peace among California's demoralized, feuding Democrats." Here, *Time* quickly enters the presidential mind, linking Truman's personal habits (his daily walks) with ongoing political events (the feuding Democrats), thereby establishing its premise for the remainder of the article: that the California speech was a referendum on Harry Truman himself.

Employing classic dramatic form, *Time* recounted Truman's slow beginning in the speech (where "he stirred up little enthusiasm") and his sluggish second argument ("the audience was unimpressed"). But Truman was "undismayed" by these rebuffs, *Time* observed, and when he got around to the upcoming '52 election, the audience "got the idea, and the applause rolled out."

Time continued this personal theme by reporting that, after the speech, Mr. Truman "changed to a dark suit" for a second event and then "roared out of town aboard the *Independence*" for Kansas City (and the floods) on the next morning. He was "wide awake and watchful" during his tour of the farmland and later ended his stay in the midwest by dedicating a new armory. As it so often does, *Time* concluded its weekly coverage by again emphasizing private feelings, recounting the President's eminently forgettable but touchingly effective remarks at the armory dedication: "When I got my warrant as corporal, I think that was the proudest day I ever spent in the military. I never was a 2nd lieutenant, much to my regret."

What has really happened here? A speech, a black-tie dinner, a trip to the farm, a ribbon-cutting. Hardly the stuff out of which history is fashioned. But it is the stuff out of which popular journalism is fashioned and, perhaps, out of which citizens' visions of politics are fashioned. Here, *Time* implicitly argues that to understand the week of September 12, 1951, in the United States one also must understand what Harry Truman saw, what he did, what he said, and, most important, what he felt. *Time* packaged Mr. Truman's feelings as attractively as they could be packaged, using its breezy formulas to relegate all nonpersonal and nonpsychological news to the dustbin.[33]

In doing so, *Time's* writers practiced their craft admirably, making an otherwise dull week passably interesting. But in doing so, they also reinforced what seems to be a distinctive model of governance. *Time's* writers, and after them television's writers, have become captivated by this psychological model. But the television industry employs more than writers. It also employs camera operators. Television is a profoundly visual medium and so it does for the eye what the print media can only do for the imagination. Consider, for example, the size of the average television screen. What can it show . . . well? When it gives viewers a wide-angle shot, for instance, the objects in its foreground are only slightly larger than those in its background. When it uses multi-camera techniques, it can move our eye around from place to place to simulate movement but it never really feels, say, like a car chase in a twelve-screen movie theater. And so television gives us the best it can—faces. Faces fit its technology and faces fit its psychology. Faces fit its politics, too.

And that is how television's pictures of politics became its model of politics. Political scientist Doris Graber has documented, for example, that in a study of more than 2,000 visual scenes in 189 news stories, close-ups of politicians were the single most dominant visual image; more than 70% of the news stories had them and most stories had more close-ups than anything else.[34] Communication researcher Montague Kern shows this to be especially true for U.S. political coverage (as opposed to news broadcast in British Commonwealth nations).[35] Political scientist Scott Keeter has detailed the unsurprising results of facial politics: Candidates' personal qualities were found to be of far greater importance to television viewers than to newspaper readers, a trend that has held constant for every U.S. election since 1964.[36]

In other words, television turns faces into arguments. Where there is a face, voters reason, there is a mind, too; where there is a mind, there are emotions. Just as the audiophile feels that he or she can now hear "more music" because of advances in CD technology, so does the videophile feel justified in ferreting out the person behind the television screen. *What's My Line?*'s own Arlene Francis proclaimed this faith to the readers of *TV Guide* in 1960: "The TV camera has an x-ray attachment. It pierces, it penetrates, it peels away the veneer. It communicates the heart and mind of man."[37]

This, then, is television's model: Know the person, know the vote. With this model, television has given us a whole new world, a world that changes how we think as well as how we see. In a strange turn, one of television's greatest inadequacies—its small space—has become a primary gateway to perception. It has made us a nation of adventurers, persons willing to explore the face-minds of politics wherever they can be found. Television also has given us the perceptual courage needed for this journey, the kind of courage philosopher Walter Benjamin once described:

> Our taverns and our metropolitan streets, our offices and furnished rooms,
> our railroad stations and our factories appeared to have us locked up hope-

lessly. Then came the film and burst this prison-world asunder by the dynamite of the tenth of a second, so that now, in the midst of its far-flung ruins and debris, we calmly and adventurously go traveling.[38]

Television deconstructs the world in another sense as well. It takes its other great inadequacy—the enormous physical distance between what it shows and who it shows it to—and makes that distance an irrelevancy. It does so through a number of devices. Network correspondents, for example, talk to the candidates "for us" and then ordinary citizens from Topeka talk to the correspondents "for us" in person-on-the-street interviews At other times, the candidate turns to the camera and speaks to us "directly." On yet other occasions, we "overhear" informal conversation between the candidate and her family, as if we were there and not there simultaneously. And the great good thing about television is that this seeming does not seem like seeming. When television brings the faces of politicians close to us, it makes us forget that it is a medium (a device that comes between). Instead, it presents itself as window first; then open window; then no window. The candidate sits on *our* sofa. And we chat.

Given television's technological determinacies, therefore, it is little wonder that "the character issue" now dominates political reportage. Each evening, we embark on television's journey to the soul and then follow its serpentine route: First to Ross Perot's Napoleonic complex, ever forward to Bill Clinton's infidelities, then onward to Bob Dole's strange coldness. Media personnel stand ready to assist us but, by now, we hardly need their assistance. Television has become our conveyance; our destination is always the same— Psyche's place. Consider these data: (a) television reporters consistently probed the personalities of anti-war activists in the 1960s, thereby turning a political movement into a psychological excursion;[39] (b) television reporters addressed personality issues far more frequently during the 1980 presidential campaign than did print reporters;[40] (c) television reporters spent almost 50% of their time profiling the families and friends of those who were hijacked on TWA flight 847 in 1985, whereas the *New York Times* gave such matters only 13% of its coverage;[41] and (d) television reporters primarily use voter profiles to talk about a political candidate's personal strengths and weaknesses rather than the candidate's stands on the issues.[42]

By now, data like these are familiar to those who study politics. They are also familiar to the American people, although the latter are of two minds about such matters. A *Times/Mirror* poll, for example, found that almost 50%

of its respondents felt that "attention to candidates' private lives . . . crowded out discussion of the issues." On the other hand, when asked if they had paid "close" or "very close" attention to Bill Clinton's extramarital dalliances, a similar number—43%—reported that they had indeed.[43] And why not, one might ask? Is not politics a human process, after all? As such, should not matters of character figure prominently into something as important as a decision about who should lead us?

This is precisely the case that Duke University political scientist James David Barber has been making for the last thirty years. In his book, *The Presidential Character*,[44] Barber offered insightful profiles of modern chief executives, combining hard evidence and imaginative projections to round out his sketches. His sketches were created *post hoc*, of course, but Barber argues that such data are generally available to the serious voter during a campaign and that they should be used to make electoral decisions.

Barber's model has become the media's model and Professor Barber himself is often used to sanctify the media's dissections of candidates. *Time, People, Psychology Today, Fortune, TV Guide, Saturday Review* and most other popular magazines reexamine the Barber thesis every four years and almost always declare it valid.[45] Scholars,[46] as is their nature, have not always been as kind to the Barber model but that has hardly affected its popularity. For their part, television reporters have largely reduced political character to face-watching and political discourse to body language. A raised eyebrow here, an ill-timed laugh there. These have become the data of choice.

Rhetorically, of course, the character model is ideal for television. With vaults of video footage at their disposal, television producers can find evidence for any claim they might wish to make. The incumbent is alleged to be worried about the polls? Show him shaking hands nervously. The challenger feels intimidated by his wife's growing popularity? Assemble a collection of his public speaking gaffes. Through it all, the character model says this to voters: "Watch television. Issues confuse, character endures." And the character model says this to reporters: "Determine your argument. Supporting evidence is everywhere."

Evidence is everywhere because character is nowhere, literally. No matter how hardy it might be from a moral point of view, character is a pure creation for the media. In the hands of a television journalist, character comes into being the moment it is discussed. It then hovers around a candidate and ceases to exist only when it no longer creates interest. Because "character" attaches to a politician's inside and not his outside, it can never be falsified completely.

But it can be altered, which is to say, its plot-usefulness can change. Bill Clinton can be an inept manager in 1994, a brilliant steward of the national economy two years later. Character is therefore elastic. Reporters can shape it and reshape it, and pollsters can call it into being merely by calling it into being: "Do you think that Al Gore secretly fears intellectuals? Agree, disagree, . . ."

Because character is a central feature of narrative, that primordial source of human diversion, it can cause a politician's story to take a sudden, unexpected turn. But this does not mean that character is all things to all people. Because it is a rhetorical creation, character can be made to seem both specific and concrete: "Supreme Court Justice Clarence Thomas is ashamed that he is black. That's why he's so conservative." In a sense, then, character has both scientific and religious features. Like science, it is rooted in empirical fact (Thomas is black); like religion, it is both value-based (he's ashamed) and predictive (don't trust insincere conservatives).

Perhaps that is why the press never issues "character corrections." If a leader does something contrary to his or her alleged character, one of two things happens: (a) a new mold for that politician is invented and, over time, is subtly reinserted into his or her storyline, or (b) more layering is added to the old model so that the politician becomes an infinitely richer object of study. With either option, media personnel are allowed to speak with the same sense of authority. Politicians themselves conspire with television reporters in these ways and more. The result is what British theorist John Langer calls the "reign of intimacy" that now controls modern television.[47]

In all cases, such intimacies are attended by television's pictures, pictures that argue eloquently against their own, mediated natures. Because television's pictures are so mesmerizing, politicians have learned how to produce their own character profiles (for example, Ronald Reagan's gorgeous 1984 convention film, *Morning in America*) and the result is precisely what one author suggests: "Television's close-ups give us a more detailed look at our leaders than we have of most of our friends."[48]

Or so it seems. In fact, television gives us nothing of the kind. The "look" it gives us is precisely that—a look. Television gives us a seeing, an ogling more often, but it provides no real friendship. Friendship, that precious metal tested constantly in the blast furnace of daily existence, can hardly be found on television. Friendship, the real thing, is tested when our friends keep us from being foolish, or help our children find jobs, or comfort us at the gravesite. I, for one, have noticed few politicians at the gravesites I've attended.

We all know that intimacy, real intimacy, cannot be found in politics. But the mass media tell a different story. The technology of television socializes its workers: Because television can only deliver close-up pictures, its employees learn to write close-up stories. The result is that voters have close-up feelings at first, far-away feelings ultimately. As political scientist Murray Edelman has warned, the requirement to make each political figure seem different from every other political figure "strains" the resources of television, but it strains us too, making us ill-equipped to deal with the intractable, character-transcending problems of politics: enmity, injustice, calamity, human privation.[49]

Although personality politics keeps the media's narrative fluid, and although it keeps politics itself tidily compartmentalized, it comes at a price. For one thing, it perverts the very notion of character. To make character specular, something that is "read" onto another, is to make people one-dimensional. Character, real character, is a built-up phenomenon fashioned each day out of life's experiences. Character, the genuine article, is best seen in the clinches. It presents itself when least expected.

Televised character is none of these things. Its roots lie in air, not in earth. It is a manufactured product, not something that grows out of lived reality. And so it is important to calculate the costs of amateurism in political psychology. For voters, overindulgence in personality politics depletes them, as they nourish themselves on less and less civics and on more and more nuance and imagery. For the media, learning the Sentiment Beat in Washington can result in media preening, in the idolatrous love of power, in reportorial laziness. For governmental leaders, psychological politics can divert them from their appointed rounds as they watch themselves being watched by the media's always engaging watchers. Despite its attractions, that is, personality politics can make a society sick.

Other Causes

Thus far, we have traced the rise in personality politics to largely technological factors. Television features people because it is only a box with wires. As such, it does better with emotions than with ideas, the former being more visual than the latter. In addition, personality politics is attractive to the electronic media for rhetorical reasons. Television specializes in narrative and is therefore always story-hungry. Because narrative requires skillfully drawn characters and because political affairs have a colorful supply of same, a match is made.

But personality politics springs from other sources as well. Philosophically, for example, there is something typically Western about this model. Its roots lie in the "Romantic assumption that style could be read to uncover the character, or soul, of individuals and nations"[50] and they lie, too, in the classic American belief that people, especially great people, make a difference. As political scientist Timothy Cook has said, the current focus of news on "individual actors within continuing stories . . . dates back to the Progressive Era's emphasis on cleaning up the system by placing well-qualified individuals in positions of power to administer in a nonpartisan manner."[51] Media historian James Carey extends this theme when contrasting U.S. news coverage to Soviet coverage. In the Soviet press, says Carey, "individuals merely personify these larger forces [capitalism, history, imperialism, etc.] which are in the saddle driving the actions of individuals. But for us [Americans], individuals act. Individuals make history. Individuals have purposes and intentions."[52]

The happy side of personality politics, therefore, is a bedrock belief in the resiliency of the individual, in a New Progressivism. But there is also something quite old about personality politics—an almost pre-modern faith in the ability of the solitary individual to conquer great odds, even great technological odds. Television does particularly well with such stories: The man ultimately identified as the Unabomber, Ted Kaczynski, stood defiantly alone, thumbing his nose at the nation's legal machinery; basketball player Charles Barkley takes on all comers with a wink and a smile; astronauts Tom Akers and Rick Heib, exhausted but inventive, finally repair the wayward satellite during the Endeavor's space expedition.

There is something even older about personality politics, an almost Calvinist determinism whereby inborn character sets one's eternal clock in motion. Television appreciates this theme, too, because essentialism makes storytelling simple. That is why television's situation comedies feature stereotyped characters—the mouthy bartender, the doe-eyed librarian—and it is also why the mass media work so hard to get an early read on the candidates' personalities during the New Hampshire primaries: Who will be The Comic? The Malcontent? The Egghead? The Warrior?

These essentialist strains are laid out with special clarity by James David Barber. When analyzing recent elections, for example, Barber found much to his liking when observing that "journalists have increasingly focused on character, attempting to judge candidates not just by what they say they want to do . . . but by who they are and thus will be."[53] Neither Aristotle nor Kant could have made foundationalism plainer. Politicians have deposited within them good seeds and bad seeds; both will bear fruit. Monitoring such processes becomes the job of the television commentator. Like 16th century prelates, they recommit themselves each evening to the principles of predestination ("Is Gore protecting shadowy financiers in China?"), limited atonement ("Can Clinton expunge our memory of Paula Jones?"), and total depravity ("Gephardt has no charisma").

In each case, reporters connect the news of the day to themes previously established, taking care to keep the storyline uncompromised and unconfusing. Why do we find such unidimensionality attractive? Political scientist Richard Merelman suggests that a large, complex society such as the United States is a "loosely bounded"[54] culture in which the day-to-day tendernesses once afforded by rural life are no longer possible. In a mass society, says Merelman, intimate disclosures become a token of group commitment ("one holds nothing back") and sharing emotions becomes a *lingua franca,* a way of reestablishing tribal connections.[55] According to sociologist Richard Sennett, the middle class is especially attracted to the myth of the "private man inside the public man"[56] that results in such a society, ostensibly because the middle class can literally *afford* to be speculative.

In addition, if social philosopher Claus Offe is correct that the traditional political structures of class, ethnicity and region are breaking down in mass society, it may also be true that modern Americans are willing to pay any price for intimacy.[57] That is, their loving Governor Pete Wilson or hating Pete Wilson may have nothing to do with governance at all. Instead, politics may simply be a convenient site for making contact with others. Life at city hall, of course, has always given people something to talk about at work. But television brings voters "closer" to their political leaders, thereby making each of them a political authority and, hence, an important communal participant.[58]

Perhaps the most direct explanation for personality politics is psychological. We are, says French philosopher Jean Baudrillard, in an age of "forced extroversion of all interiority."[59] If Baudrillard is correct, perhaps the search for political intimacy is simply a variation on a larger cultural theme. The great bloc of active voters in the 1990s, after all, either are children of the 1960s or have been "culturally contaminated" by the 1960s. They are the children of Abraham Maslow and Carl Rogers, of Consciousness IIII, of group therapy and psychobabble. They are the children of mind-expanding drugs and nude encounters, of acid rock and bralessness. They are the children of Freud, not Marx. Writing in 1968, Philip Rieff expressed their worldview well:

> Our cultural revolution does not aim, like its predecessors, at victory for some rival commitment, but rather at a way of using all commitments, which amounts to loyalty toward none. By psychologizing about themselves interminably, Western men are learning to use their internality against the primacy of any particular organization of personality. If this re-structuring of the Western imagination succeeds in establishing itself, complete with institutional regimens, then human autonomy from the compulsions of culture may follow the freedoms already won from the compulsions of nature. With such a victory, culture, as previously understood, need suffer no further defeats. It is conceivable that millennial distinctions between inner and outer experience, private and public life, will become trivial. The individual heart need have no reasons of its own that the corporate head cannot understand and exploit for some augmentation of the individual's sense of well-being.[60]

Reiff has all the 1960s code words here: revolution, internality, autonomy, freedom, well-being. Unfortunately, the 1970s and 1980s would have none of it. Politics continued to be politics: war, then peace, ecological imbalance, a deteriorating infrastructure, an unstable Mideast, banking scandals. But the *language* of the 1960s remained. More important, it crept into politics. As a "society obsessed with 'personality,' self-cultivation, and the search for uninterrupted exuberance,"[61] says James David Barber, how could it not? But it did more than creep into politics. It now threatens to dominate it.

That is, although examining the private lives of politicians has long been fair game for the press, it now seems to be the only game. During their lives, for example, numerous presidents were denounced from the pulpits of the day: George Washington for not taking communion, Thomas Jefferson for sleeping with his slaves, Andy Jackson for being an adulterer, Grover Cleveland for having a bastard child, and Woodrow Wilson for remarrying too soon.[62] But two points need to be made about these cases: (a) media outlets at the time were less intertwined and less imitative and so such attacks could not constitute a theme as easily as today; and (b) the presidents' putative behaviors, not their motives, dominated the agenda.

Things are different today. Today, all is motive. Communication scholar Eva Illouz reports, for example, that "para-scientific discourses" have grown up to interpret male-female relationships and to tell women that power imbalances are best dealt with through relabeling ("You aren't underpaid, you're misunderstood.")[63] In such a model, sexism becomes less a political crime than a semantic one. At first such a notion seems absurd, but that discounts its rhetorical power. Consider, for example, how Richard Nixon once explained Watergate:

> I'm convinced that if it hadn't been for Martha [Mitchell], and God rest her soul, because she, in her heart, was a good person. She just had a mental and emotional problem that nobody knew about. If it hadn't been for Martha, there'd have been no Watergate, because John wasn't minding that store. He was letting Magruder and all these kids, these nuts, run this thing. Now, am I saying here, at this juncture, that Watergate should be blamed on Martha Mitchell? Of course not. I'm trying to explain my feeling of compassion for my friend, John Mitchell.[64]

We have, here, a primer for intimate politics: Offer an opinion, not a fact; make it observational, not existential; make it psychological, not moral; make it personal, not institutional. Who can resist such psychodrama? John Mitchell's head was in the wrong place and so he goofed. The perpetrator of the villainy, Martha Mitchell, did not mean to sin. The criminal children of Watergate—the Hunts and the Colsons—were mentally unstable and hence forgivable. Mr. Nixon himself felt compassion and that gives him two points— one for feeling an emotion (a universal good in personality politics) and another for feeling an unselfish emotion (the best kind).

The 1991 hearings into Professor Anita Hill's charges of sexual harassment against would-be Supreme Court Justice Clarence Thomas were also a field day for the politics of intimacy. Television covered the hearings extensively and the nation's citizens became glued to their sets, some into the wee hours of the morning. Their interest in the proceedings were, in part at least, of the soap opera variety and the hearings did not disappoint:

Senator Hefflin: Do you have a martyr complex? . . .

Ms. Hill: I do not have that kind of complex. I don't like all of the attention that I am getting. I don't—I would not—even if I liked the attention I would not lie to get attention.

Senator Hefflin: Well, the issue of fantasy has arisen. You are—have a degree in psychology from the University of—Oklahoma State University.

Ms. Hill: Yes.

Senator Hefflin: And you studied in your psychology studies when you were in school and what you may have followed up with, the question of fantasies. Have you ever studied that from a psychology basis?

Ms. Hill: To some extent, yes.

Senator Hefflin: What do you—what are the traits of fantasy that you studied, as you remembered?

Ms. Hill: As I remember, it would have—it would require some other indi-cation of loss of touch with reality other than one instance. There is no indication that I'm an individual who is not in touch with reality on a regular basis that would be subject to fantasy.[65]

During the hearings, Anita Hill—the Yale-trained lawyer—went on to outline certain notions of Jungian-type repression. Clarence Thomas specu-lated about the psychosocial conditions that cause family members to become embittered with one another. Witness John Doggett, unquestionably the most adventurous of the lay psychiatrists, detailed a tolerably complete theory of how a woman's body language betrays her attraction to a dominant but distant male—himself. In between, the members of the Senate Judiciary committee walked down numerous hallways of the modern mind and the media asked mental health professionals to comment on the proceedings. For all partici-pants, the therapeutic ethos prevailed. Even Anita Hill became caught up in it: "I think he [Thomas] wanted to see me vulnerable, and if I were vulnerable, then he could extract from me whatever he wanted, whether it was sexual or otherwise—that I would be at his—under his control."[66]

The popular interest shown in the Thomas-Hill hearings makes one ambivalent. For one thing, the American people paid attention to something important—the sexual exploitation of women—and that is good. They also paid attention to something political—the nomination of a Supreme Court justice—and that is good as well. If the hearings served to heighten the nation's consciousness about sexual harassment, or the kind of consensus now possible on the Supreme Court, or even the gender imbalance of the Senate Judiciary committee, that too would be good.

But there are also questions to ask about the hearings. At what point did the viewership's political interest end and their titillation begin? Why did the size of the Thomas-Hill audience dwarf that of, say, a C-SPAN audience for a Congressional debate on pay equity? Why are the American people so obsessed by questions of political motive ("Did he mean to?") and so hard to interest in matters of political fact ("Did he?")? For what others sorts of issues would the major networks relinquish three days of air time in support of the commonweal?

As the millennium approaches, the psychology of politics is a siren song. When sung by the mass media, it is eminently sweet and distracting. But that song has consequences for any ship of state. Those consequences were forecast in 1927 by an astute observer of public life—John Dewey. He warned that "Even now, popular psychology is a mass of cant, of slush and of superstition worthy of the most flourishing days of the medicine man."[67] Perceptive though he was, Dewey could hardly have imagined a medium—television—that would later make art from slush. Such an invention would have concerned Dewey and it would have concerned one of his contemporaries, Walter Lippmann, as well.

But history would prove Lippmann wrong on at least one count. Said Lippman in 1925: "The citizen gives but a little of his time to public affairs, has a casual interest in facts but a poor appetite for theory."[68] Americans today have little time for public affairs but they are now filled with theory—psychological theory. They speak that theory fluently and unselfconsciously. They use it to explain their voting patterns and their nonvoting patterns. The theory they speak is a rich and encompassing one, for they have had master teachers: their political rulers and their rulers' interpreters—the press. It is a comforting thing, this theory, and it abides in them. But all theories have consequences. As we have seen here, personality politics is no exception.

Conclusion

Here is a hard thing to understand: Television is an arbitrary art form. Nothing—nothing—requires that it make politics personal. Instead of asking a Buffalo congressman couch questions, television personnel could film pollution in Lake Erie. Instead of discussing his boyhood in Texarkana, Ross Perot could have been forced to be clearer about gay rights when he ran for the presidency. Television presents politics as it does because doing so is the simplest and sexiest thing to do. Often, this turns politics into a synecdoche—

an endeavor that comes to stand for all human endeavors. Each evening on the nightly news, Greed, Lust, Envy, and, occasionally, Honor stride the boards. The drama of statecraft becomes the human drama, and politics is reduced to a theatrical convenience.

In some ways, personality politics constitutes a new heresy, today's counterpart to the cult of the saints that flourished in Europe in the early and middle ages. Like modern politics, the cult of the saints eroded the barrier between the private and the public by joining "Heaven and Earth at the grave of a dead human being."[69] That is, the cult reverenced martyrs and other superior individuals and "the tomb of the saint was declared public property as the tomb of no other Christian was: it was made accessible to all, and became the focus of forms of ritual common to the whole community."[70] Redirecting worship in these ways gave religion both localism and immediacy. It permitted saintly individuals to be seen and, in some cases, touched as well. Lucilla of Carthage, for example, a Spanish noblewoman, owned the bone of a martyr and was "in the habit of kissing it before she took the Eucharist."[71]

Possessing the saints in these literal and figurative ways gave concreteness to religion. It also gave some individuals heightened credibility. For instance, one church leader, Ambrose, was heavily responsible for discovering the bodies of the martyrs Gervasius and Protasius. Celebrating that fact, he once declared, "Although this is a gift from God . . . I cannot deny the grace and favor which the Lord Jesus has bestowed on the time of my priesthood; for because I have not gained the status of a martyr, I have at least acquired these martyrs for you."[72]

In many ways, Ambrose sounds like a modern television executive. Like them, he seized on the lives of exceptional individuals and linked the particular with the universal, the mortal with the immortal. Ambrose peopled religion, just as network executives try to people politics. At least in part, both do so for honorable reasons—to teach and to motivate. But the cult of the saints was not without cost. It individualized religion and therefore turned people's eyes from the godhead. More functionally, it localized religion and thereby threatened Rome's authority. By erecting a pantheon of the blessed, the cult of the saints made religion, at least in part, game-like.

Perhaps that is also true with personality politics. Despite its attractions, then, we must ask: Is it good for us? Do we really need a new cult of saints and sinners? Is it the case that we now find meaning only through what historian Luke Demaitre has called hagiotherapy?[73] When politics bends toward us by becoming intimate, can it also break? Because these questions deal with politics, they cannot be unimportant. Because they deal with television, they cannot be uninteresting. For both reasons, we must confront them.

Notes

1. R. Hart, *Verbal Style and the Presidency: A Computer-Based Analysis* (New York: Academic Press, 1984), 47.

2. "Remarks to the American Society of Newspaper Editors," April 16, 1975, *Weekly Compilations of Presidential Documents*, 11:16 (1975), 389.

3. Quoted in Christopher Lydon, "Jimmy Carter Revealed," *Atlantic Monthly*, July 1977, 56.

4. J. Carter, "Address to the Nation on Energy and National Goals," July 15, 1979, *Weekly Compilations of Presidential Documents*, 15:29 (1979), 12367.

5. F. Cormier, *LBJ the Way He Was* (New York: Doubleday, 1977), 137.

6. Quoted in M. Miller, *Plain Speaking: An Oral Biography of Harry S Truman* (New York: Berkley Medallion, 1973), 288.

7. R. Hart, *The Sound of Leadership: Presidential Communication in the Modern Age* (Chicago: University of Chicago Press, 1987). For information about the most recent chief executives, see S. Kernell, *Going Public: New Strategies of Presidential Leadership*, 3rd Edition (Washington, DC: Congressional Quarterly Press, 1997).

8. R. Hart, P. Jerome, and K. McCombs, "Rhetorical Features of Newscasts about the President," *Critical Studies in Mass Communication, 1* (1984), 260-286.

9. N. Miller, and W. Stiles, "Verbal Familiarity in American Presidential Nomination Acceptance Speeches and Inaugural Addresses, 1920-1981," *Social Psychology Quarterly, 49* (1986), 72-81. A related finding is reported by Harold Zullow and his colleagues who found that during the last 40 years, the most "optimistic" nominating speaker has always been elected president. See H. Zullow et al., "Pessimistic Explanatory Style in the Historical Record: CAVing LBJ, Presidential Candidates, and East Versus West Berlin," *American Psychologist, 43* (1988), 678.

10. M. Cuomo, "Keynote Address to the Democratic National Convention," *Vital Speeches of the Day*, August 15, 1984, 649.

11. A. Richards, "Keynote Address at the Democratic National Convention," *Vital Speeches of the Day*, August 15, 1988, 647.

12. J. Jackson, "Common Ground and Common Sense," *Vital Speeches of the Day*, August 15, 1988, 653.

13. G. Bush, "Presidential Debate of October 10, 1988," *Historic Documents of 1988-1989* (Washington, DC: Congressional Quarterly, Inc., 1989), 765.

14. K. Jamieson, *Eloquence in an Electronic Age: The Transformation of Political Speechmaking* (New York: Oxford, 1988), 67-89.

15. B. Hinckley, *The Symbolic Presidency: How Presidents Portray Themselves* (New York: Routledge, 1990), 70-73.

16. Quoted in R. Cline, "The Cronkite-Ford Interview at the 1980 Republican National Convention: A Therapeutic Analogue," *Central States Speech Journal, 36* (1985), 102.

17. Quoted in Cline, 93.

18. "A Majority of People Want a Break with the Past," *U.S. News & World Report*, March 26, 1984, 25.

19. "America Needs a President, not a Salesman," *U.S. News & World Report*, July 30, 1984, 22.

20. R. Scheer, "Playboy Interview: Jesse Jackson," *Playboy*, June 1984, 188.

21. J. Biden, "Remarks upon Withdrawing from the 1988 Presidential Race," McNeil/Lehrer News Hour, PBS, September 23, 1987.

22. Quoted in H. Hertzberg, "Monster from the Id," *New Republic*, January 18, 1988, 14.

23. J. Wright, "Partial Text of Wright's Resignation Speech," *Washington Post*, June 1, 1989, A18.

24. R. Mudd, "Teddy," CBS Documentary, November, 14, 1979.

25. "Hart's Fall: A Refusal to Accept Character as an Issue," *Philadelphia Inquirer*, May 10, 1987, E1.

26. M. Schudson, "The Politics of Narrative Form: The Emergence of News Conventions in Print and Television," *Daedalus*, 111 (1982), 97.

27. J. Meyrowitz, *No Sense of Place: The Impact of Electronic Media on Social Behavior* (New York: Oxford University Press, 1985), 270-271.

28. Meyrowitz, 290. Alan Hirsch has shown how television also emphasizes the personalities of its journalists: "The opening of these [talk] shows is revealing: *Capital Gang* prominently displays the names of the four participants; *Inside Washington* displays a montage of the participants; *The McLaughlin Group* shows the participants within the frame of a newspaper front page, suggesting that they themselves are the news. On *Capital Gang* the cult of personality runs especially high. Al Hunt frequently depicts Robert Novak as a silly hypocrite while Novak returns the favor, characterizing Hunt and Mark Shields as fuzzy-headed naifs. The participants, rather than the issues they are discussing, become the central drama." See A. Hirsch, *Talking Heads: Political Talk Shows and Their Star Pundits* (New York: St. Martin's, 1991), 70-71.

29. D. Smith-Howell, "Using the Past in the Present: The Rhetorical Construction of the Presidency," Unpublished doctoral dissertation, University of Texas at Austin, 1993, 75.

30. R. Streitmatter, "The Impact of Presidential Personality on News Coverage in Major Newspapers," *Journalism Quarterly*, 62 (1985), 68-69.

31. R. Hart, D. Smith-Howell, and J. Llewellyn, "The Mindscape of the Presidency, *Time* Magazine, 1945-1985," *Journal of Communication*, 41 (1991) 6-25. For corroborating data of this sort, see D. Graber, "Seeing Is Remembering: How Visuals Contribute to Learning From Television News," *Journal of Communication*, 40:3 (1990), 149.

32. "Words for the Faithful," *Time*, September 17, 1951, 21.

33. This, and the preceding three paragraphs, have been adapted from Hart et al., 21-22.

34. Graber, 1990.

35. M. Kern, *Thirty-Second Politics: Political Advertising in the Eighties* (New York: Praeger, 1989).

36. S. Keeter, "The Illusion of Intimacy: Television and the Role of Candidate Personal Qualities in Voter Choice," *Public Opinion Quarterly*, 51 (1987), 344-358.

37. Quoted in J. Gamson, "The Assembly Line of Greatness: Celebrity in Twentieth-Century America," *Critical Studies in Mass Communication*, 9 (1992), 6.

38. W. Benjamin, "The Work of Art in the Age of Mechanical Reproduction," in H. Arendt (ed.), *Illuminations* (New York: Schocken Books, 1969), 236.

39. T. Gitlin, *The Whole World Is Watching: Mass Media in the Making and Unmaking of the New Left* (Berkeley: University of California Press, 1980), 53-54.

40. M. Robinson and M. Sheehan, *Over the Wire and on TV: CBS and UPI in Campaign '80* (New York: Russell Sage, 1983).

41. D. Elliott, "Family Ties: A Case Study of Coverage of Families and Friends During the Hijacking of TWA Flight 847," *Political Communication and Persuasion*, 5 (1988), 67-75.

42. F. Smoller, "Presidents and Their Critics: The Structure of Television News Coverage," *Congress and the Presidency*, 1 (1988), 75-89.

43. As reported in E. Dennis et al., *Covering the Presidential Primaries* (New York: The Freedom Forum Studies Center, 1992), 54.

44. J. D. Barber, *The Presidential Character: Predicting Performance in the White House* (Englewood Cliffs, NJ: Prentice Hall, 1972).

45. See, for example, "Cycle Races," *Time*, May 19, 1980, 29; "Three Old Sagas in American Politics," *Psychology Today*, March, 1980, 61-71; "A Critic's View of Reagan's Tussles with the Truth," *People*, March 9, 1987, 40-42; "Tone-Deaf in the Oval Office," *Saturday Review*, January 12, 1974, 10-14; "Those Presidential Debates: How to Tell the Show Biz from the Substance," *TV Guide*, September 3, 1988, 28-29; and "Bush vs. Dole: What They'd Be Like as President," *Fortune*, February 15, 1988, 58-65.

46. See, for example, A. George, "Assessing Presidential Character," *World Politics, 27* (1974), 234-282; E. Hargrove, "Presidential Popularity and Revisionist Views of the Presidency," *American Journal of Political Science, 17* (1973), 819-835; R. Merelman, "The Promise of Political Psychology: A Critique and an Alternative," *Political Psychology, 11* (1990), 419-433; and R. Tatalovich and W. D. Byron, *Presidential Power in the United States* (Monterey, CA: Brooks/Cole, 1984), 393.

47. J. Langer, "Television's 'Personality System,' " *Media, Culture and Society, 4* (1981), 354.

48. Jamieson, 62.

49. M. Edelman, *Constructing the Political Spectacle* (Chicago: University of Chicago Press, 1988), 49.

50. K. Cmiel, *Democratic Eloquence: The Fight over Popular Speech in Nineteenth-Century America* (New York: Morrow, 1990), 156.

51. T. Cook, "Thinking of the News Media as Political Institutions." Paper presented at the annual convention of the American Political Science Association, San Francisco, California, August, 1990, 9.

52. J. Carey, "The Dark Continent of American Journalism," in R. Manoff and M. Schudson (eds.), *Reading the News* (New York: Pantheon, 1987), 182.

53. J. D. Barber, "The Promise of Political Psychology," *Political Psychology, 11* (1990), 180.

54. R. Merelman, *Making Something of Ourselves: On Culture and Politics in the United States* (Berkeley: University of California Press, 1984), 103.

55. Merelman, 106.

56. R. Sennett, *The Fall of Public Man* (New York: Knopf, 1977), 27.

57. C. Offe, "Challenging the Boundaries of Institutional Politics: Social Movements Since the 1960s," in C. S. Maier (ed.), *Changing Boundaries of the Political: Essays on the Evolving Balance between the State and Society, Public and Private* (Cambridge, England: Cambridge University Press, 1987), 74.

58. An extension of this kind of thinking is offered by sociologist Peter Berger and his colleagues who argue that a "pluralization of life worlds" has made modern Americans anxious in a number of important ways and that we suffer from "a deepening condition of 'homelessness' " as a result. These conditions, they say, are occasioned by our mobile, media-saturated society. Perhaps this explains why politicians try so hard to seem "domesticated"—cheerful, friendly, and unpretentious—a bulwark against modern bureaucratization and alienation. In Berger's terms, perhaps we are still looking for the whole individual. See P. Berger, B. Berger, and H. Kellner, *The Homeless Mind* (New York: Random House, 1973), 78-79, 82, 212-214.

59. J. Baudrillard, "The Ecstacy of Communication," in H. Foster (ed.), *The Anti-Aesthetic: Essays on Postmodern Culture* (Port Townsend, WA: Bay Press, 1983), 132.

60. P. Rieff, *The Triumph of the Therapeutic: Uses of Faith after Freud* (New York: Harper, 1968), 21-22. Perhaps reflecting related cultural and historical changes, even diary writing betrays such influences. Comparing 19th century to 20th century diaries, researchers found "a shift, in general, from social role and traditional institutional categories to categories of emotion, sense experience, and spontaneous action." See M. Wood, and L. Zurcher, *The Development of a Postmodern Self: A Computer-assisted Analysis of Personal Documents* (New York: Greenwood, 1988), 129.

61. J. D. Barber, "The Candidates' Analysts," in W. D. Pederson (ed.), *The "Barberian" Presidency* (New York: Peter Lang, 1989), 52.

62. E. Goldman, "Can Public Men Have Private Lives?" *New York Times Magazine*, June 16, 1963, 13, 60-61.

63. E. Illouz, *Consuming the Romantic Utopia: Love and the Cultural Contradictions of Capitalism* (Berkeley: University of California Press, 1997). In a similar vein, Sanford Schram notes that, for many people, Dan Quayle's wealth was not an onerous problem. They were only concerned that his financial *motives* were honorable: "The issue was whether he had been forthright in his use of wealth. It did not matter whether Quayle was extremely rich, only whether he was disingenuously rich." See "The Post-Modern Presidency and the Grammar of Electronic Engineering," *Critical Studies in Mass Communication*, 8 (1991), 213.

64. As quoted in R. Rosenblatt, "The Staff Ate My Homework," *Time*, March 8, 1982, 95.

65. "Anita Hill's Response to Senator Howell Hefflin," October 11, 1991, *Senate Judiciary Committee Hearings on the Clarence Thomas Nomination to the Supreme Court* (Washington, DC: Federal Information Systems Corporation, 1991).

66. Ibid. For more on the therapeutic ethos, see D. Cloud, *Control and Consolation in American Culture and Politics: The Rhetoric of Therapy* (Thousand Oaks, CA: Sage, 1998).

67. J. Dewey, *The Public and Its Problems* (Chicago: Gateway, 1946), 165. Perhaps the best example of Dewey's point lies in the rhetoric of Ronald Reagan who once probed the psychosocial dynamics of poverty and concluded that America's homeless actually wished to live in the streets. See J. C. Goldfarb, *The Cynical Society: The Culture of Politics and the Politics of Culture* (Chicago: University of Chicago Press, 1991), 154.

68. W. Lippmann, *The Phantom Public* (New York: Harcourt, 1925), 24-25.

69. P. Brown, *The Cult of the Saints: Its Rise and Function in Latin Christianity* (Chicago: University of Chicago Press, 1981), 1.

70. Brown, 9.

71. Brown, 34.

72. Quoted in Brown, 95.

73. L. Demaitre, "Insanity, Treatment of," in J. R. Strayer (ed.), *Dictionary of the Middle Ages*," Vol. 6 (New York: Scribner's, 1985), 492.

Box 2.1 Inquiries and Transitions

Television reveals its greatest power when it appears powerless, when it seems to have told all there is to tell without guile or purpose. How, then, are we to cope with the seductions of an ostensibly non-seductive medium? Who among us can resist the personal narratives television tells so well? What explains why a nation like the U.S., a nation that repudiates royalty, the maldistribution of wealth, and an excessive love of the past, cried its eyes out over the passing of Britain's Princess Diana? How did Americans become attached to this young woman who spent most of her life spending money? Why were shopkeepers in Omaha caught up in the family dysfunctionalities and palace intrigue surrounding her death? Television made all these things possible. But television takes as well as gives; it builds up certain personalities today—Winnie Mandela, for example, and Donald Trump—only to tear them down tomorrow. And so what happens to governance when voters become transfixed by larger-then-life personalities? What keeps them hopeful when their leaders prove fallible once again? Television's personality profiles charm us, engage us, and make us forget the uncomfortable; they become our favorite, exotic destinations. But who keeps the home fires burning when we are away?

Feeling Informed

The Effects of Personality Politics

As the 1992 election season rolled around, the American people were in a foul mood. Despite a successful military operation in the Persian Gulf, historic disintegrations in the former Soviet Union, the arrival of a more accommodating government in Israel, and even a subtle uptick in the domestic economy, the American people were inconsolable. They had their reasons. One of their most fabled cities had almost burned to the ground. National unemployment approached double-digits, the highest such rate in 10 years. Test scores for the nation's schoolchildren continued to be depressed (and depressing). Japanese competitive pressures threatened to overwhelm the United States financially and culturally. Only two sources of comfort emerged: the subtle imperialism of the new Euro-Disney in France and the less subtle imperialism of the U.S. Olympic basketball team.

Things were different four years later. Bill Clinton rode back into office because of a strong domestic economy and an uncanny ability to please the American people without satisfying them. But in a real sense, Mr. Clinton owed his election in 1992 and 1996 to one man—Ross Perot. In 1992, Perot helped generate the anti-incumbent fever from which Bill Clinton profited, and by 1996 Clinton had put into place much of the Perot platform— reduction of government services, a refusal to kowtow to the unions, linkage with an international economy, the embracing of high technology. Bill Clinton was a New Democrat but he was also warmed-over Perot.

Despite its leader's millions, the Perot campaigns of 1992 and 1996 were largely grassroots affairs. The ranks of campaign workers were swelled by an assemblage of malcontents—later middle-aged members of the middle class, ex-military personnel and their families, unemployed white collar workers, Southerners and suburbanites—and they worked feverishly to place Mr. Perot's name on the ballots in the 50 states. His political appeal was almost totally oxymoronic. He was an "outsider" who had made billions by milking federal and state programs, a hard-charging capitalist who had become the darling of educational leaders in Texas, a crewcut hawk who was also pro-choice. A t-shirt distributed by his admirers summed up this walking antithesis of a candidate: "He's like us, only richer."

Remarkable though Perot's achievements were historically, they were less surprising psychologically. With television now playing a dominant role in political campaigns, a Perot candidacy was not only conceivable in 1992 but almost mandatory. Two years earlier, one of Perot's fellow Texans—Clayton Williams—almost bought himself a governorship via paid advertising. Like Perot, Williams had never held political office and, like Perot, he was both self-made and opinionated. But even Clayton Williams had to muscle his way through the Republican primary in Texas (ironically by beating Tom Luce, who would later become Mr. Perot's personal advisor) and thus had the benefit of a political infrastructure. Not so Ross Perot. Mr. Perot had only his gumption, his money, and our television sets. Not a bad start for a would-be president.

Given the rise of the independent voter in the last 50 years, Ross Perot was a phenomenon waiting to happen. In 1946, when television first became commercially viable, roughly 20% of the American people declared themselves independents. Recently, that number has climbed closer to 33%.[1] Numerous explanations have been offered for this sea-change in American politics: the parties have been "bought by special interests"; national party leaders have lost contact with their state and local counterparts; and the parties have become intellectually bankrupt.[2] There is at least one other explanation: Television has given the American people a "sense of knowing" that sustains them during the political blizzard. By making politics personal, television empowers the voter, encouraging him or her to use universal criteria when making political judgments, the same criteria used when choosing a spouse or a golfing partner. Television's encouragements are subtle but, as we have seen in Chapter 2, they are also insistent. They tell us to trust our personal antennae and they tap our confidence in being able to spot a phony when we meet one.

In other words, the politics of intimacy reinforces a primitive way of learning—through other people. In 1996, that epistemology told (some) Republicans in the New Hampshire primary that Steve Forbes' ability to manage a New York City magazine was equivalent to Bob Dole's experience in managing the U.S. Senate. In an age of the political maverick, that is, one is constantly invited to ask: Why trust party hacks instead of one's intuitions? In an age of television, such an invitation is supremely attractive. It makes reading position papers, or even reading the headlines, an irrelevancy. By getting to know Mr. Perot or Mr. Forbes personally—through television, rather than through the public record—the American electorate could cleanse itself by abandoning both party structures and structural forms of thought at the same time. And so, incongruously, many Americans came to feel like lone-wolves when watching the advertising blitzes paid for by Messrs. Forbes and Perot. They came to "trust their own eyes" even though two billionaires had paid a fortune to rent their eyes.

Over the years, some authors have complained that the media's effects on campaign scheduling and financing have given them an unseemly amount of influence over political affairs.[3] Others argue that television's modes of visual presentation produce cognitive laziness among voters and thus guarantee information loss in a campaign.[4] Yet other scholars worry that television's avoidance of the issues threatens to undermine the political process.[5] These are all distressing matters, but I am distressed by something else in this chapter—the habits of thought television encourages. It is these habits that most gravely threaten the polity.

As communication scholars have argued, the medium of an age determines how the people of that age will think.[6] In a similar manner, says philosopher Guy Debord, capitalism protects itself not by selling products but by selling the habit of consumption: "By means of a ruse of commodity logic, what's specific in the commodity wears itself out in the fight while the commodity-form moves toward its absolute realization."[7] This is also true of televised politics: If today's lover disappoints, another must be sought—instantly—because a world without political love is unthinkable. In other words, personality politics is a *model*, a way of seeing the world. Because they understood that model, Steve Forbes and Ross Perot tried to rewrite American political history. Television was their scribe.

Learning About Politics

In discussing the effects of television, one must be careful not to repeat common, often thoughtless, critiques of the medium. As communication scholar Joli Jensen has argued, many of these attacks are unconscionably elitist and therefore "fundamentally disrespectful of popular experience."[8] Indeed, in many ways television is a modern miracle. It brings people into contact with new and strange ideas; it puts revolutionary happenings into historical context; it reminds us each day that we do not inhabit the planet alone. Because of television, shut-ins can get a college education, preschoolers can learn their ABCs, and the despised few, of whatever political persuasion, can share their views on cable access channels. Television can make old age less lonely and adolescence less traumatic. Television's clowns help us all laugh.

Politically, however, television's record is a mixed one. People with a grade-school education watch far more television than those with a college education (21.3 hours/week vs. 11.3 hours/week),[9] a fact that can be seen as either heartening or depressing. The upside was captured by sociologists Paul Lazarsfeld and Robert Merton in 1948 when they opined: "That the mass media have lifted the level of information of large populations is evident."[10] Communication researchers Peter Clarke and Eric Fredin put a finer point on it when they argued that the more a citizen is exposed to television news, the more he or she can recall specific pieces of political information.[11]

In this same vein, scholars have found that television was especially helpful for informing persons with "low cognitive skills" about Ronald Reagan's Star Wars program,[12] for example, and other researchers have shown that television has helped Korean immigrants adjust to social life in the United States. As communication scholar Steve Chaffee and his colleagues have stated, "the mass media are, when it comes to political socialization, agents of 'education' on a par with schooling itself."[13] Finally, John Naisbitt suggests in *Megatrends* that the mass media have leveled the playing field of politics by insuring that because we "instantaneously share information, we know as much about what's going on as our representatives and we know it just as quickly."[14]

There are more ominous findings to consider, however. In a 1986 survey, for example, respondents were presented with the names of the sitting vice president, the senate minority leader, the Speaker of the House, the Chief Justice of the Supreme Court, and several other major political figures. Less than 4% of the sample got all occupations correct.[15] On another front, if asked to tell the name of their Congressional representative today, 62% of the American people would fail that test; this same percentage—62%—would be unable to tell which party controlled the House of Representatives in Washington.[16] Another study found that even though Americans now average 12.6 years of schooling (versus 8.6 years in 1940), the same number of Americans is still functionally ignorant about political matters—about 25% of the population.[17]

Not only do we know less about politics but we also seem to care less. In 1967, 35% of the American people described themselves as "very interested in public affairs." That same statistic for 1988 was 23%. In 1967, 73% of the population read a newspaper each day; today, that number is 51% and falling.[18] In 1944, the politically ignorant were made up of those who had not completed high school, the very young, the aged, the politically apathetic, and women. In surveys begun in 1988 and continuing to today, the politically ignorant were made up of those who had not completed high school, the very young, the aged, the politically apathetic, and women.[19] Need it be added that demographic studies of heavy television viewers finds them to be drawn disproportionately from the ranks of those who have not completed high school, the very young, the aged, the politically apathetic, and women?

Detailed studies of television's messages also find them to be uninformative. Political scientist Richard Joslyn, for example, studied televised advertisements by political candidates who had achieved a rating of 75 or more from the Americans for Democratic Action. Despite these liberal credentials, "only 39 (30%) [ads] contained information adequate to identify the candidate as a liberal."[20] Perhaps political expediency accounts for such wariness. But other of Joslyn's data are equally disheartening. In a sample of 803 political commercials, only 134 (less than 17%) addressed policy questions and only 50 of these latter advertisements (6.2% of the 803) "contained specific policy positions."[21] It is little wonder, then, that political sociologist Steven Peterson reports that voters who went on record as following senate campaigns closely on television were *unable* to explain the various candidates' positions on the issues.[22]

Might television change its reportorial format to increase political learning? Use fewer talking heads, for instance? Increase human interest stories? Again, the data are discomfiting. Political scientists have reported, for example, that vivid news stories (those presenting melodramatic case studies) were generally ineffective in raising viewers' consciousness of, say, an issue like unemployment. "Overwhelmed by concrete details," explain researchers, "they [the viewers] miss the general point."[23] Similar results were reported by another group of researchers who found that highly dramatized news presentations decreased viewers' recall of information as well as the complexity with which they thought about a given problem.[24]

In essence, researchers now sing in chorus when describing television's effects on political learning: (a) "watching more television news does little to increase information or comprehension" of political information[25]; (b) people who depend on television for political information "have an increasingly impoverished sense of the political world around them as well as a growing ignorance, apathy and cynicism"[26]; and (c) studies have shown that "though [televised] news was objective and politically neutral, it was somehow failing to convey information to its audiences."[27]

In some ways, studies like these document what we have long known: To be male, white, and well educated in the United States is to be politically knowledgeable. Indeed, it is to be politically omnipotent. Television is for the rest of us. Despite the special events programming, the assorted press conferences, the omnipresent docudramas, and the all-news cable channels, television does not educate us politically, or at least not enough of us. *But being uninformed and feeling uninformed are not the same thing.*

Political scientist Russell Neuman appreciated this crucial distinction when describing the 80-80 rule of American politics: 80% of the American people will report having specific political opinions 80% of the time they are asked to share them.[28] That is, even though they know comparatively little about governance—including who makes which laws where and why—they are quick to tell anyone who asks them how the ship of state should be sailed. It is also true that American voters consistently report having the highest sense of political efficacy among democratic polities, meaning that they feel they could change public policy if the need arose.[29]

What gives them such confidence? De Tocqueville explained it culturally: Americans are brash, atheoretical puritans redeemed in part by an elegant sense of practicality. But, today, might it also be the case that Americans' familiarity with television, and television's familiarity with politics, account for their confidence? By bringing politicians close to us, the American mass media appeal to our natural cockiness about judging character. In doing so, the media also establish a model of politics that emphasizes politicians over politics and psychology over economics.

As a result, even though most "studies find relatively few Americans with a complex, well articulated, interconnected theory of politics" based on solid information,[30] many of them still feel informed about politics. Although 70% of them (between 1952 and 1984) have been willing to affirm that "sometimes politics and government seem so complicated that a person like me can't really understand what's going on,"[31] they nevertheless distinguish sharply between knowing governance and knowing politicians. Thus, when refusing to vote, they do so to "show the jerks what they think of them," not because they feel a sudden humility coming on. Through television, they have gotten to know the jerks.

And so one of the main effects of personality politics is that it creates a falsified knowledge base. Because it fills us up each day with behind-the-scenes intrigue of life on the Potomac, it cuts short our quest for real political understanding. It makes political life a weekly insert in the pages of *People* magazine and gives us absolution for not knowing how the nation's laws are made. It turns watching the nightly news into another kind of game show rather than into a vibrant lesson in the problems of self-governance. It fills us up with psychographic details about our leaders even though we ourselves live very demographic lives indeed. But false learning of any sort hides an extra tyranny. Not only does poor teaching fail to educate students, it also hides their ignorance from them. That is now the case in politics. Let us see why.

The Arrogance of the Eye

One of the more dangerous myths about television is that it is a wasteland appreciated only by the lazy and the illiterate. This myth is particularly dangerous when it comes to politics because the lazy and the illiterate are those least likely to be interested in political life. No, television is the medium of choice for all Americans from all walks of life. In fact, separate studies by researchers Scott Keeter and Doris Graber have shown that better-educated viewers are among those most likely to emphasize a candidate's personal qualities when deciding how to vote.[32]

In part this is not surprising because, as political scientist Fred Greenstein reported some years ago, U.S. citizens ranked "personal qualities" over "policy preferences" by a ratio of four to one when explaining how they made their voting decisions; Greenstein reports that these weightings held true as far back as 1948.[33] Preferences like these have hardly abated since that time, especially with television now covering politics so comprehensively. Researcher Margaret Conway and her colleagues made precisely that link when finding that high exposure to television among adolescents sharply increased their sensitivity to political personalities but had little effect on their appreciation for more abstract political issues.[34]

But distinguishing between "personalities" and "issues" violates the seamlessness of television. Although survey respondents are perfectly capable of answering issue-versus-image questions if asked to do so, television itself permits no such distinctions. With television, there are no disembodied issues.[35] Abortion means abortion protestors. Inner-city decay means Washington, D.C. mayor Marion Barry. Inflation or AIDS means drugstore interviews with their victims. This is how television brings politics to life.

And the fact that television feels the need to bring politics "to life" is itself an interesting notion. When, one might ask, did politics die? How can a system responsible for rebuilding the homes of earthquake victims, or combatting swamp fever, or feeding the homeless be declared lifeless? Nevertheless, television entertains no issue that cannot be personified. In part, that is why ecologists fought such a frustrating fight for so many years trying to get attention in the United States. Televised pictures of stagnant streams are, after all, stagnant. And so it took spiking trees in the Northwest and near-collisions on the high seas between oil tankers and Earth First vessels before the public mind could become engaged. All because of television.

And so the electronic media confuse issues and images almost completely and encourage us to do so as well. Over time, we do, for television's lessons are both powerful and repetitive. Because television is a visual medium, its pictures have a self-authenticating quality to them. The eye, that most gluttonous of all human organs, takes in all that can be taken in; it is an organ that cannot be satiated. Given the right circumstances, it will feed upon Australian-rules football at three o'clock in the morning rather than contemplate sleeplessness in the dark. It is also an organ that cannot be embarrassed. That which is seen, is.

Although television itself is a medium—a coming-between—it is a medium that deconstructs itself constantly. It asks us to look ever-closer at the intimacies it presents and then to treat those intimacies as first-order, not secondary or tertiary, perceptions. Thus, when television's Barbara Walters asks Secretary of State William Cohen what he eats for lunch, it is as if we, not she, had asked the question. When Mr. Cohen replies, it is as if we, not he, were reading his soul about matters nutritional. As British scholar Roger Silverstone has remarked, such news programs obliterate the "scars of mediation and transformation."[36]

Television, in short, encourages an arrogance of the eye. When we turn television on we become empowered in a special way. We assume control of our worlds both literally (with remote-control devices) and figuratively. With the current infinity of channels available to us, we determine which images to take in for how long. More precisely, that is, when selecting from television's pre-given menu, we are allowed to feel totally in charge. Television's technological features—its vitality, its diversity of programming, its interpersonal directness—coincide, happily enough, with the egalitarian assumptions of a democratic polity. "Live" events are particularly appreciated. In such cases, the camera goes where it *must* go (e.g., to the dropped pass in the football game or to the audience's anguished reaction when the politician misspeaks) and not where the camera operator's physical location and dramatistic biases have allowed it to go.

In cases like these, television's pictures seem raw, not cooked. Its technological limitations become the viewer's limitations and its producers' pre-thinking is hidden from us. The actors who move about on the screen either seem genuine (as, for example, when being interviewed on *Oprah*) or transparently evil, the operating premise of televised drama being that the medium should never seem smarter than its audience. In short, although they are often the tail that television wags, viewers themselves feel all-dog.

The arrogance of the eye manifests itself in a variety of ways. For one thing, it produces a kind of shirtsleeved imperialism. Popular writer Michael Korda captures its strains perfectly:

> Television, partly because it's in the home, *produces* familiarity and intimacy—and *demands* it from those who appear on the screen. . . . As everybody who has ever appeared on a television talk show knows, your best bet is to relax and be yourself. Whatever you are will come across on camera, for better or for worse. Any attempt to fake it, to act, to pretend to be something you're not will be exposed instantly. . . . Intellectuals complain that because of television, people are no longer voting on issues but on personality—but what's wrong with that? Personality is what matters, rather than the issues themselves, and anyway, the two are inseparable. . . . I have no doubt that had [television] existed in the 18th century, it would merely have confirmed what Washington's contemporaries knew: that he was the right man for the job. Character is what counts.[37]

Here, Korda intones the mantra of the television age, an age that combines the modernist strains of the 1950s with the emotional verities of the 1960s. This is an age where honesty is easy and deception is not. Let others beat their breasts about the mass deceptions perpetrated by the media, Korda argues, for they have forgotten that television makes us primitive again: keen of eye, sure of foot, stout of heart. "Those who fear television," says Korda, "fear the people—and assume they can be fooled. I have always doubted that the public can be duped. People have, in the aggregate, a sound instinct for what is real and important in a candidate."[38]

In other words, the technology of television is a de-technology, a medium that removes the between-us. Through television, we can touch persons who live elsewhere; we can read their distant hearts. Reasonably enough, attitudes like these insulate us from the massness of mass society. They let us act globally but think locally. Thus, in an era of legion manipulations, a more primitive voice can still be heard:

> *From George Bush*: "And, look, this campaign is over. There's no hard feelings about that. The American people are smart. They know a tough-fought campaign on both sides when they see it."[39]
>
> *From Gary Hart*: "I've never felt the voters really care about either one of those things [narcissism or game-playing], frankly. They're smart enough to know who you are without your telling them. You look them in the eye, you talk to them and they decide whether you're telling the truth or not."[40]
>
> *From Jack Kemp*: "The ultimate wisdom resides in people and markets."[41]
>
> *From U.S.News and World Report*: "And whatever all the flag-waving and name-calling were meant to achieve these past months, it has been neither grand nor generous. It should surprise only confirmed cynics that a great many people are fooled not one bit by such tricks."[42]
>
> *From the National Review*: "The campaign against Negative Campaigning implies that the electorate is utterly passive, manipulable, and responsive to atavistic (including racist) appeals . . . They deserve some credit for making up their own minds, especially since they seem to be making them up the way they usually do when one of the candidates is a liberal."[43]
>
> *From the Los Angeles Times*: "When the Framers wrote the Constitution 200 years ago, they set out only the barest qualifications for a President. They relied on the wisdom of the public to pick a good leader. . . ."[44]

Any refrain repeated this often is a refrain to be reckoned with. These statements look like empirical claims but they are also prayers. After all, if they were purely empirical claims—if the American people are indeed so smart—

why must these claims be repeated so often? And yet if they are prayers, which sins are they attempting to erase? As with so many true but unproven statements, remarks like these bear precious little weight when tested. If true, how do we know? If false, how can we cope? But it is especially interesting that statements like these appear so often in an age of television, for it is television's capacity for sleight of hand that often gives them the lie. Perhaps sensing that, we cling ever closer to what our eyes tell us.

Television obliges. It lets us know that even though we are, of necessity, haplessly rooted in one place and time, we can round out our perceptions by watching television. Thus, even though we can see an object from only one side at any given moment, television moves us around the object, letting us view it "from different sides and angles" even though we can never see that object "from all sides at once."[45] As Michel deCerteau explains it, "The autonomy of the eye suspends the body's complicities with the text; it unmoors it from the scriptural place; it makes the written text an object and it increases the reader's possibilities of moving about."[46] Through mediation, objects take on this full, rich, phenomenological dimension, no matter how flatly they sit on the television screen itself. Television therefore encourages a kind of visual foundationalism.

It is for these reasons—for reasons of control—that television features psychological politics and why voters feature television. As the "rational choice" theorists in political science argue, people make cost-benefit calculations when dealing with issues of governance.[47] Tracking a complex piece of legislation, that is, seems all cost and no benefit to most citizens: By the time they understand the legalisms, the bill will have been gutted by committee. Examining political personalities, on the other hand, is endlessly rewarding: (a) Because such examinations tap into our natural expertise about how people think, we stand little chance of being declared incompetent; (b) because politicians are changeful, there is always work to be done, a new psychological wrinkle to work out, and that is exciting; and (c) because political rhetoric is so often boring, we can quickly feel superior to those who use it.

And one cannot discount the phenomenology of scale where television is concerned. As communication scholar Margaret Morse has observed, "even . . . the large-screen projection [television] is no bigger than a picture window or an alternative to wallpaper."[48] Our physical dominance over the tiny figures on our television sets, says Morse, accounts for the feelings of safety we have when watching them. By towering over politicians physically, we compensate for their statutory power over us. Television, in other words, makes giants of us all.

Media scholar Chris Rawlence offers a valuable observation when contrasting theatregoers to television watchers. As Rawlence notes, a skilled stage actor will move "individual members of the audience to move others." In that sense, says Rawlence, a theater audience feels "it has the power, collectively, to shape the performance" whereas the television audience "never has the sense of itself as an audience.[49] But the home viewer is not without power. This is especially true with personality politics, where the viewer's power becomes the quieter and deeper power of the voyeur.

When conducting an in-depth political interview, for example, newscasters try to draw us in without making us audience-conscious. So, for example, when the camera comes in tight on a politician's face, "the disclosure effect becomes doubly articulated, generating an even more compelling sense of the intimate and the immediate."[50] During such moments, the audience becomes an I, a hearer but not a spoken-to. As a result, the viewer always has the voyeur's sense of safety—excitement without risk. Media scholar John Langer explains the role of the newscaster in such processes:

> The world changes but the television personality stays the same. In the case of the news, one of the conventionalized marks of this coherent stable identity which persists despite a world of flux and change, is the way the news reader is framed by the camera. The head and shoulders dominate, appearing balanced and central in glistening, unwavering focus—like the authoritative carriage of a portrait—which looks at us with calm deliberation. The "real" world, where stories come from, is, in contrast, often skewed, off balance, with shaky camera work done in the heat of the newsworthy moment. The "real" world may be unstable and unbalanced, but the world of the television news personality who *explains* that world to us is not.[51]

To sum up: Television's visual nature gives it special emotional command. With television, we can quite literally see the men and women who govern us. We can watch them tousle the hair of children in Topeka, grab for their microphones in New Hampshire. We can see them pull the ears of their beagles, light the Christmas trees with their wives, watch them bid adieu to their Stanford sophomore. Through them, we come to think of television as a window on the world rather than a rough estimation of it. Television asks us to forget that its pictures have been selected from among an infinite number of alternative images, alternative news frames, alternative camera angles, and alternative dramatis personae. It also makes us forget that all such pre-work has been done by persons unknown to us, for reasons unclear to us.

Nevertheless, television compels. It compels by presenting a world in which all can be known because all can be seen. Philosopher Michel Foucault describes the pleasures that such a transparent society promised, a society that was

> visible and legible in each of its parts, the dream of there no longer existing any zones of darkness, zones established by the privileges of royal power or the prerogative of some corporation, zones of disorder. It was the dream that each individual, whatever position he occupied, might be able to see the whole of society, that men's hearts should communicate, their vision be unobstructed by obstacles, and that the opinion of all reign over each.[52]

Learning to Decide

Although media studies are but a recent addition to the university curriculum, they are old enough to have produced a formula: Television does not tell us what to think, only what to think about. Communication scholars Donald Shaw and Maxwell McCombs first popularized this notion when finding that the topics most vigorously discussed in the mass media subsequently affected readers' personal discussions.[53] Political scientists Shanto Iyengar and Donald Kinder transported this concept to the political sphere by introducing the notion of "priming." For Iyengar and Kinder, the media generate priming effects when voters pick up the press's storylines and use them to make political judgments. So, for example, they found that media consumers became intrigued by different aspects of the personalities of Jimmy Carter and Ronald Reagan—competence and compassion, respectively—but that a concentration on their *personal* qualities was consistent in both cases.[54] Iyengar and Kinder also found that these media-based priming effects held true regardless of presidential party, news story subject matter, or the positive or negative flavor of the press coverage.[55]

Television, in other words, helps establish our judgmental criteria. It changes how we treat political information (by emphasizing personality) and thus how we make political decisions. A study of the first presidential debate of 1988, for example, looked at the impact of the debaters' "relational cues." To be fully relational, said the researchers, a candidate had to have a "cooperative attitude" and to project "equality, the absence of a superior attitude, warmth . . . friendliness, sincerity, honesty."[56] Not surprisingly, the re-searchers found that if they knew how people judged this one quality (for either Bush or Dukakis), they could accurately predict viewers' overall judgment of the debate in 71% of the cases.

A study of this sort is unnerving. One wonders whether to lament its results or the fact that it was conducted in the first place. It will be remembered, after all, that the Bush/Dukakis debate dealt with such matters as the death penalty, the national debt, abortion rights, and the possibility of a nuclear war with the Soviet Union. In light of these sobering topics, it is small solace to learn that the debaters were thought genial.

But given what we now know about television, results like these could be expected. When asked in another study to recall visual images from newscasts, for example, viewers best remembered close-ups of familiar faces. Next best remembered were close-ups of unfamiliar faces. Least remembered were what the researcher called "stereotyped" pictures (for example, farms), "establishing shots" (e.g., the outside of a building), or "vistas" (e.g., people shopping).[57] In other words, television's viewers do their watching outside-in. They study faces because they have been told that is where the political action is. For them, politics does not deal with collective behavior (the sort depicted in vistas) but with individual behavior (the sort depicted in close-ups). Television's political training therefore "homogenizes" voters in two ways: (1)it makes them prize the same limited number of qualities in political candidates regardless of the candidates' politics, and (2) it encourages "crossover" effects so that viewers evaluate political candidates just as they evaluate all other television personalities.[58]

Both conditions encourage voters to develop what psychologists Donald Horton and Richard Wohl call "para-social relationships"[59] with politicians; they come to think of their leaders as intimates simply because they spend so much time with them. Day in and day out, through agony and ecstasy, the citizenry meets its political leaders on television. These meetings are often brief—a photo opportunity here, a Jay Leno joke there—but these meetings still produce long-term knowing. The intimacy that results, of course, is not always satisfying. As political scientist Richard Brody reports, recent presidents (Nixon through Reagan) have done ten points less well in the polls than their immediate predecessors (Truman through Johnson).[60] In breeding familiarity with politics, that is, television may also be breeding contempt. Perhaps that explains why a perfect stranger could approach a U.S. senator on the street, grab him by the throat, and declaim, "I know who you are."[61]

Because television fascinates them in these ways, modern Americans live much of their lives indoors. That costs them a sense of the public place, says sociologist Richard Sennett. Personal swimming pools rather than public parks, rented videos rather than moviegoing, computer networks instead of town hall meetings—these are the ways in which people have become privatized. Sennett worries that such experiences sap our confidence as citizens:

> To speak of an end of public life is first to speak of a consequence issuing from a contradiction in culture of the last century. Personality in public was a contradiction in terms; it ultimately destroyed the public term. For instance, it became logical for people to think of those who could actively display their emotions in public, whether as artists or politicians, as being men of special and superior personality. These men were to control, rather than interact with, the audience in front of whom they appeared. Gradually the audience lost faith in itself to judge them; it became a spectator rather than a witness. The audience thus lost a sense of itself as an active force, as a "public."[62]

Although Sennett's analysis is astute, he overlooks television's ability to change the very notion of political life. Instead of shrinking the public sphere, television expands the private sphere. It also expands the leadership base. It means, for example, that General Norman Schwartzkopf of Gulf War fame could imaginably go from battlefield commander to the White House overnight. "As I watched (Schwartzkopf) give the mother of all briefings," said political pundit Hastings Wyman in March of 1991, "certainly the thought crossed my mind that he would make a delightful candidate."[63] It is not surprising that Mr. Wyman saw the road from Riyadh to the White House going smack through a briefing studio. Televised politics encourages this mixing of political and interpersonal humors, thereby making governance an increasingly indistinct occupation.

Although unblushing observations like Mr. Wyman's are popular, one does find the occasional blush. In March of 1992, for example, a radio-caller in Austin, Texas launched the ultimate salvo against Democratic candidate Paul Tsongas: "He can't project." When asked if Tsongas' rhetorical deficiencies really made a difference, the caller retreated with, "Well, it really doesn't matter to me personally but it will to the American people."[64] Our caller's argument deconstructs itself. In trying to have it both ways, he is having politics only one way, and that is television's way, too.

Our caller also demonstrates the instinctive attractiveness of the language of personality. Said another radio-caller on the eve of the Gulf War:

"Those dirty hippies [protesting the war] just want the sixties back. They miss the drugs."[65] Acerbic though it is, this critique is more than *ad hominem* or, at least, it is a new kind of *ad hominem*. Note, for example, that there is no spirited dialectic here, no cranky Old Testament God pitted against a more mellow New Testament God. The protestors' motives are not traced to some foul philosophical sewer but to a troubled, even damaged, psyche. Such a "deep read" of anti-war sentiment makes genuine argument about the war impossible. How does one respond? By championing drug use? By claiming a misdiagnosis? By defending nostalgia? In short, although psychodialogue of this sort is entertaining during drive-time, it muddles "public and private purposes, terms, and moralities"[66] and therefore turns political discourse into mere gossip.

Richard Sennett sees the language of personality as an "anti-ideological force"[67] that brackets the philosophical and the institutional. Europeans have long noted this about Americans, a people unwilling to discuss politics in the abstract *and thus in the transpersonal*. By individuating politics, Americans create a world in which one political leader may have "the force" on a given day whereas another may not. This makes the political cosmos interesting, but it also makes it capricious. But a world of whimsy is well suited to television, which justifies its existence by seeking out the hero of the moment.[68] Television's job description is therefore clear: Find two colorful personalities for each side of each dialectic; let them nip at each others heels; then call it disputation.

The language of personality has sunk deep roots in American life, especially during the last 50 years. When asked to explain why he did not vote, for example, one blue-collar worker spoke that language at warp speed:

> Well yeh, y'know, like they'll tell ya one thing, then they'll turn around an' stab ya in the back. An' they'll tell somebody else sump'm else. But they couldn't care less. They're lookin' out for number one. They'll do whatever they have ta do ta make things easier for them or ta benefit them. I don't know, it's just a political thing. An' I disagree with that policy 100% y'know. So I just stay away from it. I'll tell ya, I don't even vote. Because I—to me they're all just a bunch of power trippers. Bunch of liars is all. I mean y'know I don't like a liar. To me that's the type of person that'll stab ya in the back the first chance they get. An' I just don't like it.[69]

Our interlocutor clearly knows what he knows. Even though frightening economic conditions bore down on him when he spoke, even though state and federal regulations increasingly hamstrung him, and even though his nation was caught up in labyrinthine international alliances, our interlocutor saw only libidos in politics. That is fine with politicians, who also use the language of personality to simplify things. For them, establishing a consistent personality profile lets them integrate the nastily diverse stands they must take on the issues. That was especially true for Ronald Reagan, whose personality was so finely etched into the public mind that not even tripling the national debt could undo him. Reagan's personality—that of an amiable executioner— played well to citizens and press alike and provided a running motif to explain the many unRepublican things he did as chief executive.[70]

The war in the Persian Gulf was a case study in the language of personality. The American mass media, the White House, and even popular culture conspired to demonize Saddam Hussein. Although the war itself clearly resulted from geopolitical entanglements among oil-based economies, the rhetoric of the war was little more than psychological reductionism. Here, for example, is what George Bush said about his Iraqi counterpart:

> *Saddam-as-isolate*: "You can't negotiate with a terrorist. If a person kidnaps another, should the kidnapper be given face? Should that person be given some way out so he can have a little face when he gets back into the world? The answer is no, you do not compromise with that."[71]
>
> *Saddam-as-psychopath*: "Prime Minister John Major of the United Kingdom said it well yesterday, 'Saddam,' he said, 'may yet become a target of his own people. It is perfectly clear that this man is amoral. He takes hostages, he attacks population centers, he threatens prisoners. He's a man without pity, and whatever his fate may be,' said Prime Minister Major, 'I, for one, will not weep for him.' No one should weep for this tyrant when he is brought to justice."[72]
>
> *Saddam-as-sociopath*: "I think you just have to get the fundamentals straight. He plays with human beings as if they were pawns. Unless you stop this man, there will be no peace in the world."[73]

In some ways, this is standard denunciation of an enemy. But it has a newer, psychodynamic flavor as well. Mr. Bush describes a demon here, not a general. He reaches beyond Saddam's behavior to his motive, and then beyond his motive to his emotional state. He describes a warped individual, not a blustering despot. Mr. Bush was not alone in this approach. One publication, for example, ran side-by-side pictures of Saddam Hussein and Joseph Stalin, noted their facial similarities, and then wondered aloud if their similarities ended there.[74] Another news story reported the research of a Boston neuropsychologist who claimed that Saddam blinked 113 times per minute in a CNN interview with reporter Peter Arnett, a rate that was alleged to be dangerously high.[75] A Washington, D.C., psychologist also made the rounds of the television talk shows, declaring at one point that "for the very first time in Saddam's career, he is exactly where he wants to be—at the center of power, the focus of attention."[76]

One newsmagazine conducted a national poll that asked whether Saddam deserved humiliation or just military defeat (62% of the respondents voted for humiliation).[77] Often, the media reports about Saddam were lurid: "There's a story making the rounds among diplomats in Baghdad that one day at a cabinet meeting Saddam Hussein asked if any of his ministers had a contrary view on one of his proposals. One minister spoke up, and Saddam thanked him graciously and invited him to discuss it further in his private office. Inside, he beat him to death with a club."[78] Equally often, the news reports were lyrical:

❏ "For Saddam, a fatherless boy from a poor village in Iraq, the chance to confront the president of the United States one-on-one . . . might be in itself the culmina-tion of a dream. . . . For all his wiles, Saddam's pride makes him easily, perhaps fatally, predictable"[79]

❏ "The Iraqi president's relative ignorance of the outside world only enhances his sense of building conspiracy. . . . It is the confluence of Saddam's insularity and his pride that seems to have confounded the Bush administration . . . [B]rute force may be the only aspect of the wider world Saddam truly does not comprehend, and his pride won't let him bend to it."[80]

❏ "Saddam's last stand was Wagnerian in its madness. He backlit himself with the flames of Kuwait's oil wells, which he turned into torches. . . . One moment, he swore defiance; the next he tried to get Mikhail Gorbachev to save him. When that failed, he withdrew to his bunker, playing Hitler, who wanted to take everyone with him when he fell."[81]

Even before television, of course, the language of personality was part of politics. My argument here is thus an argument of degree and not of kind— there is simply more of it today. As political philosopher Carl Schmitt argued before the age of television, for a nation to go to war, an enemy must be *made*: "The political enemy . . . is . . . the other, the stranger; and it is sufficient for his nature that he is, in a specially intense way, existentially something different and alien, so that in the extreme case conflicts with him are possi-ble."[82] "Political energy," says Schmitt, is the capacity "to group men according to friend and enemy."[83] This principle still obtains, but today's enemies have been turned into intimate enemies.

In part, this is a semantic change, a new way of talking ourselves into battle. But in part, it may be something deeper. And more ominous. After all, in the last decade of the 20th century, there are only 180 sovereign leaders in the world and there are only so many things they can do politically and militarily. But there are myriad psychoanalytic categories available to describe what they do, myriad plus myriad ways to describe why they do it. Because the language of personality is expansionistic in these ways, it allows one person to become all persons, all archetypes. As a result, how a leader can be characterized is limited only by his or her opponent's ideological purposes and psychopathological dictionary.

The language of personality therefore adds texture and precision to political rhetoric. Thinking more optimistically, it could also be seen as an endless source of redemption—François Mitterand does not hate the United States, he has just had a bad day. But because it is used more often to vilify, the language of personality generates so many enemies that hell itself cannot contain them.

Conclusion

This chapter has examined three effects of personality politics. As we have seen, television distracts us from traditional political knowledge; it entices us with new forms of political information; and it changes the criteria we use when making political decisions. What are its long-term effects? For one thing, the American people now feel closer to political life than ever before, but that closeness sometimes results in a crisis of familiarity for them. The American people now know a great deal about politicians—their hat sizes, their sexual histories—and in that sense they "possess" them as never before. Perhaps because their own lives seem so boring in comparison, voters feed on the soap opera of politics, desperately searching "for real people, real values, real sex."[84]

Because of television, says Jean Baudrillard, there is now an "obscenity of information"[85] about all things, and that is especially true in political life. Television's polite form of "direct address"[86] builds communion between politicians and the electorate and an ideology of equality sets in. Each day, our leaders cozy up to us, and that is at first pleasant. It makes politics attractively pedestrian, a politics of the New World and not of the Old.

But personality politics also presents some knotty questions: Can the ordinary truly inspire? Will a diet of psychologizing allow us to get beyond ourselves—an obvious requirement in a democratic polity? Is personality politics anti-utopian in a dangerous sense? Although it is true, as psychologist Robert Frank has observed, that moral behavior is "more naturally summoned by persons than by institutions"[87] and although it is also true that television delivers such people to us superbly, that which is close at hand can be taken for granted.

Perhaps that has already happened. We feel smart about politics today, but do we feel generous? We can now think in the small, but can we still think in the large? Do we have the humility, awe, and sense of transcendence needed in a republican form of government? Can we still feel the great and holy mission that is democratic politics, a form of governance launched by persons of preposterous imagination and inconscionable gall! Have we forgotten how hard it is to fashion an electorate out of 275 million people and then to keep it fashioned? Has television left us with anything to wonder about?

Concerning politicians, we have never been smarter. But we have also never been sadder. Content analysts tell us that election coverage during presidential campaigns has become steadily negative over the years.[88] Survey researchers conclude that watching political news on television makes people increasingly cynical.[89] Experimental researchers report that watching a political rally in person makes 19% of the audience negative toward the speaker but that watching that same event on television upsets 52% of the audience.[90] All of this contributes to what Michael Robinson has called "videomalaise,"[91] a complex malady but one that comes down to profound disappointment. Because television now gives us our politicians warts and all (often all warts) and because, as Sheldon Wolin has observed, politicians are now more commonly regarded as technicians than as high priests,[92] it is hard to find real purpose in politics.

Television is partly responsible for that. When political leaders violate the law, they seem either oafish or treacherous, but when they violate us as people, our emotions zoom past anger and stop on demoralization. Videomalaise is therefore more than political apathy. It is rather like depression, a disease that people create for one another.

In many ways, politics is now overexposed.[93] We know too much about it and, at the same time, we do not know enough. If television's sins could be reduced to but one, it would probably be the sin of replacing political authority with political power. As anthropologist Clifford Geertz says, a society needs the "inherent sacredness of central authority"[94] to prosper. In an age of television, Geertz's claim sounds like monarchial sentimentality. Because it is so caught up with political power, television does not know how to reverence authority.

When televising a political speech in Congress, for example, camera operators sprain their sacroiliacs trying to capture the right reaction shot: Young women swooning for Congressman Bill Paxton; V.F.W. members becoming misty-eyed for his colleague Steve Largent; everyone else being charmed by the singer and later Congressman Sonny Bono. "This is political power!" the camera screams. But that same camera is mute about authority—that which authorizes the state. Political authority is too mystical for television's cameras.

So be it. If recapturing a sense of political authority is important to us, we will have to seek it elsewhere. We will have to deauthorize personality politics and look to one another for political wisdom. We can still learn from television, but we will have to choose more carefully from among its dazzling pictures and invasive biographies. We will have to recall things we have long known but have chosen to forget: That good ideas need protection; that governance is complicated; that only an informed citizenry can prosper; that people are imperfect, all of them. We will, in short, have to feel less and think more. As political philosopher Ann Norton has argued, the state has authority over us only insofar as we are its author.[95] To become our own authors, we must go beyond television. Marvelous though it is, television serves its own needs. We must learn to better serve our own.

Notes

1. G. Gallup, *The Gallup Poll: Public Opinion, 1989* (Wilmington, DE: Scholarly Resources, 1989), 174. Not all scholars are convinced that the influence of the traditional political parties has declined this precipitously. See, for example, B. E. Keith et al., *The Myth of the Independent Voter* (Berkeley: University of California Press, 1992).

2. For an insightful discussion of this latter possibility, see E. J. Dionne, *Why Americans Hate Politics* (New York: Simon & Schuster, 1991).

3. R. Schmuhl, *Statecraft and Stagecraft: American Political Life in the Age of Personality* (South Bend, IN: Notre Dame University Press, 1990).

4. See, for example, D. Graber, *Processing the News: How People Tame the Information Tide* (New York: Longman, 1988).

5. S. Mickelson, *From Whistle Stop to Sound Bite: Four Decades of Politics and Television* (New York: Praeger, 1989), 173.

6. B. Brummett and M. C. Duncan, "Theorizing and Totalizing: Specularity and Televised Spots," *Quarterly Journal of Speech*, 76 (1990), 227-246.

7. G. Debord, *Society of the Spectacle* (Detroit: Red and Black, 1982), 3-66, 3-69.

8. J. Jensen, *Redeeming Modernity: Contradictions in Media Criticism* (Newbury Park, CA: Sage, 1990), 23-24.

9. J. Robinson, "I Love my TV," *American Demographics*, September, 1990, 24-27.

10. Quoted in B. Groombridge, *Television and the People: A Programme for Democratic Participation* (Harmondsworth: Penguin, 1972), 73.

11. P. Clarke and E. Fredin, "Newspapers, Television, and Political Reasoning," *Public Opinion Quarterly, 41* (1978), 143-160.

12. M. Just and A. Crigler, "Learning from the News: Experiments in Media, Modality, and Reporting after Star Wars," *Political Communication and Persuasion, 6* (1989), 109-127.

13. S. Chaffee, C. Nass, and S-M. Yang, "The Bridging Role of Television in Immigrant Political Socialization," *Human Communication Research, 17* (1990), 284.

14. J. Naisbitt, *Megatrends: Ten New Directions Transforming Our Lives* (New York: Warner, 1982), 160.

15. S. E. Bennett, " 'Know-Nothings' Revisited: The Meaning of Political Ignorance Today," *Social Science Quarterly, 69* (1988), 476-490.

16. For a helpful review of research on political information processing see J. Robinson and M. Levy (eds.), *The Main Source: Learning from Television News* (Beverly Hills, CA: Sage, 1986).

17. S. E. Bennett, "Trends in Americans' Political Information, 1967-1987," *American Politics Quarterly, 17* (1989), 422-435.

18. Bennett, 432-433.

19. Bennett, 1988, 485. For collateral information, see L. Sigelman and E. Yanarella, "Public Information on Public Issues: A Multivariate Analysis," *Social Science Quarterly, 67* (1986), 402-410.

20. R. Joslyn, "Election Campaigns as Occasions for Civic Education," in D. Swanson and D. Nimmo (eds.), *New Directions in Political Communication: A Resource Book* (Newbury Park, CA: Sage, 1990), 104.

21. Joslyn, 104.

22. S. Peterson, *Political Behavior: Patterns in Everyday Life* (Newbury Park, CA: Sage, 1990), 230.

23. S. Iyengar and D. Kinder, *News that Matters: Television and American Public Opinion* (Chicago: University of Chicago Press, 1987), 42.

24. M. Milburn and A. McGrail, "The Dramatic Presentation of News and its Effects on Cognitive Complexity." Paper presented at the annual convention of the American Political Science Association, San Francisco, California, August 1990.

25. J. P. Robinson and D. Davis, "Television News and the Informed Public: An Information-Processing Approach," *Journal of Communication, 40:3* (1990), 116.

26. R. Neuman, *The Paradox of Mass Politics: Knowledge and Opinion in the American Electorate* (Cambridge: Harvard University Press, 1986), 145.

27. D. K. Davis, "News and Politics," in D. Swanson and D. Nimmo (eds.), *New Directions in Political Communication: A Resource Book* (Newbury Park, CA: Sage, 1990), 157.

28. Neuman, 58, 60.

29. G. Almond and S. Verba, *The Civic Culture* (Princeton, NJ: Princeton University Press, 1963).

30. R. Brody, *Assessing the President: The Media, Elite Opinion, and Public Support* (Stanford, CA: Stanford University Press, 1991), 123.

31. Neuman, 12.

32. See S. Keeter, "The Illusion of Intimacy, Television and the Role of Candidate Personal Qualities in Voter Choice," *Public Opinion Quarterly, 51* (1987), 344-358 and Graber, 1988, 83.

33. F. Greenstein, "Popular Images of the President," *American Journal of Psychiatry, 122* (1965), 526.

34. M. Conway, A. J. Stevens, and R. Smith, "The Relationship Between Media Use and Children's Civic Awareness," *Journalism Quarterly, 52* (1975), 531-538.

35. Although this proposition seems obvious to me, it is often ignored in social scientific studies. One researcher, for example, found little opinion change resulting when subjects were confronted with unexpected (hypothetical) position-taking by a political figure. Paper-and-pencil tests of this sort are interesting, but they bear little relationship to the real world of politics where such political turnabouts are accompanied by powerful arguments offered by flesh-and-blood individuals, individuals who have longstanding relationships with the citizenry. Still, studies of this sort have their uses. See J. Hurwitz, "Presidential Leadership and Public Followership," in M. Margolis and G. Mauser (eds.), *Manipulating Public Opinion* (Pacific Grove, CA: Brooks/Cole, 1989), 222-249.

36. R. Silverstone, "The Agonistic Narratives of Television Science," in J. Corner (ed.), *Documentary and the Mass Media* (London: Edwin Arnold, 1986), 81. The result of such processes, says Gillian Skirrow, is that television acquires a kind of invisibility in the British academy—it is so "natural" that it need not be studied. Needless to say, Skirrow feels that such hypernaturalism makes television an even more worthy object of study. See "Education and Television: Theory and Practice," in C. Gardner (ed.), *Media, Politics and Culture: A Socialist View* (London: Macmillan, 1979), 25-39.

37. M. Korda, "Politicians on Television: Is What You See What You Get?" *Family Weekly,* October 25, 1981, 7-8. Doris Graber has shown that Korda's views are also popular among viewers. When asked why visuals were important in a newscast, for example, 34% of her survey respondents said they added "reality" to a story whereas only 16% said they added clarification. See "Seeing Is Remembering: How Visuals Contribute to Learning from Television News," *Journal of Communication, 40:3* (1990), 149.

38. Korda, 8.

39. G. Bush, "President-elect Bush's News Conference," *Washington Post,* November 10, 1988, A41.

40. L. Eichel, "Hart's Fall: A Refusal to Accept Character as an Issue," *Philadelphia Inquirer,* May 10, 1987, E1.

41. As quoted in B. Stumbo, "Jack Kemp Still Brings Crowds Alive," *Los Angeles Times,* May 16, 1985, 1.

42. B. Duffy, "The Autumn of their Discontent," *U.S. News and World Report,* October 31, 1988, 22.

43. "The Great Denial," *National Review,* November 25, 1988, 14.

44. "America's Long March," *Los Angeles Times,* April 27, 1987, M4.

45. L. Spurling, *Phenomenology and the Social World: The Philosophy of Merleau-Ponty and its Relations to the Social Sciences* (London: Routledge, 1977), 28.

46. M. deCerteau, *The Practice of Everyday Life* (Berkeley: University of California Press, 1984), 176.

47. For a clear presentation of this orientation see O. Davis, M. Hinich, and P. Ordeshook, "An Expository Development of a Mathematical Model of the Electoral Process," *American Political Science Review, 64* (1970), 426-448.

48. M. Morse, "An Ontology of Everyday Distraction: The Freeway, the Mall and Television," in P. Mellencamp (ed.), *Logics of Television: Essays on Cultural Criticism* (Bloomington: Indiana University Press, 1990), 211.

49. C. Rawlence, "Political Theatre and the Working Class," in C. Gardner (ed.), *Media, Politics and Culture: A Socialist View* (London: Macmillan, 1979), 63.

50. J. Langer, "Television's 'Personality System,' " *Media, Culture and Society, 4* (1981), 361.

51. Langer, 357. Researcher Dennis Davis also discusses how television simulates visual "completeness" of this same sort. See "News and Politics," in D. Swanson and D. Nimmo (eds.), *New Directions in Political Communication: A Resource Book* (Newbury Park, CA: Sage, 1990), 168.

52. M. Foucault, *Power/Knowledge* (New York: Pantheon, 1980), 152.

53. D. Shaw and M. McCombs, *The Emergence of American Political Issues: The Agenda-Setting Function of the Press* (St. Paul, MN: West, 1977).

54. Iyengar and Kinder, 1987, 80-81.

55. S. Iyengar and D. Kinder, "More than Meets the Eye: TV News, Priming, and Public Evaluations of the President," *Public Communication and Behavior, 1* (1986), 135-171.

56. M. Pfau and J. G. Kang, "The Impact of Relational Messages on Candidate Influence in Televised Political Debates," *Communication Studies, 42* (1991), 124.

57. Graber, 1990, 146.

58. For more on such effects see R. Kubey and M. Csikszentmihalyi, *Television and the Quality of Life: How Viewing Shapes Everyday Experience* (Hillsdale, NJ: Erlbaum, 1990), 176.

59. D. Horton and R. Wohl, "Mass Communication and Para-Social Interaction: Observation on Intimacy at a Distance," in G. Gumpert and R. Cathcart (eds.), *Inter/Media: Interpersonal Communication in a Media World*, 3rd ed. (New York: Oxford University Press, 1986), 185-206.

60. Brody, 40.

61. This incident is reported in D. Nesbit, *Videostyle in Senate Campaigns* (Knoxville: University of Tennessee Press, 1988), 71. Effects like this may be produced by television's intense chumminess, a phenomenon that produces what researcher Robert Stam calls a "confusion of pronouns" for newswatchers. See his "Television News and Its Spectator," in E. A. Kaplan (ed.), *Regarding Television: Critical Approaches—An Anthology* (Frederick, MD: American Film Institute, 1983), 23-43.

62. R. Sennett, *The Fall of Public Man* (New York: Knopf, 1977), 261.

63. G. Spears, "Speculation Swirls around Powell and 'Stormin' Norman,' " *Austin American Statesman*, March 3, 1991, 6.

64. "The Eric Blumberg Show," 9:15 a.m., March 2, 1992, KLBJ Radio, Austin, Texas.

65. "The Eric Blumberg Show," 8:30 a.m., January 18, 1991, KLBJ Radio, Austin, Texas.

66. J. B. Elsthain, *Public Man, Private Woman: Women in Social and Political Thought* (Princeton, NJ: Princeton University Press, 1981), 342.

67. Sennett, 229-230.

68. This is political scientist Lance Bennett's phrasing. See his *News: The Politics of Illusion* (New York: Longman, 1983), 13.

69. "Joey" as quoted in M. Huspek and K. Kendall, "On Withholding Political Voice: An Analysis of the Political Vocabulary of a 'Nonpolitical' Speech Community," *Quarterly Journal of Speech, 77* (1991), 8.

70. For additional insight on this matter see K. H. Jamieson, *Eloquence in an Electronic Age: The Transformation of Political Speechmaking* (New York: Oxford, 1988), 196-197.

71. G. Bush, "Remarks and Exchange with Reporters Following Discussions with Prime Minister Margaret Thatcher of the United Kingdom in Paris, France," November 19, 1990, *Weekly Compilation of Presidential Documents, 26:47* (1990), 1865.

72. G. Bush, "Remarks to the Reserve Officers Association," January 23, 1991, *Weekly Compilation of Presidential Documents, 27:4* (1990), 73.

73. Bush, 1990, 1865.

74. *Newsweek* calls this a "tall tale" but relates it nonetheless. See "All in the Family?," *Newsweek*, January 21, 1991, 6.

75. "Don't Blink!" *Newsweek*, February 18, 1991, 12.

76. C. Dickey, "Looking the West 'Right in the Eye,' " *Newsweek*, December 10, 1990, 38.

77. C. Lane, "His Head on a Plate: Do Signs of Unrest Inside Iraq Mean Saddam's Grip on Power Is Weakening?" *Newsweek*, March 4, 1991, 40.

78. R. Nordland, "Inside Iraq," *Newsweek*, October 8, 1990, 22.

79. Dickey, 38.

80. Ibid.

81. T. Mathews, "Saddam's Last Stand," *Newsweek*, March 4, 1991, 18.

82. C. Schmitt, *The Concept of the Political*, Trans. G. Schwab (New Brunswick: Rutgers University Press, 1976), 27.

83. Schmitt, 36.

84. A. Kroker, "Baudrillard's Marx," *Theory, Culture and Society*, 3 (1985), 80.

85. J. Baudrillard, "The Ecstacy of Communication," in H. Foster (ed.), *The Anti-Aesthetic: Essays on Postmodern Culture* (Port Townsend, WA:Bay Press, 1983), 131.

86. For more on this topic, see Langer, 362.

87. R. Frank, *Passion within Reason: The Strategic Role of the Emotions* (New York: Norton, 1988), 248.

88. T. Patterson, "More Style Than Substance: Television News in U.S. National Elections," *Political Communication and Persuasion*, 8 (1991), 157-158.

89. M. Robinson, "American Political Legitimacy in an Era of Electronic Journalism: Reflections on the Evening News," in D. Cater and R. Adler (eds.), *Television as a Social Force: New Approaches to TV Criticism* (New York: Praeger, 1975), 101.

90. W. Donsbach, H-B. Brosius, and A. Mattenklott, "How Unique Is the Perspective of Television: A Field Experiment on the Perception of a Campaign Event by Participants and Television Viewers," *Political Communication*, 10 (1993), 37-53.

91. M. Robinson, "Public Affairs Television and the Growth of Political Malaise: The Case of 'The Selling of the Pentagon,' " *American Political Science Review*, 70 (1976), 425.

92. S. Wolin, "Postmodern Politics and the Absence of Myth," *Social Research*, 52 (1985), 224.

93. For more on this matter, see C. D. Livingston, " The Televised Presidency," *Presidential Studies Quarterly*, 16 (1986), 22-30.

94. C. Geertz, *Local Knowledge: Further Essays in Interpretive Anthropology* (New York: Basic Books, 1983), 143.

95. A. Norton, *Reflections on Political Identity* (Baltimore, MD: Johns Hopkins University Press, 1988), 48.

Box 3.1 Inquiries and Transitions

Perhaps this chapter overstates its case; perhaps exploring the personalities of politicians makes sense. But if such knowledge is important, how do we get it? Politicians do not normally trot out their mental health records, after all, and their ex-spouses are notoriously biased about such matters, so to whom do we turn? More fundamentally, why do we need to turn at all? Why are we so compelled to read the souls of people we have not met and cannot meet? Why do we willingly let television's reporters put candidates on the couch for us? Why can we not be satisfied with the public record the candidate has established, or failed to establish, information that can easily be obtained? Perhaps the Internet will change our habits in this regard. With so much factual information just a mouse-click away, will television's dominance over our perceptions finally be broken? Will we now become librarians rather than psychiatrists, or will we slip back into the clutches of a medium—television—that seems innocent of motive? Having grown up with television, having depended upon it for so many pleasures, can we still retrieve the power we have ceded it? Can we remain enlightened if we do not?

4

Feeling Clever

The Cold Comforts of Postmodernism

Feeling informed and feeling clever are different. To feel informed is to have a general lay of the land, to know the basics. As we have seen, voters feel informed in these ways when they come to know political people through the media. Feeling informed makes voters assured, sometimes even serene. Feeling clever also makes voters assured but it mostly makes them smug. Feeling clever is more than knowing what happens in politics; it is knowing why it happened—and how.

To feel clever is to become a political methodologist, an expert on the moves and countermoves of the public sphere. In an electronic age, it means knowing about negative advertising and focus groups, about polling statistics and press maneuverings, about soundbites and pancake make-up. It means reacting to changing political circumstances quickly and then predicting the resulting counterreactions. It means going to work each day and speaking of politics like fraternity boys speak of their sexual conquests. It means preferring Dennis Miller's political humor to Johnny Carson's, respecting comedian Dana Carvey's George Bush more than George Bush's George Bush. Feeling clever means having "an attitude."

Television also has an attitude and it has leaked into the political mainstream. Ironically enough, television's central attitude—that politics is a dastardly business—has developed because of the medium's own technological and aesthetic tendencies. Thus, because of media forces, Ronald Reagan spoke most often to friendly audiences, making it hard for the networks to assemble a collection of hecklers for the nightly news. Similarly, Gary Hart announced his candidacy for the presidency at the top of the Rockies, assuming that television could not resist covering such a luscious visual event. Echoing his approach in 1992, Bill Clinton preceded his triumphant convention in 1996 with a train trip through the heartland, thereby proving himself a fine understudy of that inveterate rustic, the late Charles Kuralt. In other words, the formats and styles wrought by television are now being rewrought by politicians.

This is also true at a textual level. Richard Nixon's meta-communicative habits of anticipating reactions to a speech even while making the speech ("You probably aren't going to believe this, but . . . " or "There are many in the press who don't like me and yet . . . ") have become epidemic.[1] The long-standing struggle between the press and the White House has jumped a level of abstraction as the arts of spin and counterspin have matured. Questions of the "How will it play?" sort have given way to infinitely more subtle queries: "If it plays poorly at first will that produce a compensatory outpouring of sympathy later on?" and "If it plays well with Group X, will that enrage their antagonists—Group Y?"

In an age of television, that is to say, one cannot possibly be too clever by half. For example, even before a single negative advertisement had been run in the 1992 presidential campaign, Republican guru Robert Teeter warned that the Bush message "would have to be sharpened" as the campaign wore on.[2] "And there is nothing wrong with such tactics," he also declared, since politics has always been a rough-and-tumble sport. Truly, here is cleverness: Being offensive about being defensive about being offensive; using a sharpening metaphor to describe a blunt instrument (negative advertising); telling representatives of a medium how they should frame a picture that had not yet been painted.

The theme of this chapter is that politics has gone postmodern. In announcing that theme, one almost instinctively heads for cover—so much has already been written about postmodernism that all else threatens to become cliché, or worse. In academia today, the battles inspired by postmodernism are being waged with a ferocity unknown to that gentle profession. And the battles have opened on multiple fronts. Because postmodernism is largely a French import, it enrages many Americanists; and because it combines outrageous assumptions with a totalistic vocabulary, it is rejected out of hand by most behavioral scientists; because it rejects philosophical endpoints and norms, it is thought godless by those who have not already declared it nonsense.

Postmodernism has the singular honor of being rejected by Marxists as well as free enterprisers, by pragmatists as well as foundationalists, by empiricists as well as phenomenologists,[3] and by many (though not all) feminists. For scholars not yet listed, postmodernism offers other insults: It is anti-definitional; it prizes discontinuity and carnivalization; it rejects all pretenses to authority; and it refuses to think of itself as an itself (as a bounded school of thought).[4]

Although the philosophical roots of postmodernism are complex, many of its strains can be traced to the often nihilistic writings of Friedrich Nietzsche. But it was probably the 1968 student riots in Paris that brought the needed intellectual and political energy to postmodern thought. The students, and more often their professors, launched blistering attacks on the modernist mindset, a mindset that championed technological development and capitalistic dominance.

In architecture, postmodern thinkers rejected the glass and steel "boxes" erected in the 1950s as tabernacles of corporate advancement; in their places, they erected far more playful, organic structures. In philosophy, Jacques Derrida and Michel Foucault wrote manifestos upending Anglo-Germanic structuralism. In literary studies, Paul DeMan and Roland Barthes radically reexamined old texts and called attention to startlingly new texts. In cultural studies, Jean Baudrillard and Jean-Francois Lyotard examined the signs and images unleashed in a fast-paced, uncertain world. Thus, although the postmodern movement is broad and deep, it does have some resonant watchwords: individuality, freedom, incompleteness, complexity, interrogation.[5]

Postmodern treatises on conventional politics are far less common, no doubt because postmodernists reject traditional statecraft out of hand. Given the purposes of this book, then, why waste our time with postmodernism? We must waste our time with postmodernism because its language has become the language of television and because the language of television has become the language of politics. At its best, postmodern thought explains some of the things people now feel when they think about governance. They have come to feel, for example, that politics is an art of image construction and not a science of community building. They often feel daunted and disoriented by the swirl of politics and they have come to accept that condition as natural.

They see history as boring, irrelevant, and submit themselves only to the discipline of the moment. They are no longer moved by the great myths of the past for they find them too ideological.

On the "positive" side of postmodernism, modern Americans do enjoy the blending of high and low cultures that television encourages, as, for example, when a former Yale president became head of the American League or when New York City's Italian American mayor appeared on *Saturday Night Live* brandishing a baseball bat to defend the honor of bat-wielding mafiosos. Today's audiences also appreciate commentators who deconstruct the president and academics who deconstruct news commentators. They enjoy the schmoozing between Hollywood's elite and Washington's elite, and they fully accept irony as the master trope of politics. In short, they subscribe, at least in part, to the postmodern credo: "Let us wage a war on totality; let us be witnesses to the unpresentable."[6]

One could spend half a lifetime embroiled in the theoretical controversies surrounding postmodern thought. As we approach the turn of the century, there is nary an academic discipline that has not given this particular devil his due. The controversies it favors lie at the epicenter of the storm known as "political correctness" and they are featured in debates about literary deconstruction, multiculturalism, critical legal studies, and much else. My approach here will be considerably less exalted. I shall avoid the highly theorized questions about postmodernism and focus instead on what voters feel when they *feel postmodern*. I shall use the term *postmodern* stipulatively, not comprehensively or exhaustively, certainly not canonically. I use it to refer to the complex of attitudes television encourages when it declares politics textual. Television makes that declaration in a variety of ways. Here, I shall count the ways.

Cynical Politics

Sociology plays a cruel trick on those who age. As if aging itself were not cruel enough, each generation creates semantic thresholds to determine cultural fittingness, to say "I am of this moment." In the 1930s, one was "in vogue," but in the 1940s, one had to be "chic." In the 1950s, "hip" replaced "cool." The 1960s "mod" became the 1970s "rad." Our list stops here, proving that its author is no longer any of these things. He can no longer just be of this moment because he has lived too many moments. He is burdened by his history, out of touch with the self-reflexive tokens of youth. He is, in his own phraseology, no longer hip.

Television compensates by tutoring us in the self-updating language of media. It does so in several ways, one of which is by making cynicism cool. Think, for example, about what being cynical says. It says that I am young but not a child, cynicism being too sophisticated an emotion for youth, too harsh an emotion for the elderly. It also says that I am a person of few commitments, ideas being too insubstantial and people too undependable to be revered. It means, in the language of postmodernism, that having "an incredulity toward metanarratives"[7] is the only self-protective route in modern times as all prior myths have been long since been interred.

Being cynical also means that I am articulate, that I can give voice to the incongruities of life, that I can speak of multiple things simultaneously. Ultimately, of course, being cynical means that I am media-savvy. It means I see the shadows dancing in Plato's cave and applaud them. I do so because applause is the universal sign of respect in an age of distanced interactions and because shadows are the only realities that modern reality permits.

Naturally, one must be careful not to blame television alone for such attitudes. Between the 1950s and the 1990s, political cynicism grew prodigiously for many reasons. In 1958, 24% of the American people felt that "government cannot be trusted to do the right thing."[8] That figure grew steadily over the years and crested at 73% in 1980, virtually a threefold increase in only 25 years. A question like "government is run for big interests only" produced similar polling results, as did "public officials don't care what people like me think." Vietnam, Watergate and, more recently, an uninspiring economy are said to explain these results. There is much to be said for those explanations, for if government cannot stop wars, maintain public morality, and put money in our pockets, it is hardly worth much.

Other studies also reveal structural aspects of political cynicism. Researchers Donald Kanter and Philip Mirvis, for example, found that young people were generally more cynical than older people, as were men more than women and minorities more than whites. Poorly educated and low-income voters were more cynical than their richer, better educated counterparts; rural residents were more cynical than urbanites. The widowed were more cynical than the married, pink collars more cynical than white collars, and union members most cynical of all.[9]

An economic determinist would have little difficulty interpreting these data: The have-nots have nothing but their cynicisms. But economics alone does not explain why *all* Americans are more cynical than before. It does not explain why some of the most successful Americans no longer vote or why they were drawn to a third-party candidacy in 1996. It does not explain why the trends cited above were just that—trends, not laws—and it does not explain why some people within a group can remain optimistic while others in that same group cannot.

My sense is that something cultural, not just economic, is happening here as everything is now overexposed in the United States—all sin, all corruption. Television's exposures flatten the perceptual landscape, making all things equally indistinct but pleasingly so. Often, these pleasures are tawdry pleasures. We come to know that some priests are pedophiles, that some corporate accountants are dishonest, that some teachers are incompetent. In each case, these are exceptions, but that is precisely what television deals with—the exceptional.

Those who live on a steady diet of television become trapped. For them, the exceptional becomes the expected and the expected perverse. In such a world, cynicism becomes an intelligent option or, at least, a realistic one. It represents "the urge of individuals to maintain themselves as fully rational beings against the distortions and semirationalites" of society, says one observer.[10] Says another: "There has been a substantial but undeniable *growth* in felt inefficacy between 1952 and the mid-1970s" and "reliance on public affairs television is, in fact, associated with lower scores on the efficacy index."[11] In the intervening years, little has changed.

The attractions of political cynicism are amply demonstrated by shows like *The McLaughlin Report* and *The Capital Gang* in which the fiercest journalistic warriors gather round the political campfire. Here is classic purgation. The ritual sword is drawn and the Blood of Politics captured in a silver vessel. In the background, one hears the yelping of dogs. We, members of the tribe, attend the campfire, in part because death fascinates but in part because ritual builds community. We rally around the commentators as they skewer yet another bloated politico. Television superintends these ceremonies of cynicism, ceremonies that produce "a common ground of the deceived gaze and of false consciousness," ceremonies in which cultural unification results from "an official language of generalized separation."[12]

The emotions displayed on *The McLaughlin Report* and *The Capital Gang*—the shouting, the name-calling, the exotic spontaneity—are truly primitive. They are pagan emotions, the sort that worried the Roman church in the Middle Ages and that eventually spawned the Enlightenment. But "the Enlightenment had never been able to form an effective alliance with the mass media," says Peter Sloterdijk,"[13] primarily because the language of television is so naturally cynical, at least where politics is concerned.

In his masterwork, *Critique of Cynical Reason*, Sloterdijk draws special attention to Weimar Germany where "the expectation of being deceived . . . had become a universal state of consciousness."[14] Such an age, says Sloterdijk, fed on the dramatic and the simplistic, and Adolf Hitler arose to translate those needs into political terms. At first it seems odd that totalitarianism could grow out of an age that prized irony—the antithesis of doctrinaire thought. Indeed, some commentators feel that the ironist's "more lighthearted" and "less self-important" stance should insulate a nation from political excess. Postmodernism "is not anxious about whether it [makes] a lasting cultural statement," says David Hoy, and hence can resist all political orthodoxies.

The postmodern individual treasures irony because it lets the individual look his or her executioner in the eye. But then there is the voice of Voltaire: "If we believe in absurdities, we shall commit atrocities." Does postmodernism foster nihilism, especially when it is abetted by television's deconstructions? Are needs for the dramatic and the simplistic, two of television's staples, pressing upon us once more? Does television turn us into Lot's wife, our eyes feasting on the political spectacle but our bodies frozen in inaction?[15] In trying to be clever like Charles Krauthammer, are we losing something important, perhaps forever?

> A few weeks ago, a producer from public television came to ask my advice about planning coverage for the 1992 elections. Toward that end, she raised a special problem: how to get young adults interested in political coverage. I offered the opinion that 19-year-olds who sit in front of a television watching politics could use professional help. At that age they should be playing ball and looking for a date. They'll have time enough at my age to worry about the mortgage and choosing a candidate on the basis of his views on monetary policy.[16]

Krauthammer's advice is characteristic of the professional cynic in another way: He urges an almost total preoccupation with the present. Indeed, the great pleasure of television is that it gives us something to do *at the moment*. We turn it on and it is fully there. We have not prepared for television but television has prepared for us—50 channels of programming at the touch of a switch. News, now. Comedy, now. Drama, now. Sports, now. This makes television vigorously ahistorical and that is one of its greatest attractions. Its total engagement in the moment makes the bitter past subside and it brackets an uncertain future as well. Television catches us up in the jumble of present events, present pleasures. One could live a lifetime in front of the television set and yet feel suspended in a single instant.

Politics, on the other hand, makes no sense without history. Although we elect our leaders to solve the problems of daily existence, we expect them to be bound by pre-established understandings when doing so. That is, if it takes financial kickbacks or faulty engineering or unfair labor practices to get a needed bridge built on time, a society will naturally seek a better solution. Even when problems press it, a society reasons, historical truths endure. Or should. But television sediments history. It focuses on history's top layer—the present, the literally superficial. That invites cynicism, as events without a history seem expedient and people without a history seem callow. With the exception of PBS documentaries and the occasional network news special, the temporal deep structure of events is removed on television. Politicians' emotions fill up the screen but, because those emotions are unmoored by historic commitments or sacred compacts, they seem grasping, as do most things that spring forth suddenly and with uncertain purpose.

Before television, it was possible to live in the present without being dominated by it. That is much harder today. Because we know so much about political affairs so quickly, we have no time to look for the grand pattern, the overarching explanation. We become tossed about on the tides of the off-hand comment, the extemporized visual. In a way, that makes us once again an "oral" society, a pre-print civilization where human memory became vital because writing was impracticable or impossible.[17] Being post-print has hardly changed that condition. And television's producers and reporters are not solely to blame. Nor are politicians, although they could surely do more to link policy to principle. No, it is technology that hides history. What Walter Benjamin has said about film applies equally well, perhaps better, to television: "I can no longer think what I want to think. My thoughts have been replaced by moving images."[18]

Our daily relationships tell us that persons who have no history are airy, weightless, not to be trusted. To understand another we want to know where they are "coming from," what had occupied their heart and mind previously. Used in this way, history is no arcane academic subject but a measuring rod people use instinctively. But for many people history is boring and so all become joined in a postmodern conspiracy that results, according to sociologist Mike Featherstone, in "the fragmentation of time into a series of perpetual presents."[19] In other words, there is not only too little history on television but too many presents as well. Television provides huge supplies of raw data about governance and does so each minute of each day, thereby precipitating an endless series of deferrals on our part: "Why become concerned today when tomorrow will be another today?"

A cynical person is a person who stands back, who resists involvement. Distrustful of both people and institutions, the cynic expects the worst and generally finds it. Perhaps without meaning to, television encourages this sort of standing back by making politics a display, a curiosity, something to be seen but not engaged. "The people did not want the [French] Revolution," said the cynic Rivarol, "they only wanted the spectacle."[20] Have we moderns arrived there as well? Are we now so saturated by affairs of the moment that we can only generate "spasms of public attention?"[21] With Ethiopian relief problems dominating the news at 6:00 p.m. and a closed Youngstown steel plant doing so an hour later, who could possibly imagine that politics makes a difference?

Only someone with an imagination. But television makes imagining difficult.[22] With television, an old theological principle applies: The immanent drives out the transcendent. By offering us so many matters to contemplate, television makes it hard, or profitless, to find the connective tissues. Television makes us atheoretical, just as it makes us ahistorical. It invites us to dwell in the moment and nowhere else. And that is where cynicism resides as well.

Textual Politics

Forty years ago, Yale political scientist Ralph Lane asked blue-collar workers what they thought of politics. Generally, they did not like it. But Lane found something else as well:

> Congressmen, as we have said, are associated with oral activity, bureaucrats with paper work. For all men, but particularly for working-class men, this wordiness has a vaguely threatening, somewhat distasteful quality. Sullivan, the truck driver, speaking of congressmen meeting their constituents, feels that in this flow of words "lots of times they've nothing to say"—a futile and embarrassing enterprise. Woodside, the railroad guard, says of the bureaucrat, "I imagine he would have the position of going through a tremendous amount of paper work." Johnson, a mechanic, and Rapuano, a clerk, distinguish between the civil servant who is out in the open doing something important

and the man in the office who is shuffling papers around. Wordiness, whether spoken or written, produces among all people—but especially among working class people—an ambivalence that, as we have seen, is likely to attach to government, particularly to a democracy.[23]

The attitudes that Lane taps here are still with us. Because of television, they are with us profoundly. For many Americans, politics is a way of speaking, not a way of living. For them, governance has less to do with Constitutional rights than with politicians' rhetorical addictions. Government produces press releases, not hydroelectric dams or interstate highways. The White House is a television studio, the State Department a xerox machine. The nation is drowning in words.

"Why bother? It's all talk," says the political truant on election day. "Discourse concerning politics" has been replaced by "discourse concerning signs," says Kyosti Pekonen a bit more verbosely.[24] But their points are the same: We cannot escape words in an age of television, nor can we escape words about words. "Politics has gone meta," says communication scholar Herbert Simons,[25] meaning that candidates now talk about their opponents' talk more than about their nation's destiny.

For example, when asked during the 1990 Texas gubernatorial race what he thought of Clayton Williams' analogy between rape and bad weather ("you might as well relax and enjoy it"), then-governor and fellow Republican Bill Clements declared, "I'm sure he'll be more careful in the future." Here is a sign of the times: Moral outrage replaced by rhetorical coaching. Ironically, the Williams campaign was ultimately dealt a death blow by a second meta-symbolic event: his refusal to shake hands with his opponent, Ann Richards, prior to a joint appearance. But the story is even more intricate, for it was later revealed that Mr. Williams had *planned* to spurn Richards' outstretched hand. And yet there is more: Williams, it turns out, had also *reflected on his planning* in front of media personnel prior to the event. Oh what a tangled web Clayton Williams wove.

If one were an unemployed farmworker watching the Williams' *contretemps* on a rented television set, one would surely declare a pox on all politicians. With politics now producing what Jean Baudrillard calls a "promiscuity of information,"[26] it insults many voters and seems silly to others. Television is partly responsible. "This must be the best speech of Bob Dole's life," the networks ponderously declared before Dole's acceptance speech in 1996, thereby trying to drum up an audience for the Republicans as well as themselves. The networks constantly hype the symbolic in these ways—the pivotal ad campaign, the do-or-die press conference—just as the commercials of a widget manufacturer offer pity to those who plan to die widgetless. Campaign coverage utters two words: Stay tuned.

Staying tuned to politics is not a horrible thing. But it does pose questions: What must people think when the media tell them how politics *works* rather than what politics *does*? What did they think of the 1988 presidential primaries when, out of 1300 television news stories, 500 were devoted to the "horesrace," 300 to "campaign strategies and tactics," and only 215 to policy differences between the candidates?[27] What did they think of the 1988 general election when the media devoted almost 30% of its coverage to such topics as dirty tricks, campaign style, debate protocols, and vice presidential candidates' electability?[28] What did they think of the nuclear freeze movement when even the venerable *New York Times* spent most of its time analyzing the movement's tactics and its members' colorful personalities?[29] What did they think when television made Roger Ailes—political assassin extraordinaire—a primary site for its coverage?[30] What did they think when a major publication declared Mikhail Gorbachev's attempt to avert the Gulf war a "peace gambit" orchestrated by a man attempting to "pose as a peacemaker" but who, in reality, was just "seeking publicity?"[31] Here is what they would think: Fie on politics.

Actually, television asks us not to think but to doublethink. When listening to the news, for example, one is often struck by the abject fear on reporters' faces that they will be late in uncovering a new political subterfuge. To stave off that fate, they turn to communications experts. Even during the Persian Gulf war, a war about truly elemental matters—who would have oil, who would live where, who would be bombed—scholars were called upon to interpret the messages coming out of Baghdad and Washington. A media preoccupation of this sort turns history into a "parade of meanings enacted through the use of language," says sociologist John Murphy.[32] It turns politics into a "literary field," according to Pierre Bourdieu,[33] thereby opening up employment to a new breed of academic specialists. This new breed presses "the networks to be less passive, to tell the public more about the candidates' image-making strategies," says scholar Dan Hallin. That "the networks have done so," observes Hallin, "is surely an advance."[34]

One wonders. It is easy to see how meta-commentaries can be good for television since they are self-promotional in effect, if not in design. By showing how politics is textual, television makes bill-passing, fund-raising, and other workaday forms of political action seem irrelevant. But are these indulgences good for us? Yes, says the rhetorical lobby: "Such coverage may help make citizens more intelligent and sophisticated consumers of the news," opines one political scientist.[35] Uncovering the "fictive impulse and restor[ing] it as a matter of appreciation," says a postmodernist, protects "society from the delusion which could be worked upon it."[36]

The American people are responsive to these inducements for several reasons. For one thing, they like competition, and so charting the punches-thrown and punches-landed in politics becomes a pleasant avocation. Americans are also technologists and so they worship the god in the machine—the computerized phone banks, the concocted visuals, the pre-coached audiences. They like it when their news commentators use game metaphors to describe politics because that makes governance safe, impersonal, pleasantly unreal.[37] Textual politics, in Terry Eagleton's terms,[38] is first a process of aestheticizing—paying attention to the brush strokes instead of the landscape—and then of fetishizing—turning political strategy into an object of veneration.

This sort of thing worries political philosopher Sheldon Wolin. In an impassioned essay, Wolin conjures up the specter of a "manufactured world of information" filled with postmodern cleverness but "dumbfounded in the presence of generational cycles of poverty, poor education, and disease."[39] By becoming preoccupied with political images, says Wolin, a nation makes political decision making harder and harder. Worse, says Wolin, it distracts us from the real levers of power in civic life. In such a managed society, argues Wolin, symbolists become the unwitting handmaidens of tyranny. Wolin is hard on the postmodernists:

> In the self-defined age of information and communication, where knowledge is said to be power, and new knowledge more power, managed democracies do need intellectuals who are adept with words and images, who realize that words are more important than beliefs, that contingency is at fault, and who are sufficiently infatuated with their own self-importance as to believe that the "founders" of the liberal utopia will be "poets" rather than the "people who had discovered or clearly envisioned the truth about the world or about humanity." Nowhere is the woman or man of language skills more useful than in the democratic elections of a managed democracy. Then true creativity flourishes to fashion a make-believe world of distortion, half-truths, lies, smears, gossip, appeals to fear, patriotism, xenophobia, racial code words, and imaginary foreign monsters (sc. "Libyan hit-squads"). It is the greatest Language Revel ever conceived.[40]

Inter-Textual Politics

One of television's most characteristic features is also its most subtle. Inter-textuality refers to the patchwork nature of the medium, the fact that any one text has buried within it the remnants of other texts. This produces a "chaos of texts" in politics, says critic Fred Pfeil,[41] but a pleasant chaos. This jumble of individual images produces something new, something that contains these images but that is more than them as well. Mikhail Bakhtin points out that most really rich messages have such "internal dialogues" built into them.[42]

During the 1996 presidential campaign, for example, the real trick for both Republicans and Democrats was mixing Perotist language ("time to fix things," "embattled middle class," "public-private partnerships") with traditional party language. This was not hard to do given television's verbal and visual features. So, for example, Democratic commercials depicted middle-Americans, not Rainbow Coalition members, and Republican commercials depicted middle-Americans, not the country club set. In a sense, Ross Perot owned all of the advertisements produced in 1996.

Through television, politics can now reach across language forms, ideologies, and cultural groupings (e.g., pictures of Hillary Clinton sitting with children in an inner-city school). It can reach across time and place as well (e.g., Ronald Reagan giving a commemorative speech at Normandy). In doing so, television creates a "confusing simultaneity of the non-simultaneous,"[43] making it hard to know what is happening when and where. Through its video archives, television can call up all persons who have lived recently, all thoughts that have ever been thought. Through its editing machines, television can then fashion them into a semiotic salad. When Peter Sloterdijk says that the media are "the descendants of both the encyclopedia and the circus,"[44] this is surely what he has in mind.

Knowing television as he did, Ronald Reagan became an intertextual giant. In many ways, he was Everyman. Political scientist Michael Rogin has written a rollicking book, *Ronald Reagan: The Movie*, showing how elements of popular culture (usually Hollywood films) found their way into both Reagan's speeches and casual comments, often without the chief executive knowing it. In his public statements, Reagan became celluloid figures George Gipp, Drake McHugh, and, memorably, Dirty Harry, all without dropping a line or revealing a juncture.

In postmodern language, Reagan "was written" by his culture rather than being his own author. This made his rhetoric democratic, a skillful blend of diverse materials.[45] But his rhetoric was Democratic as well. Communication scholar Deborah Smith-Howell found, for example, that when Reagan referred to his predecessors in the White House while on the campaign stump, 75% of his allusions were to Democrats, three in particular: Harry Truman (17.8%), John Kennedy (17.2%), and Franklin Roosevelt (12.4%).[46]

Reagan's penchant was not his alone. Televised politics often produces this smashing and crashing of symbols. Religious fundamentalists attack pornography as "anti-feminist." Gay activists emphasize their monogamous "family values." An otherwise progressive governor campaigns in front of pictures of the convicts executed under his watch. An ex-Klansman argues that he is for "equal rights" for lower-class whites. A beverage manufacturer speaks ecologically of his company's "recyclable containers" and a cigarette company speaks insurgently of its female customers "who've come a long way." In the postmodern age, says philosopher Ihab Hassan, "signs scatter like so many leaves and authorities wither in the chill autumn of our discontents."[47]

In many ways, intertextuality is what makes television interesting and enjoyable. It lets fresh images dance before our eyes and makes new associations possible. There is freedom in all this and a dose of creativity, too. In his 1992 convention film (A Place Called Hope), for example, Bill Clinton used the occasion to reposition himself in the eyes of the American people, to remove the cardboard image of Slick Willie, philanderer, trojan horse liberal, Ivy Leaguer. The film reached far and wide for contrary images, depicting Clinton as an erstwhile Junior Achiever, devoted son of an abused mother, a smalltown fellow with an open heart, a loving parent. In permitting, even encouraging, this new rhetorical mixture, television helped give the Democratic campaign a new lease on the election.

But intertextuality presents its challenges as well. Who, exactly, owns cultural images? What may be done with them? With television encouraging the "free play of signifiers," who shall police the associations it produces? Was the Kennedy family pleased, for example, that Bill Clinton was able to dredge up a picture of himself shaking hands with their martyred hero? Were the townsfolk of Hope, Arkansas, consulted before Mr. Clinton turned their town into a metaphor?

When phrased like this, critiques of postmodernism seem ludicrous. "Nobody owns referents in a media age," argue its defenders, "all persons may poach in the past." Still, one wonders. Even when retrofitted, after all, symbols have a history, an earned dignity, if you will. Was Bill Clinton implying, with his use of the Kennedy footage, that he, too, would pay any price and bear any burden in defense of liberty? Was his economic philosophy broad enough to defend the unions in their time of travail, his international philosophy catholic enough to revivify the Peace Corps, his educational philosophy ambitious enough to grant new federal aid to the nation's schools? The Kennedy image, in short, has entailments. It is indeed possible to violate the past.[48] Those who use television to sell their wares are unconcerned about such things, but that does not mean that they are unimportant. Somebody should worry about them. Perhaps us.

Politics Adrift

Watching television is delightful because it is not hard to do. We sit, the pictures move. They flow past our eyes like a primordial stream. Except for the omnipresent commercials, the breaks between television's images are very soft breaks. Game shows turn into sitcoms and then into detective shows. Tomorrow, baseball becomes the lottery and that leads to Bill Moyers. Psychologically, of course, viewers must make transitions between these different viewing experiences but television's "flow," its seamlessness, makes that easy. With remote control devices and sufficient digital dexterity, an experienced viewer can even become artful—and commercial-aversive—when assembling an evening's collage.

Politics is part of this flow and that is a problem. It is a problem because, as Michel deCerteau says, the postmodern experience has made us all "wanderers." "The story of man's travels through his own texts," argues deCerteau, "remains in large measure unknown."[49] When a viewer watches politics, as a result, the viewer becomes citizen and audience member at the same time. As a result, politics seeps out of its own space. More ominously, it comes to have no space of its own. A presidential press conference is followed by a tractor pull. A news special on starving Sudanese is interrupted by a Volvo commercial. A comedy channel lampoons the Republican convention while CBS dutifully covers it. Television's various genres are therefore linked by a Continual And. With that And, "all things can be turned into neighbors."[50]

And so: Where is politics? It is part of the cultural mix. It no longer has a special, set-apart place. No moment of time is its special time. Coat and tie, heels and hose, are no longer needed when watching the president's inaugural address. We can watch the leader of the free world while seated at home in our undershorts, belching. There is an almost Romantic strain to all this: shirtsleeved people, or no-sleeved people, in direct contact with their leaders, the old, elitist barriers torn down, all Americans swimming in television's flow. The majority leader of the senate sits next to the snake handler on *Donahue*. Surely this is what Jefferson had in mind.

It would seem pure stodginess to argue otherwise. Should not politics, the people's business, be found right where the people are found, worrying about the people's worries? "If George Bush had done a guest spot on the Home Shopping Network," some might argue, "he would have learned how to check out groceries in the supermarket." That is why it was necessary for Jimmy Carter to do woodworking and for Bill Clinton to play the saxophone. These were not just political requirements but aesthetic requirements as well. "Just as a television commercial will use an athlete, an actor, a musician, a novelist, a scientist, or a countess to speak for the virtues of a product in no way within their domain of expertise," says communication scholar Neil Postman, "television also frees politicians from the limited field of their own expertise."[51]

In addition to forcing politics into popular culture, television encourages movement in the opposite direction. The postmodern world conflates social problems and entertainment each day: A bag lady appears on *The Young and the Restless*; Robin Williams turns environmental decay into shtick; Willie Nelson sings for the farmers; HBO does both homelessness and Madonna. This sort of thing "carnivalizes" politics, says Mike Featherstone,[52] but that too seems small-minded, especially since Elton John's "Candle in the Wind" earned millions of dollars for Princess Di's charities. Such cultural events cut through the red tape of governmental programs and get relief to "those who need it most." Cultural events like these make politics seem easy.

In short, because of television, we rarely find politics in an undiluted state anymore. We are not asked to "think athletic" and then suddenly to "think political." Television makes our watching far more seamless, a world in which all things are related to all other things and in which nothing stands out. Television abhors traditional distinctions between learning and laughing, between thinking and doing, between the real and the unreal. This is what relaxation means, after all—relaxing the structures that confine us when punching a time clock or riding the subway.

Television has even invented special forms to make relaxing simpler. The "infomercial" makes corporate medicine go down more easily and the "docudrama" makes history more absorbing than it was in junior high school. Television even obliterates differences between the fictive and the nonfictive. When questioned what he thought about a segment from *The Wonder Years* that dealt with student activism, for example, a college student became apologetic: "It's not really fair to ask me, since I'm from Ann Arbor and lived here during the sixties."[53] For this viewer, at least, his real life experiences had rendered him incompetent. In his world, only television had authority.

On television, politics becomes an indistinct domain. In media scholar Margaret Morse's terms, the "interpenetration of layer upon layer of built environment and representation, the formative and the derivative, the imaginary and mundane" turns politics into an expression "of both Kansas and Oz."[54] Even if network executives really wished to be civics teachers and even if politicians truly detested celebrity, politics would still be gray because television surrounds it with technicolor.

There is, as a result, an inherent, technologically determined tension between television and politics because the former is meant to divert us and the latter to rivet us. Television is also meant to be watched, politics to be done. Television is meant for individual enjoyment, politics for institutional advancement. Television awakens us to things in general, politics to things in particular. Television tells complete stories; politics is always naggingly unfinished. Despite the best intentions of many people, then, television pushes politics to the margins.

If politics lies at the margins, what lies at the center? That question is now raging on American college campuses as professors debate matters of cultural politics. Curiously, though, those debates have made politics—the politics of statecraft, that is—hard to find. Consider, for example, some book titles:

A Poverty of Objects: The Prose Poem and the Politics of Genre
Beauty Secrets: Women and the Politics of Appearance
Bettine von Armin and the Politics of Romantic Conversation
Death and Dissymmetry: The Politics of Coherence in the Book of Judges
Friedrich Nietzsche and the Politics of the Soul
Language and the Politics of Emotion
Scenes from Corporate Life: The Politics of Middle Management
Sound Effects: Youth, Leisure, and the Politics of Rock and Roll
The City as Text: The Politics of Landscape Interpretation in the Kandyan Kingdom

Nary an academic subject matter has been missed here. Surely, then, the campuses must be afire in the late 1990s. Alas, the opposite is often true. Many college students are strangers to the voting booth. For them and for many of their professors, politics is nowhere because politics is everywhere.

When politics and culture become merged in these ways, the very notion of politics is threatened. By making politics a private and not a state-based matter, too much is walled out in an attempt to wall in still more. Sociologist Todd Gitlin cautions that these overinclusions succeed only in attenuating politics: "It is pure sloppiness to conclude that culture or pleasure *is* politics. Culture is mistaken for politics only by default—only in a society stripped of opportunities for serious politics. Let us face the depoliticization of society and not take refuge in the consolations of cultural celebration."[55]

Despite Gitlin's warnings, the feminists argue that "the personal is political" and the postmodernists scoff that "politics is mere text." College students hear such statements and, not being stupid, get the same message that television gives them: that conventional politics is boring. This is not to say, of course, that women should refrain from focusing public attention on such personal matters as reproductive rights and sexual harassment on the job. But it is to say that television is making it too easy for people to feel political but to *do* nothing about such matters, matters that can only be resolved by the force of law—which is to say, by the force of democratic politics.

In contrast, however, today's cultural products have so many political overtones that one feels one has leapt the very barricades when watching a segment of *Murphy Brown*. In other words, conservative critics like Allan Bloom, Roger Kimball, and Dinesh D'Souza have gotten the campus scene quite backwards when assailing its New Radicalism. An equally strong case could be made that, by emphasizing the purely symbolic, cultural politicians have made the campuses quiescent. Television, too, carries that message. It interweaves so many parapolitical themes into its programming that the political has taken to hiding in public. That is a postmodern effect of some magnitude.

Conclusion

This chapter presents a conundrum: If feeling clever is worrisome, is feeling unclever beneficial? In some ways, it is. After all, by deconstructing politics, clever people underestimate what politics can build. By emphasizing texts, clever people overlook the forces of good and evil that listen rather than speak. By featuring political subtleties, clever people miss obvious things about politics in a vigorous democracy: that government generally serves the people well, that most political crimes are eventually solved, that no matter how corrupt politicians may become, they are our only hope.

In an age of cleverness, such statements seem fatuous. But uncleverness is worth at least a short paean. Because they know so little, the unclever remain moderately optimistic. Because they are not consumed with images, they have time for other people. Because the unclever are functional, they are hard to distract. They therefore produce three qualities central to governance: hope, community, and a sense of purpose. This may seem like weak tea in a postmodern age, but it is tea that can nourish.

Perhaps television's greatest danger is the license it gives to citizen inaction. Postmodernism's cynicism, its concentration on "surfaces," and its strategic convolutions back people away from the political sphere. In doing so, postmodernism becomes reactionary. According to one study by political scientist Arthur Miller and his colleagues, the news media typically criticize political individuals rather than political institutions, thereby contributing to a kind of enlightened desperation in the audience. In addition, says Miller, negative news reports significantly lower our sense of political efficacy, the sense that we make a difference in the public realm.[56] In other words, the media drive us underground, thereby calling up Hannah Arendt's eerie warning: "The sad truth of the matter is that most evil is done by people who never made up their mind to be either bad or good."[57]

Feeling clever also has a personal downside. For one thing, cleverness must be earned. It takes hard work to sort through the false images and to be appropriately smug when reporting them out. Consequently, cleverness leads to defensiveness, for cleverness gained is cleverness that must be retained. The television reporter, as a result, must often feel he or she is on a postmodern assembly line, stamping out new manipulations each day. For the television viewer, cleverness requires finding pleasure in what Lyotard calls the pain of absence, in the goodness that cannot be found in social life.[58] Postmodern pressures like these lead to competitiveness, to a need for mastering the requisite brittleness expected in an age of critique. Such concerns must keep George Will and Sam Donaldson worrying that a smile, and not a sneer, will suddenly break through.

But political television's greatest problem is philosophical, not psychological. Postmodernism repudiates foundationalism, essential truths, the very sorts of truths upon which a flourishing society stands. The postmodern individual may be able to cope with a world that is "joyful, polymorphous, unhierarchial, creative, and self-constituting,"[59] but a political society cannot.

In many ways, democratic politics knows nothing but essentialism: People are happiest when they are not paying taxes; education is good; don't get the unions angry; deliver the mail on time. These are not eternal truths but people cling to them nonetheless. Democratic politics is also nothing but hierarchial. It is a system for determining what is most right and least right and what is acceptable in between. Moreover, conventional politics is dualistic in the extreme. War is either declared or not declared, the veto either upheld or overridden. In short, whereas a *theoretical analysis* may find legion contradictions in everyday life, a *functional analysis* makes little room for postmodernism when the votes are counted and the money distributed.[60]

In many ways, then, democratic politics repudiates postmodernism and television embraces it. In doing so, television offers us a world that is more comfortable with images than with principle. Following its postmodern mandate, television blends politics and culture, rewards our most cynical attitudes, and lionizes the rhetorical even when denouncing the rhetorical. Modern Americans have grown up under this aegis and it is hard for them to imagine another way. But they must begin to imagine another way, for a world in which principle is effaced is a world that cannot sustain political life. "The flight from foundationalism is at the same time often a flight from politics,"[61] says Henry Giroux. This is a flight we cannot afford to take.

Notes

1. For additional information on this characteristic of Nixon see R. Hart, *Verbal Style and the Presidency: A Computer-Based Analysis* (New York: Academic Press, 1984), 139-147.

2. "CNN Update News," July 18 and 19, 1992.

3. It may seem strange that postmodernism is at odds with phenomenology because both schools of thought seek to deal with contrary human perceptions. According to John Murphy, however, the phenomenologist holds out hope that a secret (true?) meaning can be found, a proposition that is anathema to most poststructuralists. For more on this distinction, see *Postmodern Social Analysis and Criticism* (New York: Greenwood, 1989), 49-51.

4. For a handy summary of postmodernism's most "stable" features, see I. Hassan, *The Post-Modern Turn: Essays in Post-Modern Theory and Culture* (Columbus: Ohio State University, 1987), 168-173.

5. For a useful introduction to postmodern thought, see S. Best and D. Kellner, *Postmodern Theory: Critical Interrogations* (New York: Guilford, 1991).

6. J-F. Lyotard, *The Postmodern Condition: A Report on Knowledge,* Trans. by G. Bennington and B. Massumi (Minneapolis: University of Minnesota Press, 1984), 82.

7. Lyotard, xxiv.

8. W. Miller, *American National Election Studies Data Sourcebook: 1958-1988* (Cambridge: Harvard University Press, 1989).

9. D. Kanter and R. Mirvis, *The Cynical Americans: Living and Working in an Age of Discontent and Disillusion* (San Francisco: Jossey-Bass, 1989), 146-182.

10. P. Sloterdijk, *Critique of Cynical Reason,* Trans. by M. Eldred (Minneapolis: University of Minnesota Press, 1987), 217.

11. M. Robinson, "Public Affairs Television and the Growth of Political Malaise: The Case of 'The Selling of the Pentagon,' " *American Political Science Review, 70* (1976), 418, 419.

12. G. Debord, *Society of the Spectacle* (Detroit: Red and Black, 1982), 1:3.

13. P. Sloterdijk, "Cynicism—The Twilight of False Consciousness," *New German Critique, 33* (1984), 197.

14. Sloterdijk, 1987, 484.

15. This is J. S. Nelson's image. See "Irony and Integrity: Politics in a Late-Modern Mode." Paper presented at the annual convention of the American Political Science Association, Atlanta, Georgia, August, 1989.

16. C. Krauthammer, "In Praise of Low Voter Turnout," *Time,* May 21, 1990, 88.

17. For additional information on orality and social patterns, see W. Ong, *Orality and Literacy* (London: Methuen, 1982).

18. Benjamin is actually quoting Georges Dukomel here. See "The Work of Art in the Age of Mechanical Reproduction," in H. Arendt (ed.), *Illuminations* (New York: Schocken Books, 1969), 238. An interesting research finding relates to Dukomel's observation. Researchers Peter Clarke and Eric Fredin found that people who watch television had significantly fewer reasons to give when justifying their choices in a senatorial election than did people who watched very little television. In other words, television may delight our eyes but it seems to make us mute. See "Newspapers, Television, and Political Reasoning," *Public Opinion Quarterly, 42* (1978), 148.

19. M. Featherstone, *Consumer Culture and Postmodernism* (London: Sage, 1991), 58. Yet another problem with a presentistic orientation is that it effaces the future as well as the past. Lewis Hinchman and Sandra Hinchman make this point particularly well in "In Heidegger's Shadow: Hannah Arendt's Phenomenological Humanism," *The Review of Politics, 46* (1984), 192.

20. As quoted by J. Baudrillard, *Jean Baudrillard: Selected Writings,* Ed. M. Poster (Stanford: Stanford University Press, 1988), 154.

21. C. Bosso, "Setting the Agenda: Mass Media and the Discovery of Famine in Ethiopia," in M. Margolis and G. Mauser (eds.), *Manipulating Public Opinion: Essays on Public Opinion as a Dependent Variable* (Pacific Grove, CA: Brooks/Cole, 1989), 173.

22. Although he does not connect television to the problem, Kyosti Pekonen is also troubled by the depoliticizing of politics when he says: "Politics as meaning-giving plays no penetrating role in what is happening: politics has little to do with how people imagine their future and make their identifications. It is not politics which binds people's social imagery, and the symbols of the future do not come from politics." We shall examine this theme in more depth in Chapter 5 of this book. See "Symbols and Politics as Culture in the Modern Situation: The Problems and Prospects of the 'New,' " in J. R. Gibbins (ed), *Contemporary Political Culture: Politics in a Postmodern Age* (London: Sage, 1989), 141.

23. R. Lane, *Political Ideology: Why the American Common Man Believes What He Does* (New York: Free Press, 1962), 156.

24. Pekonen, 140.

25. H. Simons, "Going Meta: Definition and Political Applications," *Quarterly Journal of Speech, 80* (1994), 468-481.

26. See D. Kellner, *Jean Baudrillard: From Marxism to Postmodernism and Beyond* (Cambridge: Polity Press, 1989), 72.

27. S. R. Lichter, D. Amundson, and R. Noyes, *The Video Campaign: Network Coverage of the 1988 Primaries* (Washington, DC: A.E.I. Institute, 1988).

28. A. Major and L. E. Atwood, "The U.S. Press Covers Two Presidential Elections." Paper delivered at the annual convention of the International Communication Association, Dublin, Ireland, June 1990, 14.

29. R. Entman and A. Rojecki, "Limiting Democracy by Containing Public Opinion: Media and Elite Politics from Watergate to the Nuclear Freeze." Paper presented at the annual convention of the International Communication Association, Chicago, Illinois, May 1991, 23-28.

30. T. Patterson, "More Style than Substance: Television News in U.S. National Elections," *Political Communication and Persuasion, 8* (1991), 149.

31. "The Tougher 'New Gorbachev,' " *Newsweek*, March 4, 1991, 44. Bruce Morton of CBS News voiced these same cynical interpretations of Gorbachev's actions on "The Evening News with Dan Rather" on February 23, 1991, 6:40 p.m. CST.

32. J. Murphy, *Postmodern Social Analysis and Criticism* (New York: Greenwood, 1989), 21.

33. Quoted in Murphy, 139.

34. D. Hallin, "Sound Bite News: Television Coverage of Elections, 1968-1988," *Journal of Communication, 42* (1992), 17.

35. B. Buchanan, "Media Coverage of Campaign '88: A Content Analysis." Paper presented at the annual convention of the American Political Science Association, San Francisco, California, August, 1990, 28.

36. J. Klinkowitz, *Rosenberg, Barthes, Hassan: The Postmodern Habit of Thought* (Athens: University of Georgia Press, 1988), 48.

37. See, for example, D. Mumby and C. Spitzack, "Ideology and Television News: A Metaphoric Analysis of Political Stories," *Central States Speech Journal, 34* (1983), 162-171, 170.

38. T. Eagleton, "Capitalism, Modernism and Postmodernism," *New Left Review, 152* (July/August, 1985), 62.

39. S. Wolin, "Democracy in the Discourse of Postmodernism," *Social Research, 57* (1990), 28.

40. Ibid.

41. F. Pfeil, "Postmodernism as a 'Structure of Feeling,' " in C. Nelson and L. Grossberg (eds.), *Marxism and the Interpretation of Culture* (Urbana: University of Illinois Press, 1988), 384.

42. M. Bakhtin, *The Dialogic Imagination,* M. Holquist (ed.), C. Emerson and M. Holquist (trans.) (Austin: University of Texas Press, 1981).

43. J. Schulte-Sasse, "Electronic Media and Cultural Politics in the Reagan Era: The Attack on Libya and Hands Across America as Postmodern Events," *Cultural Critique, 8* (1987), 127.

44. Sloterdijk, 1987, 312.

45. For more on the democratic strains of postmodern texts, see D. Fokkema, *Literary History, Modernism and Postmodernism* (Amsterdam: John Benjamins, 1984), 48.

46. D. Smith-Howell "Using the Past in the Present: The Rhetorical Construction of the American Presidency." Unpublished doctoral dissertation, University of Texas at Austin, 1993, 204.

47. I. Hassan, *The Post-Modern Turn: Essays in Post-Modern Theory and Culture* (Columbus: Ohio State University, 1987), 199.

48. For a brief but insightful excursion into such matters, see P. Ehrenhaus, "On Doing Violence to 'The Past.' " Paper delivered at the annual convention of the International Communication Association, Dublin, Ireland, June, 1990.

49. M. deCerteau, *The Practice of Everyday Life* (Berkeley: University of California Press, 1984), 170.

50. Sloterdijk, 1987, 312.

51. N. Postman, *Amusing Ourselves to Death: Public Discourse in the Age of Show Business* (New York: Penguin Books, 1985), 131.

52. Featherstone, 122.

53. As quoted in M. Delli Carpini and B. Williams, "The Method Is the Message: Focus Groups as a Means of Examining the Uses of Television in Political Discourse." Paper delivered at the annual convention of the International Society of Political Psychology, Washington, DC, July, 1990, 23-24.

54. M. Morse, "An Ontology of Everyday Distraction: The Freeway, the Mall and Television," in P. Mellencamp (ed.), *Logics of Television: Essays on Cultural Criticism* (Bloomington: Indiana University Press, 1990), 210.

55. T. Gitlin, "Who Communicates What to Whom, in What Voice and Why, about the Study of Mass Communication," *Critical Studies in Mass Communication, 7* (1990), 191-192.

56. A. Miller, E. Goldenberg, and L. Ebring, "Type-Set Politics: Impact of Newspapers on Public Confidence," *American Political Science Review, 73* (1979), 81.

57. H. Arendt, "Thinking and Moral Considerations: A Lecture," *Social Research, 38* (1971), 438. An interesting example of Arendt's point occurs when she champions "civil disobedience" over "conscientious objection." The latter, says Arendt, is purely internal and philosophical and, hence, has no *political* standing. The former, in contrast, is behavioral and, hence, relevant to the practical world. See Arendt's *Crises of the Republic* (New York: Harvest-Harcourt, 1972), 95-102.

58. Lyotard, 78.

59. This is Leslie Paul Thiele's description of Michel Foucault's politics. See "The Agony of Politics: The Nietzschean Roots of Foucault's Thought," *American Political Science Review, 84* (1990), 920. One of the most eloquent cynics of our age, Lewis Lapham seems to imply that people have learned to adjust pretty well to life in a postmodern age. Lapham's thoughts on the matter are worth quoting at some length: "Any platform that any candidate may construct the voters know to be a house of straw. . . . Unlike the custodians of political mysteries, the voters know how much they don't know. No matter how imposingly wrought the facade of permanence, the earth shifts and slides beneath their feet. One year the newspapers tell them they have the Russians for friends and the Chinese for enemies; a year later the Chinese become friends and the Russians turn out to be enemies. Somebody builds a factory and thinks he has done a fine thing for his town; a year later he hears himself reviled for having poisoned a river. Somebody else sets out with the noblest of intentions to work for racial equality; after having pursued the twists of logic into the maze of affirmative action, he finds himself arguing on behalf of racial privilege. Who could have imagined, even ten years ago, that a decision to winterize one's house would be a matter of foreign policy? Nothing remains as it was, and the voters know that their lives tremble in the balance of decisions taken by people whom they have never seen and whose names they don't know how to pronounce. Knowing themselves to be transients in a world of ceaseless change, the voters also know that no politician can resolve their doubts or put to rest their entirely reasonable fears." See "Political Discourse," *Harper's*, August, 1980, 8, 9.

60. My remarks here reflect an undisguised pragmatism, the sort that John Dewey championed. Dewey was uninterested in all forms of "mentalism" and argued that "the main facts of political action . . . are [always] facts of human behavior accessible to human observation." At least when writing as a political theorist, Dewey distrusted all talk of philosophical essence, the will of God, spontaneous social contracts, and even human reason. He would have been even less impressed with postmodernism. See *The Public and Its Problems* (Chicago: Gateway, 1946), 20.

61. H. Giroux, *Schooling and the Struggle for Public Life: Critical Pedagogy in the Modern Age* (Minneapolis: University of Minnesota Press, 1988) 61.

Box 4.1 Inquiries and Transitions

Who can resist cynicism? That is the question of the age. Can the affluent resist? Not really, for is not cynicism a useful way of signaling class membership, of copping an attitude, of displaying a chic materialism? Can the downtrodden resist? Not really, for is cynicism not also a reasonable refuge for persons promised one thing only to have a lesser thing delivered? Can youth resist? Not really, for is cynicism not a cultural style, a way for the body-piercing set to signal their superior confusions to one another? Can the middle class resist? Not really, for does not cynicism compensate for the affluence, youth, and easy-outrage thus far denied them? And so all today are cynical coconspirators; all are devotees of Chris Rock and Dennis Miller. But why? Who wins and who loses when people find community only in their rejection of communal possibilities? What seeds are sown for the future in such a condition? And then there is this question: When television finally drives us all from the civic project, who will fight the wars and teach the children and build the roads and feed the elderly? Is the world-after-cynicism a world we can live in? Not really.

CHAPTER 5

Feeling Busy

The Frenzy of Establishment Politics

During a recent political campaign, *Washington Post* writers Richard Morin and Dan Balz conducted a disturbing set of interviews with representatives of the "20-something" generation in Sacramento, California. Doug Dollar, a 23-year-old cabinetmaker, had never voted and doubted that he ever would. "I think it's a game," said Dollar. Gustavo Ferrer, in contrast, once considered voting but ultimately decided "It's not worth my time." Christy Berger likewise did not vote because of her family responsibilities and college classes but admitted that her attitude toward politics was "very wrong." Sherri Bounds also felt guilty but her guilt did not preclude her from "thinking about me, my schooling, my friends, my work" rather than about her civic responsibilities. "In two hours of discussion about their generation," said Morin and Balz, "these young people spoke passionately about problems . . . but when the subject turned to politics, the conversation faltered, their mood turned cynical. They hold politicians in contempt; have little or no connection to the political parties; are not excited by [the candidates]." Morin and Balz added one more piece of information to their report: "Members of the group said they get almost all of their political information from television."[1]

The causal interpretation—that television makes the young stupid about politics—must be resisted. Television does something far more profound, and unsettling. It redefines politics. As we saw in Chapter 2, television makes politics personal rather than economic. As we saw in Chapter 3, television features psychological relations rather than power relations. As we saw in Chapter 4, television confuses politics with culture. This chapter traces how television makes politics a speculative rather than a real-life activity, an individual rather than a collective matter. Both redefinitional moves have phenomenological consequences for the American people, as viewers and as voters.

This chapter takes the matter of definition seriously, treating it not as some sort of semantic housecleaning but as a guide to the very lives we lead. My argument is that when politics loses its specificity for a society, it loses its capacity to guide that society. The youthful malaise reported by the *Washington Post* is troubling, therefore, not because the young people it surveyed found politics and then rejected it but because they were unable to find it at all. For them, politics was a rarified business practiced by empty suits in Sacramento, California and Washington, D.C., persons far removed from the troubles that plagued them. Although these young people were vitally concerned about education, the environment, abortion rights, and the economy, they had somehow come to believe that politicians were either (a) unable to solve such problems or (b) irrelevant to such problems. In the short run, society can cope with the first belief, but the second belief opens the door to anomie.

Is television responsible for all of this? Clearly not. But it is ironic that these young members of "the television generation" could not locate politics even when it threatened to suffocate them. Said 24-year-old Eleanor Alvarez: "This generation went through the latchkey syndrome, we went through parents divorcing constantly, and now single women raising the home. . . . We went through a lot. That's why our concerns are more social than politically oriented."[2]

The distinction between the social and the political Ms. Alvarez makes here is a distinction that would mightily vex legislators who had worked tirelessly in behalf of Ms. Alvarez's parents to pass Aid to Dependent Children legislation, Equal Opportunity employment laws, and No-Fault Divorce bills. On more philosophical grounds, it is a distinction that would also interest political theorist Hannah Arendt. For Arendt, there were three important dimensions of life—the Private, the Social, and the Political. Private life, said Arendt, dealt with matters of day-to-day sustenance; it was a "barbarous" realm that drove *animal laborans* to fulfill elementary bodily needs. In ancient Greece, Arendt notes, the Private was an apolitical world populated by women and slaves, persons who had no access to, and hence no concern for, the "beauty" of the public sphere, a sphere in which one could display a "heroic contempt" for life's necessities and hence be free to perform great public deeds.[3]

For Arendt, politics meant transcendence, a going-beyond the everyday. It also meant going beyond the popular: "The *polis*, with its emphasis on speech and action, could survive only if the number of citizens remained restricted."[4] Because she was so fascinated by the ancient Greeks, Arendt equated citizenship with action as did they, an equation that seems almost quaint by the laid-back standards of modern politics. Also quaint is her sharp distinction between the Private and the Political. With legislation on the family, the church, and the workplace now choking legislative dockets, Arendt's assumptions about the perfection of private life now lies in ruins. But it is Arendt's third and most uncertain dimension—the Social—that especially complicates the definitional problems mentioned above and that recommends further examination of television's role in political life.

In her writings, Arendt defined the Social variously. At times it appears to mean something like Society (as in high society), at other times something like Accepted Understandings (cultural norms) or simply social relationships.[5] Most predictably for Arendt, the Social oscillated somewhere between the Private and the Political, exalting the former and impinging, however faintly, on the latter. Had Arendt trained her withering intelligence on television, she might have had an easier time explaining the Social, and she might have concluded, as do I, that *television makes the private viewing of political activities feel like genuine participation.* Television allows one to become, in Arendt's terms, a parvenu, a dabbler in politics. It gives us a sense of the State without placing responsibility upon us for the success of the State.[6] It lets us live in the Private world—the world of the *Washington Post*'s 20-year-olds—and yet feel close enough to the Political world to reject it.

Television, then, does not create political alienation. Economic disparity and social injustice do that. But television does make political alienation articulate and it makes that articulateness a sufficiency. These are television's twin philosophical legacies. Each is worth at least one tear.

The Simulated Actor

Here is a curiosity: Americans are among the most opinionated people in the world and yet they do not vote. Or at least not enough of them. In 1960,

62.8% of U.S. citizens cast ballots in national elections but in 1980 only 52.5% did.[7] In round numbers, that means that in just 20 years well over ten million persons found something better to do with their time than vote. More people joined their ranks in the ensuing decade. The 1988 election, for example, produced the lowest voter turnout since 1924 (about 50%) and also produced the highest level of dissatisfaction ever recorded by opinion pollsters.[8] And despite the Perot-induced furor four years later, the numbers generated by both poll watchers and poll takers were only marginally improved, and they dropped back down once again in 1996.

Decline in voter turnout has become something of a Rorschach test for researchers, each finding something different in its inky blackness. Scholars with an economic bent, for example, note that people vote less faithfully when the money supply is tight, ostensibly because such conditions show how irrelevant politics has become.[9] In contrast is the philosophical interpretation of E. J. Dionne, Jr. who claims that "What is needed, and desperately, is a resurgence of common citizenship that animated the early civil rights movement."[10] Different still is political scientist Richard Brody's interpretation, which contends that no single, *personal* variable (such as employment status) explains voter decline in the United States.[11]

Francis Fox Piven and Richard Cloward are equally sure of their case. They argue that voter disinterest results from onerous voter registration procedures, procedures that discriminate against the poor, the homeless, the immigrant, the rural dweller, African Americans, and so on. The "social-psychological model [of voter decline] confuses causes and consequences," argue Piven and Cloward.[12] For them, it is not negative attitudes that sap voter motivation but the inability to participate in the electoral process that produces political alienation. Anecdotally, at least, Piven and Cloward's case is compelling, as 87% of those who do register eventually cast a ballot.[13]

Perhaps the most balanced interpretation of non-voting is offered by researcher Ruy Teixeira who has examined the effects of such sociological variables as geographic mobility, party decline, and non-holiday voting traditions on voter turnout. Teixeira focused especially on the demographic shifts that took place in the United States between 1968 and 1980, shifts that resulted in (a) a younger voting pool, (b) fewer "traditional" spousal relations, and (c) an electorate that had fragile communal ties because of their changing employment patterns. During these years, says Teixeira, "Americans became disconnected from the political world, thereby found elections and their outcomes less meaningful and, as a result, turnout rates went down."[14]

Deprived of a common ethnic or religious heritage, having only a comparatively short history as a nation, and having stoutly separated its corporate and
public sectors, the United States produced a political individual who "must,
by and large, mobilize himself or herself to go down to the polls and cast a
ballot."[15]

Although most writers wring their hands when confronting these data,
not all do. From his typically Olympian perspective, for example, columnist
George Will is able to find the silver lining in the electoral cloud when
observing that "in a good society, politics is peripheral to happiness. You want
high turnouts? Try 86.2, 83.5, and 88.8. Those were the rates in three elections
in Germany, 1932-33."[16] Predictably, Piven and Cloward are unimpressed
with such preachment, arguing that "no one has satisfactorily explained why
the 'politics of happiness' is so concentrated among the least well off."[17] Not
to worry, says columnist Charles Krauthammer. Time heals all wounds, even
those inflicted on the commonweal by political indifference:

> Low voter turnout means that people see politics as quite marginal in their
> lives, as neither salvation nor ruin. That is healthy. Low voter turnout is a
> leading indicator of contentment. . . . Let others struggle valiantly to raise the
> political awareness of all citizens. Let them rage against the tides of indiffer-
> ence. They will fail, and when they do, relax. Remember that indifference to
> politics leaves all the more room for the things that really count: science, art,
> religion, family and play.[18]

My argument is different still. I suggest that television provides viewers
with so much vicarious political experience that they often feel too tired to
vote. I suggest, further, that even when voters feel politically alienated, they
do not necessarily feel politically *inert* because of television. Each day, the
nation's media drench them in politics: photographers popping flash bulbs,
the President running from his helicopter, crowds milling about at abortion
clinics, minicams waving unsteadily as the candidate jogs past, talk show
guests ranting when they are not raving, U.N. diplomats scurrying away from
over-eager reporters, a new charismatic whipping up the crowds. Here is
energy aplenty. Here is stuff to quicken the pulse. Even at home, in an
overstuffed chair, watching politics can be draining.

Television can be draining because it can also be energizing. Phenomenologically, at least, the energy it produces may not result in voting but it
can make people feel aware, one-with-their-times. Ruy Teixeira may well be

correct when noting that "the sharp decline in campaign newspaper reading" is often strongly correlated with voting downturns,[19] but that is not to say that these readers-turned-viewers feel politically marginalized in every case. For the reasons mentioned previously in this book—television's intimacy, its omniscience, its unstinting cleverness—the electronic media bring viewers up to speed quickly and then keep them at speed. As a result, viewers today almost never feel compelled to admit fundamental political ignorance. Or political lethargy. They have their explanations for not voting down pat: They would vote if they wished to vote. They know the score. They certainly know the candidates. They have met them on television, 15 seconds at a time, weeks on end. With such a wealth of experience, how can voting be anything but an afterthought?

The political energy television affords relates in a curious way to what Paul Lazarsfeld and Robert Merton have called the "narcotizing dysfunction" of the mass media.[20] The notion here is that television dulls people's sensibilities to such an extent that fully rational thought is no longer possible. A phenomenological approach looks at the matter differently. It assumes that if television is a narcotic, it is an upper. It may produce political lethargy but it does not necessarily produce *feelings* of lethargy. Like cocaine, political television feels empowering.

"Those who watch more television," says researcher Michael Morgan, "are less likely to say they voted, by an average margin of about 10 percent."[21] "The relationship holds up," Morgan continues, "despite statistical controls for age, income, education, sex, race, political orientation, party identification, and other powerful factors."[22] All of this may be true, but the story does not end there. Although television keeps some people from the voting booth, it offers two things in return: a sense of participation and a sense of completeness. Not everyone who sits at home on election day, in other words, is angry.

Perhaps this is why so many people became fascinated with Ross Perot's notion of an "electronic town hall." In presenting his idea, Mr. Perot was completely in step with his times, his times being both televisual and cybernetic. But he was also in step with the phenomenology of his times. Here, at last, was a device for removing the remaining bit of tissue between thinking and doing. Now, with the merest touch of a keypad, a citizen could create empirical evidence of his or her political existence.

Perot's idea, of course, was but a methodological addendum to the American people's growing fascination with themselves, a fascination best evidenced by opinion polls. Today, not only do politicians wish to know what the people feel as soon as they feel it but the people, too, wish to know what they feel even, in some cases, before they feel it. As a result, poll-watching has become addictive. According to one set of researchers, nearly one third of all primary news stories now mention polling data,[23] with television putting flesh on the statistical bones via person-on-the-street interviews.

Optimists look at opinion polling as a way of giving voice to the voiceless, as an emancipatory adjunct to modern politics. A more pessimistic reading is that opinion polling is little more than proxy citizenship, a suburbanization of politics that keeps people away from the muss and fuss of the *polis*. From such a perspective, polling turns politics into a purely specular art form, something akin to the dazzling architecture of the Bonaventure Hotel in Los Angeles. The mirrored sheathing of the Bonaventure's exterior, says Fredric Jameson, both attracts us (because it is reflective) and repels us (because it is opaque). The Bonaventure, says Jameson, is autoreferential, a building "which tends to turn upon itself and designate its own cultural production as its content."[24]

So it is with polling. Polls let us see ourselves with little or no effort but, because they are so ephemeral, polls keep us from leaving a permanent mark on the political edifice. In that sense, polling breeds dependence rather than independence in the electorate, substituting perceptions of perceptions for direct political action. Equally, polls hide the structural and economic forces controlling the public sphere. Having said that, one cannot discount the popularity of specular politics. Christopher Hitchens explains why: "At a dinner party, one is seldom told—and one is never to ask—how and especially why a given guest voted in the last primary or national election. Instead, one spends the evening at a certain clever, cool remove from the stuff of democratic politics—swapping back and forth across the table numbers gleaned from the CNN or ABC or Times Mirror poll."[25]

Yet another way of thinking about polling is to see it as a conversation among the citizenry overseen by television. But if polling is a conversation it is a strange one, for its participants know nothing of one another and do nothing with one another. Instead, polling makes their speech numerical, integers that know neither reason nor passion. Polling also restricts speech, permitting no individuation, no serendipity, only a steady murmur of "very much" and "just a little." Increasingly, polling is a conversation that leads only to more conversation, rarely to political action. Polling is thus dandified politics, the sort of thing practiced by 19th century pedestrians eager to learn the code of polite society. Such passersby, says Richard Sennett, "move[d] in silence, in isolated protection from each other, and release[d] themselves through fantasy and daydreaming, watching life go by on the streets."[26]

Television viewing is often little different. It simulates political interaction and offers those simulations as surrogates for political involvement. Often, of course, television's simulations do a brilliant job of awakening viewers to the world around them, of making people less self-centered, less risk-aversive. In the 1990s, a viewer must work hard to remain as xenophobic as his or her forebears, as resistant to new ideas and attitudes. In fact, there is even a bit of evidence to suggest that high exposure to television news makes people more willing to engage in informal political discussions,[27] although that same study also found that heavy television watching correlates with *less participation* in politics (voting, passing out handbills, going to political rallies, etc.). A more worrisome finding is that reported by two University of Chicago researchers who found that television watching slows viewers' physiological responses, creating in them an intense state of physical and emotional relaxation. These findings held constant even when subjects were watching the evening news![28]

For a variety of reasons, critic Robert Schmuhl is worried about the new phenomenon of "cocooning" whereby people sequester themselves with a gaggle of personalized electronic media in order to tune out the world around them.[29] Can we expect such people to withstand the "introspective flight from reality" that so worries Hannah Pitkin?[30] Will they be motivated to join in the "plurality of equals who speak and act together" that Hannah Arendt says is central to a free and pluralistic society?[31] Indeed, will more than 5% of them ever contribute to a political campaign? More than 4% of them send a letter to a government official? More than 2% of them demonstrate for a political cause?[32] Ultimately, can they avoid becoming a nation of Chance the Gardeners, Jerzy Kosinski's delightful, but addle-brained, protagonist in *Being There*, who rose to fame and fortune by doing nothing more than watch television? For his part, Chance was delighted with his success, not because it gave him more power but because it gave him more time to watch television. Surely citizens today have more options than that.

The Flourishing Individual

One of the subtlest effects of political television is that it gives viewers the feeling that someone else is minding the store and that they, consequently, can turn to other pursuits. Television de-politicizes its viewers because it so fully politicizes everyone else. As we saw in Chapter 2, television makes politics personal. In doing so, television reduces the scale of politics by encouraging us to think about individuals instead of governmental systems, about isolated events rather than structural inevitabilities. Television, then, is example driven. It introduces the struggling dirt farmer in Iowa, the out-of-work machinist in New Jersey, and uses them to stand for some larger trend. It tells of their hopes and dreams, of their sons and daughters, of their remembered high school glories, of the local bars they frequent. In doing so, television follows the classic dramatic formulas of discussing one thing rather than many things and of setting the scene but then letting the actors act.

Because it follows these rules so faithfully, television is theory resistant. The viewer is rarely asked to think large thoughts—case-transcendent thoughts—but is focused instead on real people situated in real time. Because television is an entertainment medium, it assumes that dramatic force comes from identification, from the ability to see in others what we half-sense about ourselves. And so the television text is pure sociology. It tells us who is watching by what it presents: Bikini-clad skydivers during football timeouts; middle-class alcoholics on *Oprah*; darling young black children in McDonald's commercials.

Television is predictable in these ways because its audiences are stable. And so we can project that in mid-June of 2010, *60 Minutes* will present a three-part show consisting of (a) the dilemmas posed for the U.S. economy by troubles in the Middle East; (b) the changing mores of corporate America perpetuated by the rise in female CEOs; and (c) a profile of an aging, but beloved, rock star. That same mid-June show will most assuredly not investigate a disease unique to Sri Lankans or a new cosmological theory emerging from Berkeley's physics department.

The people seen on television are therefore new and not-new at the same time. Last year's child stuck in the Texas well is different from, and yet similar to, this year's child with AIDS in Indiana. "The news," in this sense, is only partly new. Often enough, it merely picks up old storylines and rejuvenates the characters. In part this is because people themselves are patterned—they live, they laugh, they die. But television does more than just tape the proceedings. It also helps create the proceedings by faithfully following its dramatistic rules. Viewers therefore know that they will meet old-new people each time they turn on their sets. That is why watching television is comforting.

What does this mean for politics? It means that television is "busy" in two senses: (1) it is busy like cheap wallpaper is busy—many and different faces poke out at us from the screen each evening—and (2) it presents so many people doing so many political things that viewers feel licensed to concern themselves with other matters. Consider some of the relevant research. An "Earth Day" documentary places responsibility on individuals, not on corporations, for ecological disaster.[33] The highly touted show *Roots* depicted black history as a case of individual perseverance rather than a systemic nightmare.[34] The lone whistleblower, not the Washington bureaucracy, is lionized for cleaning up the workplace,[35] and the wayward driver, not the auto industry, is said to be responsible for all traffic accidents.[36] In *The Cosbys,* black problems were shown not to result from underemployment or industrial relocation but from not following dad's advice.[37] The media conduct far more polls about political personalities than they did about, say, U.S. policy in Nicaragua.[38] And when covering natural disasters, the media typically focus on individual preparedness, not on how governmental agencies respond to such calamities.[39]

As mentioned earlier, there is a touch of romanticism involved when the single individual stands above all else. According to sociologist John O'Neil, "Television . . . is democratic, maverick, lawless" in these ways, favoring "people without titles, private individuals, common folk, comic children, ethnics. Thus, television is especially concerned to portray the private cop or detective who goes for his man with more passion and concern for speedy justice, more wit, and strength than the fat, bureaucratic legal and criminal system."[40] The world of television is therefore almost pre-political. The people it depicts are part of a hands-on polity. When they do battle, they clash directly with others, *mano a mano.* When they fail, they are undone by a conglomerate so imperious that it will not even submit to an on-camera interview. But aligned against that conglomerate is the Hero. For such an individual, John Dewey would say, the state is an impertinence.[41]

Because television produces these political cameos so skillfully, viewers get the impression of a crowded public sphere. Politicians contribute to that impression as well. Ronald Reagan, for example, had an especially deft touch. From his very first address as president where he lionized Martin Treptow (a World War II hero) to his 1982 State of the Union speech where he praised (and then introduced) Lenny Skutnik, who had jumped into the Potomac River to save plane crash victims, Mr. Reagan well understood the usefulness of an example. All presidents do. In an age of media, both Republicans and Democrats have their thousand points of light. As political scientist Barbara

Hinckley says, "Washington and Jefferson appear briefly on stage during appeals for tax reform or budget cuts, to remind the audience of America's past greatness, while Apollo astronauts and black sports champions carry the past promise to the present. In this particular portrayal of government, presidents make policy alone after reading their letters from sleepless Americans."[42]

When watching politics, then, the American people are treated to an endless series of inductions, as today's cast of characters fades into tomorrow's. Television's logic is therefore a logic of instances. New datum replaces old datum and conclusions become irrelevant. Such a logic leaves viewers philosophically at sea as they grapple for some overarching truth. But television's personalities buoy them up, releasing them from the old fixities of party and bureaucracy. "Only extraordinary conditions can enable charisma to triumph over the [party] organization"[43] in the United States, predicted Max Weber in 1911. Political parties will prevail, said Weber, because continuity prevails over emotionality.

Weber had clearly not anticipated television. Television, we would later learn, finds only grayness in political parties. Viewers find the same thing, and so more and more of them register as independents.[44] In part they do so because television has shown them how much the single individual can accomplish. Unfettered by tradition, released from statutes and charters, people like Ted Turner, Roseanne Barr, Oliver North, and Dennis Rodman become television's favorites.

The American people seem happy with cameo politics of this sort. Why not let them enjoy it? There are several reasons. For one thing, television's rugged individualism obscures the inevitable continuities that guide political decision making, continuities not capturable on videotape. There is a hint of Marxism in this premise, but one need not posit conspiracies of consciousness to remember that the people *not* seen on television also have a great deal of power. By attending to people's idiosyncrasies, says Jean Baudrillard, we lose sight of the regularities that underlie almost all decisions made in the modern state.[45] Still, television has its rebuttal ready for Baudrillard. As Michael Milburn and his colleagues report, the most popular explanation for international terrorism among heavy television viewers is psychological ("terrorists are deranged") rather than political ("they have been aggrieved").[46] This effect, reports Milburn, held regardless of how much formal education viewers had previously received.

And there are other danger signs. For people who watch small amounts of television, says Michael Morgan, party affiliation, social class, and region of the country—traditional political variables—count most in their political decision making. Heavy viewers, in contrast, exhibit what Morgan calls a "mainstreaming" effect, a term that sounds ominously like mindless conformity.[47] According to Shanto Iyengar and Donald Kinder, television's melodramatic case stories tend to *lower* viewers' concern for political issues, ostensibly because they cannot generalize from the particularities presented—"it's his problem, not mine."[48]

This same effect is found in other media presentations. Susan Whalen details how dramatizing the grievances of individual union members camouflages their common problems.[49] In a similar vein, Richard Campbell and Jimmie Reeves have shown how most coverage of drug abuse features the struggles of individual addicts, not the social conditions sustaining the drug culture.[50] In a broader context, Arthur Miller and his colleagues have traced how consistently the media direct criticism at individual officeholders and how rarely they scrutinize the traditions that keep them in power.[51] Interestingly enough, note Iyengar and Kinder, when the news plays down the activities of officeholders, viewers are *more likely* to view the problem being dramatized as serious.[52]

Cameo politics, therefore, has a curious effect. Rather than drawing people into the public sphere, it tells them that another sentry is already on duty. This has long been one of the problems with voluntarism in the United States, observes sociologist Robert Bellah. "Because of its individualistic component," says Bellah, populist politics "tends to be discontinuous, oriented to single issues, opportunistic and thereby easily coopted, local, and anti-institutional."[53] Furthermore, says Bellah, voluntarism tends to decrease interest in party politics. At first that may seem all to the good, until one recalls what a political party does: it focuses on long-term issues; it reaches across regional jealousies; and it promotes itself, which is to say, it promotes itself above any of its constituents. Most important, a political party keeps track of a limited set of agendas; it remembers things. Television, in contrast, is notoriously forgetful.

Naturally, a case can be made for the politics of individualism. Popular talk shows like *Ricki Lake* or *Rosie O'Donnell*, says communication scholar Mark Pollock, "make it possible for their viewers to see and hear people who would not otherwise be seen or heard."[54] At first, this "big tent" theory of the mass media is attractive, until one remembers that circuses, too, are held in tents. What starts out on television as a serious political discussion often devolves into curiosity-shopping for viewers. Because television producers live solely for the moment (Nielsen ratings being a literal matter of the moment), they are easily drawn to the odd individual and social cause. And it is all well and good for television producers to argue that ideas die unless they are humanized, but what happens if the identification fails to "take?" If a spokes-person displeases an audience, must the social cause be dismissed as well? When a reductionistic rhetoric fails, is anything left?

Cameo politics is a staple on television because it draws an audience. In bending to the iron law of attention—that which is similar to me, galvanizes me—television commits no crime and often strikes a political spark or two. But being interested in political personalities and developing a political conscience are not the same thing. It is the universal, not the particular, that distinguishes political thought. Communities, not personalities, build polities. It is good, says Bhikhu Parekh, to search for moral perfection, to follow the life of the mind, to strive for personal happiness or eternal glory. But these are not political things, says Parekh, for a genuinely political philosophy begins with community, with the freedom to interact, not with the freedom to be left alone.[55]

All too often, I have argued, television leaves us alone. It removes us from the public sphere by making it seem that the public sphere has come to us. This sort of remote control politics is entertaining, but it is surely not the stuff out of which vital, participatory communities are built. Politics can only succeed when enough people care, and care enough, to make it succeed. Despite its best efforts, television does not consistently promote that end.

The Languishing Community

Perhaps the single most important thing to remember about watching television is that it can be done alone. It often is. Once the Zenith delivery agent leaves and once the cable company has done its work, no one else is needed. For the reasons already advanced, television's aloneness need not translate into loneliness. Its sparkling personalities quickly enter our lives and connect us to the world at large. They help us build emotional bridges to other persons, other cultures, and give us a sense of participation in the world around us. From a political point of view, it must be said, this sense of participation leads more often to quiescence than to genuine political involve-ment, and yet that too has its advantages in a large and heterogeneous society.

As I have mentioned elsewhere, the media often do a service when they help us sublimate raw political passions.[56]

But just as the mass media feature political personalities, they also feature diverse pressure groups and that makes building a sense of national purpose difficult. Each evening, television presents its own version of the rainbow coalition, although television's coalition often does not coalesce: feminists, environmentalists, neo-Nazis, corporate apologists, trilateralists, devil worshippers, Clinton Republicans. Through such assembly work, television responds to the postmodern challenge, confronting the American people with their sumptuous diversity. In so doing, television places new social issues on the agenda and provides a forum for previously disenfranchised groups.

Still, there is the warning of Ihab Hassan: "I have no prophecy in me, only some slight foreboding, which I express now to remind myself that all the evasions of our knowledge and actions thrive on the absence of consensual beliefs. . . . This is our postmodern condition."[57] In other words, a "busy" public sphere causes viewers to wander through the televisual maze looking for someone with a matching ethnic, religious, and psychographic profile. In Jurgen Habermas's lexicon, television "refeudalizes" politics.[58] Just as in medieval Europe, each contending group is now allotted its own acre of airtime, leaving precious little time for larger communal concerns.

The "free play of signifiers" runs riot in such conditions, as traditional American watchwords are redefined and redeployed. "Freedom of choice" becomes the right to have an abortion. "Family values" cloaks the savaging of homosexuals. "States rights" is the token for decreasing federal aid to education. And "rebuilding the U.S. economy" means everything else: corporate glass ceilings, union-bashing, exploitation of Mexican laborers, the suppression of Zionism in Israel.

According to many writers, such contrariety is central to a vibrant democracy. For political scientist Iris Young, searching for "a civic public in which citizens transcend their particular contexts, needs, and interests to address the common good" is a fool's errand. Such a unitary goal ultimately "will suppress difference, and tend to exclude some voices and perspectives" from public participation, she argues.[59] Moreover, says sociologist Alain Touraine, a highly contested public space reveals "the fragility, the contradictions, and the conflicts present in the dominant order once believed to be so powerful"[60] and thereby opens the door to crucial political changes. In addition, says Roland Barthes, the "disease of thinking in essences"[61] stifles the imagination, as the old social and political bromides are repeated *ad nauseam* and asked to consolidate a people who have long since lost their grasp on a center that holds.

Television is implicated in all of this. That is perhaps best exemplified by the death of communal language. John Kennedy's historic phrasing, "Ich bin ein Berliner," is now antique. In today's political forum, Kennedy would be roundly vilified. Imagine, if you can, Newt Gingrich singing "I am woman" to the annual convention of N.O.W. or supplicating the N.A.A.C.P. with "Word, brother." Charges of paternalism, if not imperialism, would ring forth. Mr. Gingrich would be accused of trying to colonize his audiences' consciousness.

In other words, a highly individuated discourse has taken hold in the United States, a discourse that permits nobody to speak for anybody. Language that might have been termed empathic in earlier times ("I know how you feel") is now political death. An ideology of particularism prevails and it censures all unthinking attempts to build cross-group coalitions. Language that is too communal ("All Americans know that . . . ") is used sparingly and language that is too universal ("As citizens of the world, we must . . . ") is eschewed altogether. In their stead has grown up a thick argot that touches every conceivable base:

> As a white, heterosexual, middle-class, able-bodied, not old woman, I cannot claim to speak for radical movements of Blacks, Latinos, American Indians, poor people, lesbians, old people, or the disabled. But the political commitment to social justice which motivates my philosophical reflections tells me that I also cannot speak without them.[62]

Although this passage reflects the hypercorrectness of the academy, media politics is often not far behind. The Thomas-Hill hearings of 1991 were a case in point, blending as they did so many diverse political ingredients. A highlight of the hearings was watching Senator Orrin Hatch tiptoe through the landmines of race, gender, and sexuality when questioning Clarence Thomas. In doing so, he presumed no knowledge unavailable to the average white citizen in his home state of Utah:

❐ "Now I want to ask you about this intriguing thing you just said. You said some of the language is stereotype language. What does that . . . mean?

❐ "As I recall it, there were two black men talking [in a television program] about this matter, and one of them said, 'She's trying to demonize us.' I didn't understand it at the time. Do you understand that?"

❒ "Okay, Hill said that he [Thomas] discussed oral sex between men and women. Is that a black stereotype?"
❒ "Is [this] a black stereotype, something like 'Long Dong Silver'?"[63]

Feigned though it was, Hatch's witlessness here exemplifies the care that must be taken when speaking in an oversocialized culture. Not to be outdone was Senator Joe Biden, who had his female aides sit behind him during the proceedings, a kind of visual warranting of his feminist sensibilities. But scenery can only take one so far in politics; eventually one must speak. Biden did so, often with excruciating effort:

> Well, you said at the—your very first—almost your first utterance yesterday when you first appeared, that you can't imagine what you could have said that could have caused Anita Hill to say what she has said. But if there were anything she ever misunderstood—I'm paraphrasing, I don't know the exact quote—then you're sorry. Now let me ask you this. On its face, that seems to me to be a completely reasonable statement for one to make. I don't think it—speak for myself—things that I might say, jokes that I might tell, with a male trusted aide that I've been with for 20 years, might not be the same joke that I'd be willing to tell with the female members of my staff. And I suspect that were I a woman, there are certain things that I could say to the females on my staff that I couldn't say to the males on my staff. Now, I'm groping to try to figure out how we got to where we are in terms of this discrepancy, among the men on your staff, did you ever kid about, make reference to, say you saw, deal with, any of the subjects that Anita Hill says you dealt with, spoke to, mentioned to her?[64]

Biden's self-interruptions, his temporizing, and his tramp through the sociological thicket raise an interesting philosophical question: If an efficient language of community can no longer be spoken, can community be said to exist? The importance of this question was once dramatized by the scuffle between U.S. Representative Pete Stark of California and then Health and Human Services Secretary Louis Sullivan. Stark claimed in a moment of pique that Secretary Sullivan was "a disgrace to his profession and his race" (Sullivan is a black physician).[65] The resulting furor was intense, and Stark ultimately apologized for his choice of words. Lost in the exchange, however, was Stark's charge that Sullivan was refusing to require American tobacco companies to help pay for the costs of smoking-related illnesses, illnesses suffered disproportionately by African Americans. For Stark, this was either a case of interest-group protectionism (re: the tobacco lobby) or group abandonment (re: Blacks) on Sullivan's part. For Stark this was politics, the language of *collective* life.

The subtlety of his distinction was lost in an age of individualistic politics. Stark's main point crashed to the ground around him, but it was he who understood what Hannah Arendt meant when she said that, yes, Adolf Eichmann had failed as a human being but he failed even more grievously as a public citizen.[66] Representative Stark could also understand why John Dewey preferred Cromwell and Napoleon to Jesus and Shakespeare. The former pair, said Dewey, "must have had a private life, but how insignificant it bulks in comparison with their action as representatives of a state."[67]

I make no brief here for racial insensitivity. Representative Stark clearly overstepped his bounds. But it is worth noting that the *communal* strains in his critique were lost in the resulting melee. By giving so much attention to the individual in political life and much less to the broadly communal, the mass media have, in Hannah Arendt's terms, championed strength over power: "While strength is the natural quality of an individual seen in isolation," said she, "power springs up between men when they act together and vanishes the moment they disperse."[68] And it is not hard to sympathize with television's bias because strength is so visual: blocked doors at an abortion clinic, podium-thumping in the Senate chamber. To get a snapshot of power, however, one must look elsewhere.

Conclusion

Perhaps the most important thing to remember about watching television is that it is a cumulative process. Its real power comes not from an isolated program here or there but from the steady drumbeat of its day-in and day-out telecasts. The more habitual television watching becomes, the more taken for granted its images, and the more it affects how we think and what we think about. Because we often watch television in a distracted state, we are only half aware of the pictures dancing before our eyes. In like fashion, television's spoken text rarely invites studied reflection on our parts. Instead, its "flow" carries us along. As we drift lazily across the social and political landscape, we pay less and less attention to any one programming segment and are therefore more and more susceptible to the psychological aggregate building up within us. And because the television set is on so often in the average American home, its sights and sounds become almost atmospheric.

Current political analysts too often forget such processes. In focusing so heavily on the extraordinary political event—the mass demonstration outside the White House, the quadrennial convention oratory—commentators forget the humbler, but insistent, political images that sweep over the American people each day. Because these images pop up unlabeled and unheralded, they typically seem inconsequential. And yet when *Law and Order* reruns introduce us to one more corrupt city councilman, or when David Letterman interviews the 12-year-old who bested the vice president in a spelling bee, or when Somalian relief aid breaks down because of international antipathies, viewers are once again invited to believe that politics does not work. Because these images appear disjointedly, with no overarching text to summarize them, they seem innocent of politicization (really, de-politicization).

No useful phenomenology of politics can fail to reckon with such additive effects of the mass media. As this chapter has argued, political television is now so "busy" that viewers respond by watching the political system rather than working for it. Heretofore, observers had posited a vigorous public sphere (composed of a small number of dedicated professionals) that was contrasted to a much larger group that seldom thought about politics and that did even less about it. The argument here is different. It claims that television creates a middle way between the active and dormant cultures. By parading diverse political actors across the screen, television gives viewers a sense of participation. Whether these actors win or lose a particular struggle seems not to matter very much, nor does it seem to matter whether we like them, singly or collectively. It is their energy, their commitment, that is transformed into our own emblems of involvement.

Obviously, this is a speculative argument. Nobody knows for sure what happens when people watch television. But we surely know these things: that the American people are not shrinking violets when it comes to politics; that opinion polls and audience call-in shows are immensely popular; that political themes interpenetrate all forms of popular culture; that, in study after study, the American people remain convinced that what goes wrong in governance can be fixed but that politicians do not have the solutions. In other words, the American people seem attracted to and yet repelled by politics. Television, I think, contributes to both feelings.

The most worrisome thing we know, however, is that it is becoming harder and harder for the American people to acknowledge an overriding sense of community. Perhaps that is because the crime rate is higher than ever, because the economy is an uncertain thing, or because the melting pot no longer melts in the United States. But television hardly helps matters. Rarely, for example, does it show people pulling together. Instead, it shows Group A pitted against Group B, the former frustrated, the latter disheartened. Because these images are so persistent, it makes for a lonely politics, the sort that E. J. Dionne Jr. has described:

> Gays wanted an end to laws against sodomy ("leave us alone"); feminists wanted an end to laws against abortion ("leave us alone"); blacks wanted an end to laws enforcing segregation ("leave us alone"); there were many battles against the censorship of music, books, and alternative papers ("leave us alone"); dictatorships everywhere were called upon to lift barriers against emigration and to end torture and the imprisonment of political dissidents ("leave *them* alone").[69]

Because these images are so rife on television, children today are finding it hard to see possibilities for collective action, according to Henry Giroux.[70] Their parents are no more buoyant, and that gives the Democrats and Republicans fits when trying to fashion political platforms that are strong yet elastic. When a senator or governor holds forth during a campaign about the beliefs of "the people," virtually everyone descends upon them with a single, angry question: *Which people?* In a pluralistic society, this has always been an important question. Too often, it has been ignored or trivialized by those in power. But it is only one question, and a democracy houses many questions. As Martin Luther King, Jr. used to say, it is effete to dismiss politics, the business of community. That is no less true in an age of media.

Notes

1. R. Morin and D. Balz, "Children of the Tuned-In Find Politics a Turnoff," *Washington Post,* June 17, 1992, A1, A16.
2. Morin and Balz, A16.
3. S. Dossa, *The Public Realm and the Public Self: The Political Theory of Hannah Arendt* (Waterloo, Canada: Wilfrid Laurier University Press, 1989), 63.
4. H. Arendt, *The Human Condition* (Chicago: University of Chicago Press, 1958), 43.
5. For a thorough exegesis of Arendt's various meanings, see H. Pitkin, "Conformism, Housekeeping, and the Attack of the Blob: Hannah Arendt's Concept of the Social." Paper presented at the annual convention of the American Political Science Association, San Fra ncisco, California, August 1990.

6. For an alternative way of appreciating the distinctions being raised here, see C. Maier, "Introduction," in C. S. Maier (ed.), *Changing Boundaries of the Political: Essays on the Evolving Balance Between the State and Society, Public and Private* (Cambridge: Cambridge University Press, 1987), 12-20.

7. J. Citrin, "The Changing American Electorate," in A. J. Meltsner (ed.), *Politics and the Oval Office: Towards Presidential Governance* (San Francisco: Institute for Contemporary Studies, 1981), 34-35.

8. E. J. Dionne, *Why Americans Hate Politics* (New York: Simon & Schuster, 1991), 317.

9. S. Peterson, *Political Behavior: Patterns in Everyday Life* (Newbury Park, CA: Sage, 1990), 63-64.

10. Dionne, 338.

11. R. Brody, *Assessing the President: The Media, Elite Opinion, and Public Support* (Stanford, CA: Stanford University Press, 1991), 107.

12. F. Fox Piven and R. A. Cloward, *Why Americans Don't Vote* (New York: Pantheon, 1988), 119.

13. Piven and Cloward, 18-19.

14. R. Teixeira, *Why Americans Don't Vote: Turnout Decline in the United States* (New York: Greenwood, 1987), 91.

15. Teixeira, 8.

16. G. Will, "More People Voting Isn't the Answer to Anything," *South Bend Tribune*, September 6, 1991, A6.

17. Piven and Cloward, 13.

18. C. Krauthammer, "In Praise of Low Voter Turnout," *Time*, May 21, 1990, 88.

19. Teixeira, 91.

20. P. Lazarsfeld and R. Merton, "Mass Communication, Popular Taste, and Organized Social Action," in W. Schramm (ed.), *Mass Communications* (Urbana: University of Illinois Press, 1948), 492-503.

21. M. Morgan, "Television and Democracy," in I. Angus and S. Jhally (eds.), *Cultural Politics in Contemporary America* (New York: Routledge, 1989), 243.

22. Ibid.

23. S. R. Lichter, D. Amundson, and R. Noyes, *The Video Campaign: Network Coverage of the 1988 Primaries* (Washington, DC: A.E.I. Institute, 1988), 65.

24. F. Jameson, "Postmodernism, or The Cultural Logic of Late Capitalism," *The New Left Review*, 146 (July/August, 1984), 82.

25. C. Hitchens, "Voting in the Passive Voice: What Polling Has Done to American Democracy," *Harpers*, April 1992, 46.

26. R. Sennett, *The Fall of Public Man* (New York: Knopf, 1977), 196.

27. R. Allen and C. Kuo, "The Impact of Symbolic Social Reality on Political Orientations." Paper presented at the annual convention of the International Communication Association, Dublin, Ireland, June 1990, 25. The importance of this finding is reinforced by another set of researchers who have shown that "as the number of reported conversations about the news increases from nine to ten or more across the week, [a subject's] comprehension score almost doubles" on current events tests. See J. P. Robinson and D. Davis, "Television News and the Informed Public: An Information-Processing Approach," *Journal of Communication*, 40:3 (1990), 116.

28. R. Kubey and M. Csikszentmihalyi, *Television and the Quality of Life: How Viewing Shapes Everyday Experience* (Hillsdale, NJ: Erlbaum, 1990), 98.

29. R. Schmuhl, *Statecraft and Stagecraft: American Political LIfe in the Age of Personality* (South Bend, IN: Notre Dame University Press, 1990), 99-102.

30. Pitkin, 27.

31. W. Allen, "Hannah Arendt: Existential Phenomenology and Political Freedom," *Philosophy and Social Criticism,* 9 (1982), 177.

32. These are the current, depressing facts about citizen politics as reported in Russell Neumann's *The Paradox of Mass Politics: Knowledge and Opinion in the American Electorate* (Cambridge, MA: Harvard University Press, 1986), 11.

33. M. Delli Carpini, M. and B. Williams, "Is Dan Rather More Real Than E.T.? 'Fictional' and 'Non-fictional' Television Celebrates Earth Day." Paper presented at the annual convention of the International Communication Association, Dublin, Ireland, June 1990.

34. E. Rapping, *The Looking Glass World of Nonfiction TV* (Boston: South End Press, 1987), 154-157.

35. R. Merelman, *Making Something of Ourselves: On Culture and Politics in the United States* (Berkeley, CA: University of California Press, 1984), 113.

36. J. Gusfield, *The Culture of Public Problems: Drinking-Driving and the Symbolic Order* ((Chicago: University of Chicago Press, 1981).

37. H. Gray, "Television, Black Americans, and the American Dream," *Critical Studies in Mass Communication,* 6 (1989), 376-382, 383-384.

38. W. L. Bennett, "Marginalizing the Majority: Conditioning Public Opinion to Accept Managerial Democracy," in M. Margolis and G. Mauser (eds.), *Manipulating Public Opinion: Essays on Public Opinion as a Dependent Variable* (Pacific Grove, CA: Brooks/Cole, 1989), 346-347.

39. L. Wilkins and P. Patterson, "Media Coverage of Disasters and Hazards: The Political Amplification of Risk." Paper presented at the annual convention of the International Communication Association, New Orleans, LA, May 1988, 8.

40. J. O'Neil, *Plato's Cave: Desire, Power, and the Specular Functions of the Media* (Northwood, NJ: Ablex, 1991), 182.

41. J. Dewey, *The Public and Its Problems* (Chicago: Gateway, 1946), 41.

42. B. Hinckley, *The Symbolic Presidency: How Presidents Portray Themselves* (New York: Routledge, 1990), 56.

43. M. Weber, "The Nature of Charismatic Domination," in W. G. Runciman (ed.), *Weber: Selections in Translation* (Cambridge: Cambridge University Press, 1978), 248.

44. For additional data on this matter, see A. Ranney, *Channels of Power, the Impact of Television on American Politics* (New York: Basic Books, 1983), 106.

45. J. Baudrillard, *Jean Baudrillard: Selected Writings,* M. Poster (ed.) (Stanford, CA: Stanford University Press, 1988), 15.

46. M. Milburn, B. Cistuli, and M. Garr, "Survey and Experimental Studies of the Effect of Television News on Individuals' Attributions About Terrorism." Paper presented at the annual convention of the International Society of Political Psychology, Washington, DC, July 1990.

47. Morgan, 251.

48. S. Iyengar and D. Kinder, *News That Matters: Television and American Public Opinion* (Chicago: University of Chicago Press, 1987), 42.

49. S. Whalen, "The Institutionalization of Relations of Power through Practices of Speech: A Theoretical Inquiry," Unpublished doctoral dissertation, Pennsylvania State University, 1989, 160-161.

50. R. Campbell and J. Reeves, *Cracked Coverage: Television News, the Anti-cocaine Crusade, and the Reagan Legacy* (Durham, NC: Duke University Press, 1994).

51. A. Miller, E. Goldenberg, and L. Ebring, "Type-Set Politics: Impact of Newspapers on Public Confidence," *American Political Science Review,* 73 (1979), 72.

52. Iyengar and Kinder, 125-126.

53. R. Bellah, "Populism and Individualism," *Social Policy,* Fall 1985, 30.

54. M. Pollock, "The Social and the Political on TV: Implications of Hannah Arendt's Political Philosophy for Analyzing Televised Politics." Paper presented at the annual convention of the International Communication Association, Chicago, Illinois, May 1991, 22.

55. B. Parekh, *Hannah Arendt and the Search for a New Political Philosophy* (London: Macmillan, 1981), 16-17.

56. See R. Hart, *The Political Pulpit* (West Lafayette, IN: Purdue University Press, 1977).

57. I. Hassan, *The Post-Modern Turn: Essays in Post-Modern Theory and Culture* (Columbus: Ohio State University, 1987),181-182.

58. J. Habermas, "The Public Sphere: An Encyclopedia Article," in S. Bronner and D. Kellner (eds.), *Critical Theory and Society: A Reader* (New York: Routledge, 1989), 141.

59. I. Young, *Justice and the Politics of Difference* (Princeton, NJ: Princeton University Press, 1990), 118.

60. A. Touraine, *Return of the Actor: Social Theory in Postindustrial Society*, Trans. M. Godzick (Minneapolis: University of Minnesota Press, 1988), 57.

61. As quoted in J. Klinkowitz, *Rosenberg, Barthes, Hassan: The Postmodern Habit of Thought* (Athens: University of Georgia Press, 1988), 73.

62. Young, 14.

63. "Clarence Thomas' Response to Senator Orrin Hatch," October 12, 1991, *Senate Judiciary Committee Hearings on the Clarence Thomas Nomination to the Supreme Court* (Washington, DC: Federal Information Systems Corporation, 1991).

64. "Clarence Thomas' Response to Senator Joe Biden," October 12, 1991, *Senate Judiciary Committee Hearings on the Clarence Thomas Nomination to the Supreme Court* (Washington, DC: Federal Information Systems Corporation, 1991).

65. "Lawmaker Assails Health Chief," *New York Times*, August 3, 1990, A16.

66. A paraphrase from Dossa, 138.

67. Dewey, 29.

68. Arendt, 200.

69. Dionne, 53.

70. H. Giroux, *Schooling and the Struggle for Public Life: Critical Pedagogy in the Modern Age* (Minneapolis: University of Minnesota Press, 1988), 15-16.

Box 5.1 Inquiries and Transitions

Why is it so hard to write a book about the feelings associated with watching television? Television clearly makes us feel things, but why is it so hard to put those feelings into words? When we watch the weather report before going to bed, we feel oddly satisfied. Why? When we watch people pull one another's hair out on *Jerry Springer*, we feel illicit but strangely entranced. Why? When we watch a great quarterback thread the needle to a wide receiver, we feel a sudden jolt of energy, perhaps even a sense of dominance. Why? Not only is it hard to trace the sources of these feelings but it is also hard to even admit to them. Why? Why does television usually seem like the wind to us, something there but unimportant? Why do we prefer to think of it as a microwave oven with pictures? By actively denying television's power, we perhaps reach for some of the influence we have already ceded it. But is denial our best strategy? If television is making us feel politically involved even though we are not, if it is filling up our lives with confection and not nourishment, and if it is making us feel alone when we so need community, is it not a medium of feeling and, hence, a medium to be studied imaginatively? Indeed it is.

Feeling Important

The Temptations of Alternative Politics

O ddly enough, politics can disappear precisely when it seems most present. And most passionate. The chapter explores the influence of the mass media on the politically engaged-but-disenfranchised. It asks whether social movements have been aided or undone by the mass media, especially television, and it reports a mixed result. On the surface, of course, television seems to have been an aide to controversy. McCarthyism was dealt a death blow by the Senate's decision to televise its hearings; the Vietnam war was abandoned because its backers lost Walter Cronkite's confidence; the gay rights movement was born largely because television was an attending physician; Earth First!'s theatricality has been the stuff of a video age. Indeed, the average American cannot think of counter-establishment politics without first remembering a photojournalist's picture: of freedom walkers being hit with water cannon in the 1960s; of anti-war protestors festooning national guardsmen's rifles with flowers in the 1970s; of anti-nuclear activists lying across railroad tracks to prohibit the delivery of fissionable materials in the 1980s; of anti-abortionists' 10-year-old children being carted off to jail in the 1990s.

And yet there is more to be said about the matter. Like all blessings, television's blessings are not unmixed. What it gives, obviously, it takes away, subtly. As more and more viewers become accustomed to television's routines, the subtlety of its influence only increases. As more and more political move-ments become attracted to the feelings of importance television provides, the magnitude of its influence increases as well. There is at work, I believe, a powerful set of phenomenological forces that undo what movements try to do via media exposure. These forces are not, as some might argue, the products of political conspiracy. They are the products of an aesthetic conspiracy. Television does what all dramatists do—it simulates. In broadcasting the story of alternative politics, television remakes that story. It cannot do otherwise.

But this is not to say that television does not advance social causes as well. Each day, important problems are announced by movement leaders, rebroadcast by media personnel, and thereby moved toward resolution. But these processes are not inevitable. To think of a problem is not necessarily to share it and to share it is not necessarily to solve it. In any event, television is now deeply implicated in all such decision making. How it is involved, and why it is involved, are the matters at hand.

The Rhetorical Establishment

My central claim is that a Rhetorical Establishment has grown up in American life. This Establishment is populated by congeries of people that vie for our attention, adherence, and affection. Members of this Establishment burden our ears daily, causing us to think new thoughts, try new options, develop new prejudices, send new money. Their habitat is the public forum and their tools include speechmaking and lectures, the television interview, the radio call-in show, the outraged editorial, the denunciatory pamphlet, and the impromptu press conference. Normally, there are audiences aplenty for even the least well-established members of this Establishment, all of whom are adept at delivering new information to audiences who cannot get it for themselves and renewed passion to audiences who have become listless.

Some members of the Rhetorical Establishment are well paid for their labors, although many are not. (Looking at the fee structure of any of the national lecture bureaus will determine who's who.) Whether rich or not-so-rich, however, and whether religious, political, scholarly, or consumerist in orientation, this Establishment presses on, sustained by a nation with an incurable media habit, with a love of larger-than-life personalities, and with the willingness to entertain endless social possibilities.

Most often, members of the Rhetorical Establishment emanate from six arenas: (1) conventional politics, (2) organized religion, (3) popular journalism, (4) higher education, (5) social movements, and (6) what might be called "advocacy aesthetics," that collection of painters, writers and musicians who use their art to dramatize political issues. This band of salespersons struts about in the public marketplace daily, arguing loud and long with one another, hoping to get a minute of airtime here, passage of a piece of legislation there, bullying their ways into sacred forums with some new proposal for social betterment. After emerging from the rhetorical arena, the most successful members of this fraternity socialize amiably (regardless of political orientation) in the dark cocktail lounges of turn-of-the-century hotels, while the lesser among them repair to corner cafes to order pasta and total up the suasory victories they have claimed that day.[1]

Like any viable establishment, the Rhetorical Establishment provides a livelihood for a great many talented and committed persons. Even if their salaries are not grand, their personal commitments and the blessings of the gods for whom they witness are normally enough to sustain them, as is the encouragement of the hundreds and thousands of poorly paid aides who do research for them and run copiers for them and buy coffee for them. These latter persons form a huge Under-establishment and take as their task the echoing and re-echoing of the messages they are expected to disseminate. Working for the Rhetorical Establishment, as well as being part of it, is hard work and it demands great dedication. Its members must often cope with insufficient resources for their labors, with recalcitrance from the forces of power they would replace, and with the feelings of impatience that are natural in any long-term effort. And because of the sheer amount of verbal repetition persuasion requires, professional advocates must also cope with an endemic sense of déjà vu.

Still, members of the Rhetorical Establishment constitute a long and impressive list: Nadine Strossen, Ted Koppell, John Paul II, John Kenneth Galbraith, David Broder, Marion Barry, Greta Van Susteren, Jonas Salk, George Steinbrenner, Rudolph Giuliani, Toni Morrison, Sister Souljah, Lester Thurow, Edward Bennett, Robert Schuller, Gary Wills, Holly Near, Kweisi Mfume, Arthur Schlesinger Jr., Alice Walker, Bill Moyers, Michael Novak, Helen Caldicott, Andrea Dworkin, John Silber, Jack Kemp, Susan Molinari, Spike Lee, James Gilden, Salman Rushdie, Phyllis Schlafly, Edward Kennedy—these are the Scions of Public Opinion in the United States. When they speak, people listen.

But who makes up the Rhetorical Establishment at a given time is less important than the essential condition under which it operates: For a variety of reasons, the mass media allow some people to speak more frequently than others. Although virtually all cultures produce rhetorically prominent people as well as political mutes, in American society those at the top are quickly institutionalized by being included in the nation's most hallowed rituals, by being listened to respectfully on matters about which they are expert (and a good many about which they are not), and by being given special access to the mass media for personal use.

Others are not so fortunate. Social historian Eugene Genovese reports, for example, that at one time in the nation's history, African Americans were punished for speaking what was then considered "proper English," ostensibly because such linguistic habits were seen as a primitive power grab—if I allow you to appropriate my language today, tomorrow you will want my wife.[2] In a similar vein, Robert Goodin reports that the disadvantaged more often speak hyperbolically, compensating for their sorry economic situations with unusually vigorous forms of oral expression, thereby signaling their exclusion from the social equation.[3] In other words, American society is rhetorically stratified, just as it is socially and economically stratified.

Becoming part of the Rhetorical Establishment is not easy. Society doles out media power as it doles out any precious resource—slowly and selectively. A simple comparison between the 21,000 activist groups listed in the *Encyclopedia of Associations* and their relative coverage in the *New York Times Index* quickly indicates that many are called to Establishment status but few are chosen. That same *Index* also reveals that last year's candidates for membership are often not found in this year's volume. Topics of political concern change rapidly, as do the dispositions of the Establishment's gatekeepers (the press), and the fickleness of the nation-as-audience. As with any self-regarding institution, therefore, acceptance into the Rhetorical Establishment is a precious thing, protected by high thresholds for admission and by the sudden, imperious, purging of its membership rolls.

Over time, membership in the Establishment can change dramatically. Recently, for example, Russell Jacoby has complained that there has been a precipitous drop in the number of "public intellectuals" in American life. He argues that academia has become a kind of black hole that absorbs the social and political energies formerly dispensed in the public sphere by such persons as Lewis Mumford, Mary McCarthy, Irving Howe, and C. Wright Mills.[4] Jacoby may be right that this change has resulted from a New Conservatism (or a New Selfishness) but it may also be the case that the performance standards of television have simply proved too daunting for academicians. For similar reasons, says Jeanne Kirkpatrick, corporate executives rarely find themselves in the Rhetorical Establishment because they are "likely to say something inept, which is then repeated and ridiculed by the guardians of the symbolic environment."[5]

Kirkpatrick's remarks point up a curious feature of the Rhetorical Establishment: Its constituency is sometimes out of sync with other power blocs in society. Although Bill Gates, for example, has long been part of the Rhetorical Establishment, so too has his new nemesis—Ralph Nader. Although Texas governor George W. Bush's millions brought him into politics only recently, Jesse Jackson has been there for some time despite his humble origins. Although industrialist Warren Buffett has passed up every opportunity to speak in behalf of America's rich, Mother Teresa willingly grabbed the microphone in behalf of the world's poor. Leaders of women's groups, not leaders of men's groups, are part of the Rhetorical Establishment; black spokespersons, but not (yet) Hispanic or Asian spokespersons, have achieved special public regard; presidents of some, but not all, public universities have been accorded high rhetorical status, as have presidents of some, but not all, private colleges.[6] In other words, it is the *ability to sustain media attention*, not ideological correctness, that most readily ensures membership in the Rhetorical Establishment.

The result is a pronounced arbitrariness to who is, and who is not, admitted. Some expend superhuman effort to be accepted and yet fail to be taken seriously; others drift effortlessly, almost magically, into its embrace. Some are admitted to this select company as individuals; others are inducted corporately. Some receive temporary status because of politically charged situations, while others transform early partisanship into permanent Establishment status. Some join the rhetorical elite by championing a cause that finds favor with the media, while others simply wear down the press with their persistence. Some apply moral pressure and are admitted quickly; other, longer-standing groups are repeatedly, and unceremoniously, dismissed.

This may make it seem that membership in the Rhetorical Establishment is an entirely arbitrary matter, completely a function of whoever is drafting the latest edition of its Blue Book. This is only partially true. A rough estimation of the Establishment's current membership can normally be obtained by scanning the pages of the daily newspaper. There, candidates for membership play out their political dramas, vying with their rivals for favored standing. In one era, industrial unionists like George Meany dominate the public stage whereas at other times agricultural unionists like Caesar Chavez take the bows. Counterculturalists like William Kunstler command the lecture circuit in one era, whereas neofascists like David Duke do so a decade later. Old Right partisans make espionage the most heinous offense of the 1950s, whereas feminists make rape a *political* crime twenty years later.[7]

The constituency of the Rhetorical Establishment is therefore a variable thing although, like any Establishment, it changes slowly. For example, television viewers are accustomed to hearing from the American Enterprise Institute on contemporary political matters but only rarely from the Hoover Institute. What causes such waxings and wanings? There are many factors, one of which, quite logically, is rhetorical skill itself. In the 1950s and 1960s, for example, any cause with which activist Saul Alinsky was associated was destined for societal effect. Similarly, although many Americans had long been concerned with the plight of the world's poor, it took an entrepreneurial genius like Bob Geldorf to blend rock music with social activism in the 1980s.

But rhetorical skill alone is not sufficient to ensure success. Social change is a slow thing, so simple, human endurance is also necessary. In addition, press routines greatly affect who will and who will not be favored with Establishment status. Having a national office in Washington, D.C., or New York City makes it more likely that a group's press releases will be read or that its spokesperson will be asked to do a live studio interview than if that organization is headquartered in Omaha. Similarly, a group is best assured that its message will be disseminated if its leader is photogenic—or bizarre—rather than bland, and if its staff fraternizes with—or is colorfully hostile to—media personnel.

Historical forces also conspire to preserve the Rhetorical Establishment. As political and religious groups solidify their constituencies over time, and as communication networks develop among them and between them and other groupings, institutional habits also develop. Such habits ensure that some organizations, some topics, and some individuals continue to dominate the public dialogue.[8] Money, too, perpetuates a Rhetorical Establishment. Groups like the National Rifle Association or Common Cause persevered because they had adequate, or more-than-adequate, financial backing, whereas groups like Stop Forced Busing or Jews for Jesus faded when their funds faded.

But money alone does not ensure high rhetorical status, largely because the "free media" (what used to be called the news) compensates selectively for a group's comparative insolvency. Genuine longevity, then, is a product of many, often whimsical, forces. That seemingly crucial element—having something to say—is sometimes not one of those forces, a conclusion evidenced by the inability of American environmentalists to be admitted to a prominent position in the Rhetorical Establishment after more than 25 years of intense activism.

Having obtained a rough idea of who makes up the Rhetorical Establishment, it is useful to ask why such an Establishment exists at all. Why are people attracted to it, both as members and as audiences? Psychologically, the Rhetorical Establishment is appealing on multiple fronts. Perhaps the simplest way to appreciate this appeal is to consider a formal definition: *The Rhetorical Establishment is that portion of the American populace professionally devoted to effecting political change and that achieves considerable prominence for so doing.*

There are, here, a host of attractive features. For one thing, this Establishment often has organizational—and thus social—solidity. Its members are linked with others in some important cause and they are separated from those who toil at more mundane jobs. Members of the Rhetorical Establishment work almost exclusively with ideas and with the power of their imaginations. Because a media presentation is a plastic thing, it can be molded and remolded and molded again as its various drafts travel down the rhetorical assembly line. Moreover, whole teams of people participate in its molding—thinkers, stylists, editors, designers, printers, technicians, reporters—and all share in the joy of watching New Words and New Images being formed. Framing a resolution, staging performance art, drafting an op-ed piece, splicing a documentary, hawking a book, choosing a location for a new shoot—all of these activities involve manipulating symbolic materials, materials whose flexibility gives them endless social possibilities.

Thus, the Rhetorical Establishment is an ideal working environment for social dreamers, persons whose creativity exhausts the most tireless political foe and whose symbolic resources are able to expose the most heinous injustices. And the fact that so much of this activity is group activity provides important social reinforcement, even when a press conference is poorly attended or when the usefulness of a minority plank expires at convention's end.

Those who inhabit the Rhetorical Establishment, as well as those who work for it, are change oriented and that is another reason for their emotional sustenance. As I have indicated elsewhere, rhetoric often operates as a kind of waystation for the patient,[9] as a device for reifying certain ideas in attractive ways. So, for example, Martin Luther King Jr. buoyed up the spirits of his people in the 1960s on the basis of his rhetorically skillful dreams, dreams that did not come to pass for many years after his death (and many of which have still not come to pass). But his public presentations made these unrealities seem real and it gave his followers a sense of change even when there was none. That happened because the *act* of communication—what philosopher J. L. Austin calls an illocution[10]—sometimes becomes a kind of surrogate victory in itself as, for example, when a new topic is added to a traditional religious agenda (as King did with his *Letter From a Birmingham Jail*) or when a new speaker is invited to stride across a traditional political stage (as AIDS activists did at the 1992 Democratic convention). When a person is initiated into the Rhetorical Establishment in such a dramatic fashion, it becomes news.

In other words, media politics is typically seen as a harbinger of things to come, and it therefore becomes a refuge for the terminally hopeful, persons who read important messages into the social fact of some particular communicative event. The mere setting up of a media event often has meta-rhetorical importance as a result. For example, when a well-known political candidate agrees to debate lesser rivals during a primary, it is a sure sign that that candidate's campaign is in trouble. In other words, political discourse functions as a social commodity that can be traded for, taken back, or given out by members of the Rhetorical Establishment. So, for example, Lyndon Johnson traded his presidential speeches to Republican states for pro-Vietnam votes in Congress in 1965; Richard Nixon punished the people of Massachusetts by refusing to speak there during his presidency; and Ronald Reagan frequently addressed women's groups early in his presidency even though he did nothing to advance their political aims.[11]

Another attraction of the Rhetorical Establishment is the social prominence it affords. Today, especially, its members are rewarded with ample amounts of media attention. Those with an incurable case of electronic narcissism—people like liberal James Carville and conservative Arianna Huffington—are part of an elaborate network of personalities that meets constantly in studio Green Rooms. Although ideologically separated by miles, they are emotionally separated by inches. They flatter each other with their mutual presence and yet vie, sometimes openly, for a greater share of the media pie. For many, then, television exposure is a commodity of incredible importance. Five units of airtime propagates ten units more, and that ten an additional twenty. For the ideologue, each such addition means that "the issue" has again found its way onto the nation's agenda. For the egotist, each such addition ensures further media attention and, presumably, greater political effect as well. For members of the Under-establishment, each such addition becomes an emotionally satisfying reward and a powerful rationale for continued hard work.

In critic Michel Foucault's terms, the mass media have therefore become a "site" for the dispensation of political authority, just as the hospital and the medical laboratory confer special status on the personnel who work there.[12] For a movement leader to be interviewed on the *Newshour with Jim Lehrer* is to say "I count too," the electronic equivalent of animals marking their territory. Naturally, such appearances typically ensure nothing, that is, nothing, but they do "keep alive a collective feeling of political efficacy."[13] There is importance to such events precisely because they are *events*. As such, they have empirical standing ("*20/20* has finally had a show on abuse of the elderly"), and thereby fully exist. Indeed, in an era of videotape recorders, they exist doubly if not trebly, silicon tokens that can be passed from movement member to movement member.[14]

Despite its phenomenological subtleties, then, membership in the Rhetorical Establishment is also tangible, a commodity possessing what the economists call "use value." So, for example, researchers Michael Robinson and Andrew Kohut found that better-known newscasters (i.e., persons higher up in the Establishment) are typically thought more believable when reporting the news than are their more anonymous counterparts.[15] Similarly, another study showed that Jesse Jackson received considerably better news coverage during the 1988 primaries (he achieved a 78% positive rating between January and April), ostensibly because his Establishment status shielded him from the slings and arrows of outrageous newscasters.[16]

Outrageous editorialists are another story. Robert Bartley, long-time editor of the *Wall Street Journal*'s editorial page, once issued a stinging rebuke of Ralph Nader. By sputtering when doing so, however, Bartley eloquently testified to Nader's dramatic ascension in the ranks of the Rhetorical Establishment. For example, in addition to critiquing Nader's insensitivities to corporate America, Bartley also questioned his publishing ventures, his choice of housing, his charitable donations, and even his sexuality.[17] And so it would seem that Claude Offe is somewhat mistaken when claiming that social movements cannot negotiate with the political elite because they have nothing to trade.[18] Television now offers supply-side possibilities. Because of it, an interview with Ralph Nader can become symbolic capital for consumerists. And in an electronic age, symbolic capital is indeed a kind of capital.

The Marxian take on all this is somewhat different. Marxists would call attention to the processes of commodification that attend any such system of bartering (someone, after all, makes money from Farm Aid concerts and emancipatory rap lyrics). But the usefulness of media coverage cannot be denied. Because of it, movements can now be exported quickly, a phenomenon evidenced in the United States in the late 1960s (when the student movement took its marching orders from the much-televised civil rights movement) and in the world at large in the late 1980s (witness the satellite-assisted "democratization" movements in Eastern Europe and Asia).

The underlying premise of the Rhetorical Establishment—that power can become electronic—is also a premise very much in keeping with New Class attitudes. According to Peter Berger, the New Class is composed of people who work with symbolic materials. They are teachers, office workers, reporters, artists, and so on.[19] Because of the work they do, they prize any device that manipulates symbols: stereos, computers, television. Also because of the work they do, they are likely to be impressed by anyone capable of mastering the symbolic universe, persons ranging from the populist-classicist Placido Domingo to the product-endorsing Michael Jordan.

It is out of this New Class that most of the recent social movements have been born. These New Movements are no longer drawn from the (economically) downtrodden and the alienated, says sociologist Claude Offe,[20] but consist of persons concerned about matters of *identity* (gay rights, the women's movement, racialists) and *purpose* (educational reformers, trilateralists, the "green" movements). Converts to the new religious movements in the 1970s and 1980s came almost exclusively from such New Class members,[21] not from among the blue-collar workers so central to the labor and ethnic movements of earlier years.

Thus, although it is hard to imagine an old labor leader like George Meany being compromised by the chance for a soundbite, New Movement leaders have much greater respect for the media's gratuities. But theorists of the New Class have missed an important insight. Although the Rhetorical Establishment, like all of U.S. society, is no doubt tilted to the middle-and upper-middle classes, it also includes spokespersons for the poor (Operation Breadbasket), the homeless (Whoopi Goldberg), and the disenfranchised (C.O.Y.O.T.E., a prostitute-support group). Thus, whereas Carl Boggs complains that some recent social movements "choose to operate at a distance from the political system itself,"[22] the more accurate claim is that many of them have become enmeshed in the Rhetorical Establishment, even while forsaking traditional lobbying activities.

Despite its several attractions, however, there is ample reason to question the usefulness of the Rhetorical Establishment for political movements. As Henry Giroux argues, it is now possible to imagine "a discourse of critique that is simultaneously a practice of political impotence."[23] Media exposure, like all else, can become a dangerous compulsion, a space of containment rather than one of liberation.[24] In other words, instead of silencing dissident groups, the Rhetorical Establishment can "voice" them and thereby de-radicalize them. Instead of marginalizing society's critics, it can make them part of its discussions.

In an electronic age, it is becoming necessary to rethink the central problem that Walter Lippmann, Harold Lasswell, and Daniel Bell worried about 40 years ago: the Information Revolution. According to them, citizens who proved incapable of absorbing the vast amounts of information generated and stored in the modern age would fall by the political wayside. Today, the greater danger may lie in a Media Revolution in which mass exposure ensures nothing more than mass exposure and in which media imperialism becomes a quaint, but misleading, political myth.

The advent of the Rhetorical Establishment therefore demands that we ask a new set of questions about politics. Although that establishment serves a number of important advantages, it also retards social change on occasion and, worse, hides the effects of that retardation. Needless to say, questioning the utility of the Rhetorical Establishment is not to call into question the good will of its members, or their social concern, or their political dedication, or their consummate professionalism. Instead, it is to be reminded that there are other forces of influence in the world besides media forces. Above all, it is to become concerned that television can lull us to sleep as well as awaken us. The former function is especially worrisome.

Lost in the Language of Politics

One of the most basic problems associated with the Rhetorical Establishment relates to language itself. That is, despite its enormous social influence, rhetoric is, after all, only rhetoric—words written, symbols generated, pictures displayed, logos designed, letterhead utilized. That rhetoric can hearten the depressed, inform the unknowing, and whip up the winds of social change goes without saying. And when such persuasion is delivered by members of the Rhetorical Establishment, it can be an impressive thing indeed. But all too often, political and economic forces conspire to exploit these users of political television.

A paradigm example is outlined in my book, *The Political Pulpit*.[25] There, I note the constant rhetorical intertwining between representatives of organized religion in the United States and elected government officials. The rhetoric of God and country they cooperate to produce has served, I maintain, an important social good by creating a kind of "established religion" in the United States without also creating religious sectarianism or a national orthodoxy. Congressional invocations, convention benedictions, Memorial Day services, military chaplaincies, and much else remind Americans daily that they are doing the special work of the Lord and that America is truly a redeemer nation.

Despite the obvious political advantages of such accommodations in a nation hosting more than 2,000 different religious denominations, the rhetoric of civic piety also *inhibits* substantive religious/political relations in the United States. That is, because such ceremonial presentations give a sense of participation to Christian and Jew alike, each becomes less likely to intrude into the policy-making arena itself. Heartened by the honorific roles assigned them and by their easy conversational access to influential public officials, mainstream religious leaders are surprisingly docile politically. Some clerics, of course, decry this rhetorical arrangement. People like Father Daniel Berrigan in the 1960s and, after him, Gerry Falwell and Ralph Reed, forswore this contract between religion and government by involving themselves directly in political lobbying. Because their religious agendas were really social agendas and, hence, political agendas, they made what many felt was an unseemly fuss.

Although their substantive political success was modest at best, the Berrigan/Falwell/Reed defiance is instructive. It shows that joining the Rhetorical Establishment often produces political quiescence in its members and allows important governmental decisions to be made by less visible persons. After all, there are at least three possible responses powerbrokers can make to any charge: agreement, denial, and (perhaps most likely) respectful acknowledgment that the charge has been made.

It is this latter possibility that is especially galling to religious activists. They come to understand that the rhetoric of petition-and-reaction often becomes a smokescreen for the legislation that others will implement. They come to realize that being invited to join the Rhetorical Establishment implies a policy-making role for the invitee but ensures nothing more than that he or she will move about in polite company. They come to realize that the standard definition of politics contains no *constitutive* role for media artistry. Ultimately, in short, they are required to ask the politically unnerving question: *Once I control the media agenda, what is it, exactly, that I control?*

Because media appearances can be emotionally charging for speaker and audience alike and because it is often so hard to tell when a bottom line has been reached in politics, members of the Rhetorical Establishment often become distracted from the policy arena. Operating on the deterministic notion that if discourse is fixed first, policy will be fixed second, they become, in effect, rhetorical police. Good examples of this were the feminist activists in the 1970s who purged sexist language from schoolbooks, newspapers, and legal documents and sexist images from situation comedies, soap operas, and popular advertisements. Predictably, the powerbrokers of the day fought them tooth-and-nail, thereby raising the stakes so that whatever rhetorical victories the feminists achieved would be seen by them as policy victories.[26]

All the while, however, three other things were happening: (1) members of the feminist Under-establishment were beginning to define linguistic triumphs as genuinely political triumphs; (2) working-class women were becoming alienated from the women's movement because its ostensible goal—ungendered discourse—seemed so removed from the often brutish lives they led; and (3) society's (male) powerbrokers were gradually giving way to these rhetorical onslaughts while still retaining a stranglehold on jobs, money, information, and mobility. As political scientist Murray Edelman has observed, it is often possible in politics to give the rhetoric to one disputant and the decision to the other.[27]

Objections could, of course, be made to this line of reasoning. "Altering the media agenda *is* effectual," some might contend, "a necessary first step in a protracted struggle." "Any victory builds solidarity in a young movement," still others could respond. Although these are solid tactical assumptions, joining the Rhetorical Establishment can also cause a leader to sell out too cheaply. This is exactly what Malcolm X accused Martin Luther King Jr. of doing 25 years ago. By accepting early membership in the Rhetorical Establishment, Malcolm argued, King had become trapped in the traditional language of change in American life. By speaking that language, Malcolm warned, King was asking for less than he should ask for, was asking more politely than was honorable (given the incivility of the opposition), and was asking less often, less dramatically, and less specifically than was strategically wise.

Were he alive today, Malcolm X would note with irony that African Americans as diverse as Vernon Jordan, Bernard Shaw, Johnnie Cochran, and

Henry Louis Gates, Jr. are now fully accepted members of the Rhetorical Establishment and yet that black unemployment is still high, black educational opportunities still bleak, and affordable housing still appallingly deficient. Malcolm X would argue that although some rhetoric makes a difference, some puts us to sleep.

Jacques Ellul made much this same point in his writings. He argued that modern society is being overrun by politicization—the sense that "something is being done" via discourse. Much is always being done, Ellul would note, but what is being done is often sharply at odds with the popular language of society.[28] Were he to survey the U.S. landscape today, for example, Ellul would be struck by the confidence exhibited by radio talk-show callers. Such shows, Ellul might note, give a sense of action to listeners who are removed from real political action and suggest that problems are being solved *because they are being talked about.*[29]

Each day, however, the Rhetorical Establishment presents a countermodel to Ellul's joyless formulation. Each day, leftists and rightists, sexists and feminists, Klanners and divesters, protectionists and interventionists, prochoicers and pro-lifers, agriculturalists and industrialists, polluters and environmentalists catch their audiences up in a whirlwind of discourse. Such spokespersons give visibility to their ideas, prove that their cause is just and generate camaraderie sufficient to get them through the hard times. By making access to the Rhetorical Establishment comparatively easy for some groups (like women, gays, and blacks) and comparatively difficult for others (like atheists, John Birchers, and I.R.A. supporters), society passes out legitimation without having to pass out—immediately, at least—fundamental political changes. During such interim moments, some argue, the established media serve us well. But there are other moments in politics too, and they are also part of the Rhetorical Establishment's story.

Lost in the Celebrity of Politics

Problems related to the Rhetorical Establishment also stem from the snares of media celebrity. As with any totem pole, the Rhetorical Establishment provides a great deal of attention to a limited number of individuals, thereby breeding jealousy and contentiousness among them. An even greater danger is the individuated politics it produces. For example, when the media turned against the leaders of the peace movement in the 1960s, says sociologist Todd Gitlin, they simultaneously discredited the movement.[30] By focusing heavily on persons at the top of the movement's hierarchy—people like Tom Hayden, Abbie Hoffman, and Mark Rudd—the media narrowed the conceptual and political focus of the movement right from the beginning, making it difficult for viewers to think beyond the admittedly colorful people who danced before their eyes each evening on the news.[31] In converting "leadership into celebrity," says Gitlin, the mass media reward flamboyance and make politics inert.[32]

Because media protocols determine celebrity, the radical voice is often muted. John Fiske, for example, makes the rather conspiratorial argument that genuinely dissident voices are not heard at all via the mass media but are only "translated" for the viewer by more accommodating persons.[33] Perhaps this explains why Louis Farrakhan, who consistently refused to trim his sails, had such a difficult time entering the Rhetorical Establishment.

Celebrity, then, promotes centrism. Rarely, for example, does *60 Minutes* present a segment on the atrocities done to Native Americans or on the regressiveness of taxation laws. Persons caught up in such issues are not, in the eyes of the media, demographically useful. Moreover, such persons are more likely to be reduced to mute rage than sprightly chatter by their problems and so probably could not meet the aesthetic requirements of political television. And so the American media describe largely middle-class crimes each week—fraudulent bank examiners, unfair college entrance exams, toxic swimming pools. Problems such as these are to some extent soluble and the persons who root them out typically articulate. To a real extent, the Rhetorical Establishment helps to ensure that American politics is played between the 40-yard lines.[34]

Celebrity promotes centrism in another way. Because the people spearheading political movements are of such interest to the media, and because the media make movements and their leaders isomorphic, political groups are often tied to the inevitable misfortunes of their champions. In other words, because Martin Luther King Jr. *was* civil rights for so many people in the United States, his personal idiosyncrasies bore directly on civil rights legislation. So, for example, when Reverend King's extramarital dalliances were brought to light (or widely suspected), many became cynical about his political dreams as well. Had King's identity not been so closely tied to racial justice in the United States, his extramarital affairs could have been forgiven, or at least

treated as irrelevant. But his standing in the Rhetorical Establishment permitted no such option. As a result, his movement suffered when he suffered.

Lost in the Pluralism of Politics

The Rhetorical Establishment seems somewhat unique to the United
States. Although many other countries have voracious media institutions, no
other society has had to contend with pluralism on the American plan. And
it is pluralism, above all, that inspires political movements. Because of the
"complexity of a programmed society," says Alain Touraine, our experiences
tend to form "a mosaic rather than a pyramid," all of which makes "individuals,
goods, and ideas circulate much more intensely than [they did in] earlier
societies."[35] The Rhetorical Establishment therefore resembles a spinning
color wheel that refracts the various political shadings of the American polity.
But when a color wheel spins fast enough, grayness results. And so a two-part
dilemma is presented to would-be activists in a media age: (1) be silent and
risk being ignored, or (2) talk and risk being absorbed by centrist discourse.[36]

Because of pluralism, members of the Rhetorical Establishment are often
sharply competitive with one another. They now form a vast political network,
each with its own goals and philosophies but also with its own membership
rolls, fund-raising activities, annual conferences, and press routines. "We
[now] have protest movements in the name of everything," says Alain
Touraine.[37] In the 1960s, C.O.R.E., S.N.C.C., S.C.L.C., N.A.A.C.P. and
countless other groups competed with one another for the right to speak for
African Americans. Today, countless religious groups and environmental
organizations do the same for their constituencies. As a result, rhetorical
coordination has become an important challenge to all political groups.[38]

Because of the great number of voices now included in the Rhetorical
Establishment, an *atomizing of distress* is produced. So, for example, "Labor"
has been transmuted into the Boston Police Association, the Brotherhood of
Locomotive Engineers, the Retired State Employees Association, the National Association of Social Workers, the United Farm Workers, and literally
thousands of other constituent groups who toil in behalf of the nation's
workers. No doubt, each such group adds precision to the story that Labor
tells and each ensures that workers' rights are better monitored and more
insistently articulated than in the past. But anarchy, too, can attend pluralism.

The sweeping generalizations of a Samuel Gompers or an Upton Sinclair can be heard no longer. As a result, sanitation workers in Duluth cannot identify with air traffic controllers in Dallas. By turning the mosaic of labor into a cameo of local concerns, television again proves its resistance to grand theory.

Other commentators view the atomizing of distress as a byproduct of capitalistic domination. Media institutions *are* institutions, Marxists note, and it is thus in their interest to divide pressure groups so as to conquer them (or at least diminish them). In performing such work, say the Marxists, the mass media dance to the tune of corporate America. By producing a hundred variations on the Labor theme, by only assessing the specific grievances of specific workers, television thereby deconstructs the economics of work in the United States. "The issue is wages," say the pipefitters; "The issue is working conditions," say the electricians. As each such position is articulated, systemic critique is finessed, in part because Americans genuinely fear revolutionary change and in part because the American mass media are so unblinkingly committed to pluralism.

Perhaps one of the clearest examples of the atomizing of distress occurred during the Senate hearings investigating the fitness of Clarence Thomas to sit on the Supreme Court. Predictably, given the politics of race in the United States, the hearings deeply divided the civil rights community, created unusual political struggles among Southern Democrats, and, in part because of the Anita Hill revelations, pitted men against women as well. The hearings proved a field day for members of the Rhetorical Establishment, with Clarence Thomas becoming not one person but many: an African American, a Republican, a divorcee, a bureaucrat, a self-made scholar, a Southerner, a suspected anti-abortionist, a natural rights theorist, a beneficiary of affirmative action, and a lusty or virtuous male (depending on whom one believed). Each of these roles inspired commentary from a different interested party. Each lobbyist who spoke out inspired three more to do so as well.

Pundits at the time credited Thomas' elevation to the Supreme Court as a stroke of genius on President George Bush's part. By turning members of the Rhetorical Establishment against one another, Mr. Bush stood safely above the fray as the process played itself out. And so during the crucial Anita Hill hearings, the President played golf in Maryland, relaxed at Camp David, and visited with his family over the Columbus Day weekend. Back in Washington, an internecine war was waged between interest groups. They asked the members of the Senate Judiciary Committee to stand in behalf of poor black men from the rural South who had successfully pursued the American dream or in behalf of poor black women from the rural Southwest who had been victimized by sexual harassment. In October of 1991, there was distress enough for any and all tastes in the nation's capitol.

And so pluralism is really quite untidy. But does a vigorous modern democracy have any other choice but to foster pluralism? No doubt it does not. Pluralism has been the United States' finest political legacy and will surely continue to be so. Still, pluralism has its phenomenological side effects: If a people's affections are too finely splintered, they will come to feel numb as a result. Thus, it is good to remember that pluralism can be a step, if only one step, on the road to nihilism, because a government that stands for everything can become a government that stands for nothing. No establishment should be allowed to establish that without our conscious permission.

The Silent Establishment

Perhaps the harshest way of viewing the Rhetorical Establishment is to see it as the disingenuous gift of society's true powerbrokers, a gift designed to convince Establishment members that progress is being made when, in fact, only rhetoric is being made. The implications of such a gift become clear when we acknowledge the existence of another Establishment in American life, what I choose to call the Silent Establishment. It is within this second Establishment that genuine power lies, even though its members characteristically flee the public stage. Typically, they do not grant interviews, do not make public speeches, cannot be seen on the nightly news, make few ceremonial appearances, and do not author memoirs. Theirs is an anonymity of power. They distribute scarce resources without seeming to have done so and their names are virtually unrecognizable to the average person: Levin Campbell, William J. Bauer, Harrison Winter, Leslie Arps, Walter Stratton, Robert Herres, John Wicham, Jr., William J. Lucas, Charles Dallara, Timothy Lankester, Stephen Higgins, William von Rabb, Diane Steed, Martin Davis, David Kearns, John S. Akers, James Goldberg, David Bloom, Thomas Quinn.[39]

Who are these individuals? International monetarists, the heads of the nation's most influential law firms, members of the joint chiefs of staff, tertiary-level government bureaucrats, heads of successful American corporations, powerful Washington lobbyists. Collectively, these persons determine much; some argue they determine all. Their power is not rhetorical in any public sense, although it is no doubt rhetorical in many private senses. Their bottom line is a genuine bottom line—that is, an economic bottom line—and so they are never distracted by the vagaries of public exultation. When they think of power, they rarely think of words and when they think of the mass media, they think of an enemy, not of a friend.

Like the members of the Rhetorical Establishment, they are extraordinarily enterprising but, unlike them, they are enterprising about enterprise. They spend their days shifting capital, not opinions; they enforce their wills by legal contract, not by rhetorical contract; they treat armaments as realities, not as metaphors. Their world is drab compared to that of the Rhetorical Establishment but they find security in drabness and, more important, they find profit there, too. The decisions they make affect millions even though they rarely see these people—except occasionally, as in Vietnam, or cynically, as in Bhopal. When they need rhetoric done, they hire it out. More often, though, they are quiet. The stillness of their world is interrupted only by the faint, rhythmic pulsations of financial, military, and legal machinery.

The relationship between the Silent Establishment and the Rhetorical Establishment is a complicated one. The simplest view is that the former is the latter's ventriloquist. That is, some observers feel that the Rhetorical Establishment is ultimately centrist because its financial base is set by the same moneyed forces that control munitions production (and hence geopolitics) and agricultural economics (and hence American eating habits). Because the mass media are *businesses*, such critics argue further, they artificially restrict the range of discussable political options, ensuring that no system-threatening rhetoric is ever allowed to counteract the images generated by its advertisers. As political historian F. J. Lea notes, there is a dangerous "overlap of concentrated ownership" in many mass media industries that must be watched carefully.[40]

But economic determinism alone cannot explain why the Rhetorical Establishment operates as it does. After all, the political range represented within it approximates that represented in American society itself. For the American people, pluralism has always dictated centrism, not because it is right but because it is easiest. Being required to watch a six o'clock news story on petrochemical cleanup problems does not make Exxon executives happy, but it makes them far happier than having their Houston headquarters bombed. Thus, there is a sense in which the Silent Establishment encourages the work of its chief rival because the latter operates so effectively as a receptacle for politically charged issues. The ultimate consequence is that the

Rhetorical Establishment can move society forward only gradually. Were the American people themselves not such committed gradualists, that would be a fate of some consequence.

Perhaps it is also true that if the Rhetorical Establishment did not exist, the Silent Establishment would have invented it. Why? For one thing, the Rhetorical Establishment provides a contrast effect: Its radical members stand as evidence of where society would go were they given the chance to make it go there. Typically, their outspokenness causes the average American to look for less radical alternatives. The head of General Motors, whoever he is, becomes far more attractive when his main rival is seen as Operation Rescue's Randall Terry. In addition, the Rhetorical Establishment performs a useful surveillance function for those in power. Because its criteria for admission are suitably liberal, because it is comparatively easy in a democratic society to get one's issue on the media agenda, the Rhetorical Establishment provides constantly updated information on the persons and ideas who would supplant those in power.

Sometimes the Silent Establishment speaks, although its speech is normally reduced to print and presented in the third person (as, for example, in courts of law). Sometimes the speech of the Silent Establishment bears the intertextual markings of its most radical critics. For example, communication scholar John Llewellyn[41] has found that the company newsletters of Eli Lilly Pharmaceuticals and the Ball Corporation of Indiana borrowed the voices of their political opponents, creating an undesignated but still familiar "Them." Manipulations of this sort contribute a sense of dialectic to what little rhetoric the Silent Establishment produces, making it appear socially aware and yet unbent in pursuit of its traditional goals. That strategy also creates a kind of "artificial negativity," says Timothy Luke,[42] giving the appearance that political alternatives are being considered when, in fact, they are often being ignored. A tangled web indeed.

Conclusion

Throughout this chapter, I have tried to maintain a suitably generous perspective on the Rhetorical Establishment. As we have seen, its problems are quite real and yet its potential for good is considerable. Because of it, countless persons who suffer deprivation are given new hope each day.

Because of it, too, grievous social ills are identified and important political initiatives undertaken. In these ways and more, the Rhetorical Establishment serves the American people well.

And yet Marx's voice must also be heard, especially because television's simulations so often displace it. It is all too easy, argues Todd Gitlin, for political movements to confuse the "values, myths, symbols and information" they command with the structural resources they do not command.[43] It is all too easy, says poet Audre Lord, for white American feminists to forget that "the women who clean your houses and tend your children while you attend conferences on feminist theory are, for the most part, poor and third world women."[44] And it is all too easy, says social theorist Guy Debord, to be seduced into believing that "that which appears is good" and that "that which is good appears."[45] The underlying logic of the Rhetorical Establishment is a logic that places great faith in the utility of publicity. It is discomfiting in the extreme to call such a logic into question.

But question it we must, precisely because media experiences are, for the viewer, *experiences*. Watching a Nelson Mandela speech, for example, is a powerful event. Crowds of people gather and press upon one another; Mandela's arrival becomes imminent; excitement builds; hopes are renewed. Finally, the timber of his voice resonates, the force of his gestures motivate. His conclusion moves some to tears, others to shout his acclaim. Even when carried on television, such an event is a doing, a tangibly completed act.

But we must also ask this: How many colleges and universities divested their funds in apartheid-abetting corporations because of Mr. Mandela's U.S. tour in June of 1990? That question seems small-minded, for surely the Mandela tour meant much to many. But it did not necessarily mean divestment *even though it felt like divestment*. Phenomenologically, that is, movement events simulate accomplishment. This is especially true when they are sustained across time. The more often we hear an idea articulated, the more real that idea seems; the more ardently a plan is endorsed, the more it seems that we already live under its guidance. So despite the good it did, the rhetoric of divestment might also have staved off divestment by substituting feelings for actions. Surely that is a curious thing.

It is also dangerous. Race relations constantly prove that. Because there is a Rhetorical Establishment in the United States, and because minority leaders are well represented within it, it often seems—to middle- and lower-class whites in particular—that discrimination has ended and that reverse discrimination is now a national policy. That is, for almost 30 years the nation's media have described black unemployment, teenage pregnancy rates among Hispanics, and educational discrimination against Asians. But those same media have also announced (with television, *shown*), that school lunch programs are plentiful, that A.T.& T. courts minority employees, that O. J. Simpson is rich. Naturally, these selective examples misrepresent what daily life is like for people of color in the United States. But examples do argue. On television, they often argue powerfully.

And so letters-to-the-editor consistently reflect resentment about the "minority gains" of the last three decades. And so Jesse Helms wins a senate seat, and George Bush a presidency, by attacking quotas in hiring. And so legislation to help the homeless languishes because white Americans believe—wrongly—that blacks dominate that community of unfortunates. Empirically speaking, it is manifestly *not* profitable to be born poor, malnourished, and African American today. But because of the Rhetorical Establishment, blacks have established a kind of symbolic dominance in certain quarters.[46]

Leaders of some political movements report a parallel effect: The rhetoric of minority accomplishment sometimes misleads minority members themselves, causing them to forget how dire their straits really are. "Surely that problem must be solved by now," argue many, "we've been talking about it for years." Perhaps this is what media scholar John Brenkman means by the "logic of mediation" operating in politics.[47] According to him, the mass media collect the private discourses of individual citizens, present those discourses in the public sphere, and thereby make them seem universal rather than particular truths. Movies like *Roots*, *The Color Purple*, and *Driving Miss Daisy* have surely done much to give heart and hope to all Americans, as well as to make them think. But despite the feelings of importance such narratives generate, politics is complete only when it is completed—statutes written, votes taken, funds encumbered. Any rhetoric that makes us forget those facts deserves scrutiny.

In isolating a Silent Establishment in the United States, we have made no great discovery. This collection of individuals has wielded influence in the nation since its beginning. Perhaps it always will. But several things are worth noting for the future. One is that the Rhetorical Establishment can easily serve as a refuge from—rather than a stimulus for—social change. And this is more than simple co-optation because the psychology of the Rhetorical Establishment is a complex psychology. Belonging to it taps one's need to be noticed, to feel loved and admired, to celebrate with friends, to experience a sense of forward movement, to be creative. These feelings are indeed important. But when they become the only feelings one craves, they become politically debilitating. Perhaps the only real antidote to such a disease is awareness of its danger signs, a function this chapter has attempted to fill.

In shedding light on the Silent Establishment, this chapter has followed the path of Saul Alinsky who often traveled to the suburbs with his followers to picket the private homes of corporation CEOs.[48] Admittedly, this was an unseemly tactic, but Alinsky felt that it was the only way that persons of this sort could be brought into the public dialogue. If there was to be a Rhetorical Establishment in the United States, Alinsky reasoned, *all* persons of influence should be included within it. In a society with a vigorous free press, Alinsky's goals can be reached. Each time a whistle is blown on bureaucratic waste, or corporate double bookkeeping is publicized, or military overspending is documented, or questionable legal arrangements are unearthed, or lobbyists' pay-offs are revealed, more and more persons will be required to speak. And when they are, they will come to realize that ideas which cannot be expressed civilly ought not to be pondered at all.

This is sociologist Herbert Spencer's line of argument. He contends that some people are publicly virtuous not because they are law-abiding but because they cannot easily justify their would-be violations to others.[49] Spencer's is hardly an exalted goal, but where the Silent Establishment is concerned, it is a practical goal. In the final event, it is only when all persons explain their actions and when all persons reveal their goals that the Rhetorical Establishment will begin to serve us truly.

Notes

1. Sociologist Alberto Melucci has argued that these "cross-movement networks" have greatly proliferated in recent years and that they consist of numerous professional and semiprofessional workers dedicated to a wide variety of social and political movements. In some senses, they can be seen as a kind of institutionalization of 1960s activism. See A. Melucci, "The Symbolic Challenge of Contemporary Movements," *Social Research*, 52 (1985), 798.

2. See E. Genovese, *Roll Jordan Roll: The World the Slaves Made* (New York: Vintage, 1976), 434.

3. R. Goodin, *Manipulatory Politics* (New Haven, CT: Yale University Press, 1980), 117.

4. R. Jacoby, *The Last Intellectuals: American Culture in the Age of Academe* (New York: Basic Books, 1987).

5. J. Kirkpatrick, "Politics and the New Class," in B. Bruce-Briggs (ed.), *The New Class?* (New Brunswick, NJ: Transaction, 1979), 34. Although this chapter concentrates on the attractions of membership in the Rhetorical Establishment for leaders of alternative political groups, traditional politicos in Washington are also making greater and greater use of the media. For details, see J. Foote and D. Davis, "Network Visibility of Congressional Leaders: 1969-1985." Paper presented

at the annual convention of the International Communication Association, Montreal, Canada, June, 1987, 10; and S. Hess, *Live from Capitol Hill! Studies of Congress and the Media* (Washington: Brookings, 1991), 106-107.

6. Whether or not membership in the Rhetorical Establishment is constant across cultures is an interesting question. According to Teun van Dijk, minority members are more likely to become (mute) actors on Dutch television than they are *spokespersons*. The contrast to the American situation is sharp, perhaps reflecting the very different processes of pluralization at work in the United States and the Netherlands. See T. van Dijk, "Mediating Racism: The Role of the Media in the Reproduction of Racism," in R. Wodak (ed.), *Language, Power and Ideology* (Amsterdam: John Benjamins, 1989), 214-215.

7. The rhetoric of diseases is also interesting. For no particularly clear reason, some maladies receive special publicity when their cause is championed by popular figures like Will Rogers or Jerry Lewis, while cures for equally fatal illnesses are shunted aside because of the rhetorical shortcomings of their champions. Similarly, AIDS stimulated massive social concern when its horrors were spotted by Americans rather than by Africans and when its cure became a political crusade for gay activists (who have been part of the Rhetorical Establishment in the United States since the 1960s).

8. Several studies have reported on the differential media coverage afforded groups by such encrustations. For information on how tradition, provincialism, economics, and ideology affect coverage, see, serially, R. Stanfield, "The Golden Rolodex," *National Journal*, March 10, 1990, 552-557; D. Hallin, R. Manoff, and J. Weedle, "Sourcing Patterns of National Security Reporters." Paper presented at the annual convention of the American Political Science Association, San Francisco, California, August, 1990; B. Ginsberg, *The Captive Public: How Mass Opinion Promotes State Power* (New York: Basic Books, 1986), 130-135; and S. Reese and L. Danielian, "The Structure of News Sources on Television: A Network Analysis of CBS News, Nightline, Macneil-Lehrer, and This Week with David Brinkley." Paper presented at the annual convention of the International Communication Association, Miami, Florida, May, 1992, 15-16.

9. R. Hart, "A Commentary on Popular Assumptions About Political Communication," *Human Communication Research, 4* (1982), 377.

10. J. L. Austin, *How to Do Things with Words* (Oxford: Oxford University Press, 1962)

11. For these and similar data, see R. Hart, *The Sound of Leadership: Presidential Communication in the Modern Age* (Chicago: University of Chicago Press, 1987).

12. M. Foucault, *The Archaeology of Knowledge* (New York: Pantheon, 1972), 50-51.

13. C. Boggs, *Social Movements and Political Power: Emerging Forms of Radicalism in the West* (Philadelphia: Temple University Press, 1986), 48.

14. Although the radical left might decry all such appearances as perfunctory, media scholar John Fiske seems more correct when noting that there is always some element of "semiotic excess" given off whenever an alternative voice is heard on a conventional medium. See J. Fiske, *Television Culture* (London: Methuen, 1987), 91.

15. M. Robinson and A. Kohut, "Believability and the Press," *Public Opinion Quarterly, 51* (1988), 174-189.

16. S. R. Lichter, D. Amundson, and R. Noyes, *The Video Campaign: Network Coverage of the 1988 Primaries* (Washington, DC: A.E.I. Institute, 1988), 65.

17. R. Bartley, "Business and the New Class," in B. Bruce-Briggs (ed.), *The New Class?* (New Brunswick, NJ: Transaction, 1979), 60.

18. C. Offe, "Challenging the Boundaries of Institutional Politics: Social Movements Since the 1960s," in C. S. Maier (ed.), *Changing Boundaries of the Political: Essays on the Evolving Balance Between the State and Society, Public and Private* (Cambridge: Cambridge University Press, 1987), 71.

19. P. Berger, "Different Gospels: The Social Sources of Apostasy," *This World, 17* (1987), 9.

20. C. Offe, "New Social Movements: Challenging the Boundaries of Institutional Politics," *Social Research, 52* (1985), 840.

21. R. Stark and W. Bainbridge, *The Future of Religion: Secularization, Revival and Cult Formation* (Berkeley: University of California Press, 1985), 394-424.

22. Boggs, 75.

23. H. Giroux, *Schooling and the Struggle for Public Life: Critical Pedagogy in the Modern Age* (Minneapolis: University of Minnesota Press, 1988), 204. Media scholar Ted Glasser makes an additional point when noting that rhetorical opportunity and rhetorical effectiveness are often very different matters: "[I]ndividuals in a liberal democracy have only the right to speak *in* public; to speak *to* the public requires communication, and communication is not a public right but a private privilege." See T. L. Glasser, "Communication and the Cultivation of Citizenship," *Communication, 12* (1991), 241.

24. One person attracted to politics-by-media was Axel Traugott, the brother of a hostage taken in the TWA hijacking case in 1985. In celebrating the mass media as he did, Mr. Traugott showed unquestionable political wisdom. But in being unable to think beyond the mass media, he also effaced himself as a political actor: "We felt that the only way we could exert any influence on the process was by generating as much publicity as possible. Our politicians are quite sensitive to public opinion." No doubt they are. But they are sensitive to much else as well, a fact too often ignored by the Rhetorical Establishment's apologists. See D. Elliott, "Family Ties: A Case Study of Coverage of Families and Friends during the Hijacking of TWA Flight 847," *Political Communication and Persuasion, 5* (1988), 71.

25. (West Lafayette, IN: Purdue University Press, 1977).

26. A sharply different perspective from mine is provided by political scientist Iris Young, who argues the importance of symbolic interventions in alternative politics, especially in such areas as "language, jokes, style of advertising, dating practices, dress, norms of childrearing, and countless other supposedly mundane and trivial elements of behavior and comportment." See I. Young, *Justice and the Politics of Difference* (Princeton, NJ: Princeton University Press, 1990), 87.

27. For perhaps the best version of Edelman's remarks on this score, see his *Political Language: Words That Succeed and Policies That Fail* (New York: Academic Press, 1977).

28. See J. Ellul, *The Political Illusion* (New York: Vintage, 1967).

29. Political scientist Ann Norton provides a useful addendum to this discussion when commenting on how political myth often depends on *unrepresentative* examples of human prowess for its force. Extrapolating from her discussion, one can almost make the perverse observation that today's economically privileged viewer derives a kind of "pleasure" when witnessing the impassioned rhetoric of society's unfortunates. These negative examples highlight-by-contrast the economic lot of those who are better off and thus establish once again that "the system works" (for some). See A. Norton, *Reflections on Political Identity* (Baltimore, MD: Johns Hopkins University Press, 1988), 61-62.

30. T. Gitlin, *The Whole World is Watching: Mass Media in the Making and Unmaking of the New Left* (Berkeley: University of California Press, 1980), 159-160.

31. Carl Boggs describes an even more subtle effect of political celebrity: By substituting individuals for ideas, the mass media "localize" politics, substituting well-wrought cameos of movement leaders for genuinely enlightened civic discussions. Such a strategy, says Boggs, "defers coming to grips with the global crisis until a later period when, presumably, the cumulative impact of small-scale political successes will add up to a national presence." See Boggs, 225.

32. Gitlin, 3.

33. See J. Fiske, *Television Culture* (London: Methuen, 1987), 294-295.

34. Examples of a society's most basic beliefs typically occur during times of crisis. Thus, it is not surprising that groups opposing the Persian Gulf War were generally *not* shown prominently

on U.S. television during the early stages of that conflict. See T. Cook, "Domesticating a Crisis: Washington Newsbeats, Human Interest Stories, and International News in the Persian Gulf War." Paper delivered at the Social Science Research Council Workshop on Media and Foreign Policy, Seattle, Washington, September 1991, 19.

35. A. Touraine, *Return of the Actor: Social Theory in Postindustrial Society*, M. Godzick (trans.) (Minneapolis: University of Minnesota Press, 1988), 106, 108-109.

36. Todd Gitlin discusses such matters in greater depth. See Gitlin, 290-292.

37. Touraine, 1988, 111.

38. The rise in the number of pressure groups corresponds to the rise in media institutions themselves. It is hard to determine what caused what: Did the increasing number of media forums permit a greater plurality of voices to be heard? Or did the rise in social action groups in the 1960s create a market for more and more political programming (call-in radio, for example)? Or is there now a more complex relationship between media and movements such that broadcasting institutions, having expanded perhaps too rapidly and with too uncertain a sense of purpose, found themselves with increasingly large news holes to fill and more and more candidates needed for the now-endless parade of talk show guests? Each of these explanations is incomplete, but together they show that media and movements now need each other as never before.

39. These names and others like them can be found in such standard reference works as *U.S. Government Manual, The Europa Yearbook, Washington Representatives, Encyclopedia of Associations, World Almanac and Book of Facts, Standard and Poor's Corporate Directors,* and *The American Bar Reference Handbook.*

40. F. J. Lea, *Political Consciousness and American Democracy* (Jackson: University of Mississippi Press, 1982), 108.

41. J. Llewellyn, "The Rhetoric of Corporate Legitimation: Public Relations and Philanthropy as Social Responsibility." Unpublished doctoral dissertation, University of Texas at Austin, 1990.

42. T. Luke, "Culture and Politics in the Age of Artificial Negativity," *Telos,* 35 (1978), 56.

43. Gitlin, 24.

44. A. Lord, "The Master's Tools Will Never Dismantle the Master's House," in C. Moraga, G. Anzaluda, and T. Bambara (eds.), *This Bridge Called My Back: Writings by Radical Women of Color* (Watertown, MA: Persephone, 1981), 100.

45. G. Debord, *Society of the Spectacle* (Detroit: Red and Black, 1982), 1:12.

46. Political scientist Kent Jennings shows how pernicious these effects can be when he describes the ways in which many whites look at black advances: "The major villain is redistributive public policies that are seen (rightly or wrongly) as squeezing the middle classes in terms of high taxes on one hand and inaccessible government benefits on the other. . . . Minorities are rather widely perceived to be recipients of unjust *benefits* as well (22% in 1974, 36% in 1981). Indeed, by 1981 the proportion naming blacks as being overrewarded approached the proportion naming them as underrewarded (11% and 16%, respectively)." See M. K. Jennings, "Thinking about Social Injustice," *Political Psychology,* 12 (1991), 193, 194.

47. J. Brenkman, "Mass Media: From Collective Experience to the Culture of Privatization," *Social Text,* 1 (1979), 94-109.

48. Alinsky recounts these and other strategies in his *Rules for Radicals: A Practical Primer for Realistic Radicals* (New York: Vintage, 1972).

49. H. Spencer, "Politics and Rhetorics," *Social Research,* 37 (1970), 567-623.

Box 6.1 Inquiries and Transitions

Is there any real alternative to the Rhetorical Establishment? Given the danger of being caught up in its web, could a movement leader in good conscience refuse to sell out for a news conference here, a media event there? In a vast and complex nation like the United States, are direct actions alone (boycotts, strikes, legal maneuvers, etc.) still dependable political tactics? Ultimately, is it better to have rhetorical power than no power at all? And what of the chronic problems—disease, malnutrition, redlining, pollution? Given how fickle the mass media are, given how bored they get with truly fundamental problems, how can their agenda be directed away from the New and the Odd to the Old and the Chronic? What responsibility do the media have for ensuring that their coverage of social problems ultimately translates into something real, something solved? More optimistically, is the Rhetorical Establishment a good thing, a sign that the democracy is taking its problems seriously, even if it must deal with these problems one at a time? If the Rhetorical Establishment suddenly ceased to exist, that is, would we be content with the silence that follows?

7

Residual Feelings

Actor Kirk Douglas is many things but he is not a reliable student of politics. Reflecting on the interface between politics and television sitcoms, he once declared: "Dan Quayle reacts to Murphy Brown's baby as if he were real and then Murphy Brown reacts to Dan Quayle as if he were real!" Douglas's remarks reflect a pre-electronic bias, an artificial separation of perceptual experiences no longer separable in an age of television. Douglas' remarks also fail to remember that politics itself is just another kind of imagining. That is, when John Kennedy proposed his New Frontier in the 1960s and when Bill Clinton proposed to completely overhaul the nation's healthcare system, they spoke of realities that were not. Mediated politics has always operated in just such a world of proposing. And so it is not hard to see how even the unborn child of a non-pregnant actress could genuinely bedevil the vice president of the United States.

This book has explored an unlikely thesis: that television redefines how we feel about politics. Not what we *know* about politics, but how we *feel* about politics. Not *what* we feel about politics but *how* we feel about politics. Television, in a sense, has ushered in a Second Renaissance, substituting mass emotion for mass subservience to the church in Rome. Television has also ushered in a Second Enlightenment, requesting that the brain, too, serve the dictates of the heart.

Television's revolution has been both quiet and bloodless. The feelings it encourages have crept up on us, insinuating themselves into our lives without self-commentary. This has resulted in a curious sense of political competence on the parts of many Americans—they know all that is worth knowing about their elected officials and they know how the game of politics is played. Knowing what they know, many Americans have become alienated. By not voting, they demonstrate their political competence. Often, television ratifies their feelings.

Here, I have attempted a "deep read" of televised politics. By locating the power of television in the emotions, the book differs from those that trace television's influence to the decisions made in corporate boardrooms or to newsgatherers' reporting practices. Its approach differs also from those that locate political power in the independent actions of elected officials, in regnant economic and social theories, in bloc voting routines, in PAC-based financing practices, or in the other conventional tools of political influence: barter, patronage, and gerrymandering.

No doubt, such forces are important. But television is also important and, as has been argued here, we need a new way to talk about it. Because feelings float loosely through us, they are often hard to capture, much less articulate. That is especially true with feelings about politics because government is so great and voters so puny. Politics throws whole nations into bloody revolution and causes other nations to rework folkways patiently established over centuries. Voters, on the other hand, tend their lawns each Saturday and worry about getting the kids to the Brownie meeting on time. As a result, they are naturally tempted to let the lions of power roar in some distant jungle.

Television arrests that temptation, bringing politics ever closer to them. By making politics familiar, television becomes a breeding ground for both awe and contempt. But because it is a visual medium, television appears to relinquish its power over us, making us masters of all we survey. We take the measure of the events that flash before our eyes. We assess their meaning and significance as well. In a sense, then, television is a bashful suitor. It woos us by refusing to intrude upon our reverie. But television also supplies the reverie we so crave and thus has its way with us even in its moments of greatest diffidence.

In many ways, visual politics is a radical phenomenon. It operates in its own special world with its own special rules. It explodes the old axioms of party discipline and geographical distinctiveness, replacing them with the new dictates of nuance and imagery. Television also gives the viewer a new sense of autonomy, at times an imperialism, about politics. Phenomenological forces like these can empower voters as well as inform them. But they can also make governance seem a world apart and encourage citizens to abandon the commonweal.

Television now offers a complete model for politics. Like any good model, television's model outlines the vectors of the political process, explains their interrelationships, and predicts their effects. Like any good model, television's model is non-falsifiable: It explains matters comprehensively and definitively. The model is also self-protective, forcing new data into old explanatory pathways whenever possible. When that becomes impractical, television finds ways to stress its traditional themes even as it admits variations on those themes.

To imply that "television" does all of this by itself is inaccurate. Viewers, you and I, are active agents in the model's perpetuation. Voters, you and I, speak the language of television during election season, searching for the kinds of political information our eyes, especially, demand. We evaluate politics as television has taught us to evaluate it; we discard information that makes us uncomfortable. In these ways and more, television teaches us how to think.

Negotiating With Television

In this book, I have identified five feelings that make us especially uncomfortable: detachment, ignorance, obsolescence, inertness, and impotence. Television works to overturn these feelings. Its textual practices, its rituals and incantations, give evidence of that effort. The result is that television acts as an emotional referee in political life, ruling out some emotions, ruling in others. But television's prized emotions are counterfeit, I argue. By opting for them we cut ourselves off from genuine political involvement. Here are the tradeoffs television offers:

1. *Become intimate, not involved.*

Speaking of the rise of a "bourgeois culture of feeling" at the turn of the century, historian Carl Schorske says that the New Citizen was enticed into a world of "narcissism and introversion, passive receptivity toward outer reality, and above all, sensitivity to psychic states."[1] We moderns have continued these traditions. We now know everything about our political leaders—their alcoholic stepfathers, their personal overindulgences—but that has hardly bound us to them. Instead, it causes us to search our television screens for displaced aggression or the freshly warped libido. Our politicians are now objects to be studied, not leaders to be followed.

The power television gives to the psychological was in evidence some years ago when CBS commentator Andy Rooney disparaged blacks and homosexuals. Public reaction was swift and negative. Rooney was temporarily suspended by CBS and he then quickly offered an apology. Speaking briefly on 60 Minutes, Rooney plumbed his emotional depths, telling viewers how the controversy had caused him moments of self-doubt ("I've always had in the back of my mind that I was doing some little bit of good"), put him off his normal writing pace ("I didn't feel like doing anything, including nothing"), and made him uncommonly introspective ("What do I say to defend myself? Do I say that I am not a racist? Sounds like saying 'I'm not a crook.' How do I apologize to homosexuals?"). Rooney went on to recount his personal wave of emotions—the fear he had felt during times of racial strife, his son's pride in him, his loneliness during his recent suspension, and his consummate humility ("What do I do about the kind words heaped on me by friends and strangers?").[2]

During his speech, Rooney never declared himself at fault nor did he offer to make amends to the affected communities. His remarks were self-serving in the extreme. But because they were broadcast on television, his remarks let him simulate political action without having to take political action. According to political scientist Dana Villa, a "first-order narrative" like Rooney's is a powerful, contemporary, way of circumnavigating the rather messy world of political principle, a classic example of the "fragmentation" produced in the postmodern world.[3] Besides, real apologies are hard to make.

2. Become informed, not involved.

This book has analyzed the dangers of watching television, not those of creating television programs. Where others have critiqued television producers' biases, I argue that the medium itself frustrates citizen involvement. Television's great scope, its ability to circumnavigate the globe every 30 minutes (on CNN), constantly puts us in the know. It delivers an endless stream of political personalities to us, and this stream carries its own meta-message: If we (the networks) know this much, surely we must know every-thing. And so even for viewers who only half-watch the news, knowing political personalities has become a way of knowing everything.

The opposite case has been made—that people are now so overwhelmed by political information that they feel impotent. As one set of researchers notes, "People [in interviews] explain that they do not have the energy or interest to follow public affairs very closely. They are puzzled by why they should follow issues over which they have no control."[4] But I find much greater bravado when such interviewees discuss *politicians.* In 1997, U.S. citizens knew very little about campaign finance irregularities, but they did know that it had something to do with Attorney General Janet Reno, and that either enthralled them or outraged them. For such citizens, there is nothing to politics but politicians.

Television is consumed by the present and that, too, deflects political involvement. Television keeps viewers on-line, trapped in an endless string of facts and anticipations. By staying tuned, people *stay* tuned, unable to break the habits of nowness television engenders. This is not just true for political junkies. In an era of personality politics, few can resist television's endless series of disclosures. Admirably, political philosopher Thomas Pangle is one who can: "We cannot possibly rest satisfied with the sorts of challenges that originate in our own age and culture, because what we seek is precisely critics whose spiritual footholds are outside our cave, outside our own time, outside the basic matrix of our moral outlook."[5] Television, I am arguing, is unlikely to provide said footholds.

3. *Become clever, not involved.*

Clever people are also immunized from political participation, in part because they are so frustrated and in part because they look at politics from so many vantage points simultaneously. They have a special intricacy, a capacity for distinguishing the real from the unreal, and so they live in the world and not-in-the-world at the same time. They cannot be counted upon politically because they cannot count upon themselves, so distrustful are they of appearances, of feigned stabilities. In the postmodern world, they are so busy adjusting to "the wild ride of discontinuity"[6] that there is only time for dizziness. Moving forward—moving anywhere—becomes impossible.

Taking any sort of action (even entering an elevator) requires either faith or foolishness. Clever people are too clever to be foolhardy and too complex for the simple pieties underlying political commitment. Television's strategy-centered reporting, its visual gymnastics, and its cerebral meta-commentaries turn politics into a simulation within a simulation, a space where only the clever can survive.

But Jean-Jacques Rousseau would be unimpressed with television's cleverness. For Rousseau, it is "simpler men" who ultimately act. They are not distracted by the complexities of city life nor by the city-in-a-box we now call television. Their schemata are simple, their emotions uncomplicated. They act because they do not over-think. Says political scientist Ruth Grant:

> People of this sort may be found anywhere, but they are more likely to be found among simple people who have not obscured the voice of conscience with a fog of sophistication, philosophic speculation, and the false moral ideal of balanced moderation. A Rousseauan political science would predict, for example, that the French peasants would be more likely to hide persecuted Jews in their homes, while the Parisians would rationalize collaboration with the Nazis.[7]

4. Become busy, not involved.

This phrase may seem an oxymoron, but it seems apt as television makes watching and doing the same thing. In an era of cable television and extended-cable, of stacked satellites and mixed-media computers, politics follows us everywhere. As a result, modern campaigns are awash in technology and thus never really end. In what is surely a sign of the times, Bill Clinton's first comment about his new home at 1600 Pennsylvania Avenue focused on its primitive communications technology. The oriental rugs in the upstairs parlor and the *Coq au Vin* for dinner were nice, Mr. Clinton seemed to be saying, but how can one run a presidency without celluloid and silicon?

Clearly, one cannot. Because of television, viewers are now so saturated by the political that it has become a background mist for them. Viewers breathe in so much of it, from NBC's *Today* show in the morning to its *Tonight* show later on, that to say such viewers are politically uninvolved is to insult them phenomenologically. Given current trends, more people will soon participate in opinion polls than will vote. The former is a simulation, the latter an inalienable right. In a mediated age, that distinction seems irrelevant.

Too often, political lethargy is made to seem like a moral failing. In this book, I have stressed its technological components. In complex and subtle ways, watching television constitutes political action for many. Thus, when confronted with their lack of civic energy, nonvoters do not simply slither off into the underbrush. They often make a fight of it, displaying familiarity with the issues and candidates and arguing (implausibly, it would seem) that alienation is a powerful kind of politics. A more precise rendering is this: Watching television is indeed an activity; like any favored activity it produces feelings of effectuality. To ignore those feelings is to misdiagnose why political participation is now so low for so many Americans.

5. Become important, not involved.

Political philosopher Bhikhu Parekh observes that young lovers entwined on a park bench instinctively back away from one another if the conversation suddenly turns political.[8] They immediately establish a public space for their conversation, a space that neither inhabits physically so that both can inhabit it conversationally. Politics is always reduced to a space-between—to a state, if you will—but television confuses that fact. By making "media presence" valued merchandise, television creates a space in which all persons can seem political. The result is a rhetorical establishment made up of diverse person-alities and pressure groups who use the media to achieve political ends.

Television, as a consequence, has become a factory for importance. Being interviewed by sportscaster Bob Costas makes a young athlete feel important. Having their demonstration covered on the six o'clock news makes AIDS activists feel important. Reporting live from the scene of battle makes an otherwise sedentary news anchor feel important. Such people become part of television's rhetorical establishment, part of its space-between. Being "on" television in these ways feels wonderful, but only if an audience can be posited, only if one imagines oneself being seen by a great many strangers. By making airtime a valued commodity, television seems to have shifted the political locus in the United States.

The result? Many of television's most visible personalities are ignored when the political bottom line is calculated, whereas many of those seen least often on television—those who run Aramco Oil, for example—acquire hid-den political influence.[9] In other words, rhetorical efficacy is now too often confused with political efficacy. In any polity, it must be remembered, money, law, and might determine almost everything. Television is a fourth force but only a fourth force. That fact is often hard to remember in a media age.

Citizen involvement is a fifth force. Sometimes, it seems like no force at all. In this book, I have laid part of the blame for that at television's door. Some years ago, Michel Foucault worried about the development of a society in which citizens were controlled ("disciplined" in his terminology) by centralized, state-based overlords.[10] My worry runs in the opposite direction. I worry that watching politics gives *us* a panoramic sense and that we are rendered impotent as a result. Because of television, we now see all and know all. When people like ourselves appear on television, acting as we might act, we seem to *do all* as well. Television takes viewers into the vestibules of power in Washington, into a thousand boudoirs. Why would people who see so much need to act at all?

That, I think, is the question of our age. Never before has a democratic people been so tempted to abandon the commonweal. Never before has a technology been powerful enough to make the very notion of political involvement seem oddly surreal. Never before have citizens been offered so many reasons to think of the state as an alien force. Never before has voting seemed so anachronistic or political disaffection so virtuous. The fact that pundits chose to *celebrate* a 55% turnout rate in a recent American election is an odd testament to our condition.

There are many explanations for this alienation—some demographic, some political, many of them economic. Here, I have added television to the list. In doing so, I have tried to spread the responsibility widely. Politicians, media personnel, and viewers themselves must be included in the arc of blame. All overburden a marvelous technology. All let it do too much of the political work that is rightfully theirs to do.

If television is part of the problem, can it be part of the solution? What problem? some ask. One set of researchers claims that television is too often blamed for problems that are not of its making. In their studies, they find that television's informativeness varies from issue to issue, but that it is helpful at times for stimulating political concern among uninterested voters. Decrying the "uninformed voter paradigm" that has guided so much previous research, these researchers conclude that "individuals do not slavishly follow the framing of issues presented in the mass media" but "are capable of constructing richly human conceptualizations of public issues from their personal and media experiences."[11]

Anyone who listens regularly to the bigotry found on drive-time radio is
more than familiar with these "richly human conceptualizations." Mindlessly
praising conventional wisdom hardly seems the way to go. As might be
expected in a nation long addicted to modernism, however, a number of other
solutions have been proposed. American commentators, being American
commentators, have typically looked to either law or science to fix what is
wrong with politics. Examining the terrain broadly, one observer offers a
laundry list for increasing citizen involvement: Hold more state and local
referenda, change campaign finance laws, disestablish the political parties,
liberalize voter registration procedures, organize a national reform movement.[12] Another scholar has detailed media options more directly: "Require
candidates to debate in more substantive formats; make candidates appear in
person in their television commercials; ban political advertizing; tell reporters
to forget about the trivia of campaign horse races and produce substantial
news stories about the great public issues instead; make officials gladly reveal
facts that damage them politically."[13]

These are the conservative solutions. The liberal approach is that of
Raymond Gozzi and W. Lance Haynes who argue that *viewers*, not television,
must be changed. The media's programming biases are so well entrenched,
they argue, that it is naive to think of undoing them. The answer is to learn
doublethink. Say Gozzi and Haynes:

> The wise person in the electric epistemology will possess the ability to discover
> progressions and to apply patterns to produce understanding, yet must be
> tolerant of ambiguity and accept incompleteness. The rigid standards of
> writing, which demand completeness on the fixed page, can no longer hold.
> The capacity to simulate and detect simulation, to believe and doubt simul-
> taneously, to operate in a universe of only relative fixity, must rise to the call.[14]

We can do better than trying to forge a link between John Dewey and the
Mad Hatter. But Gozzi and Haynes' focus on the television audience is helpful.
It is helpful because there is no other option. To expect politicians to stop
dissembling or to forego the sumptuous array of new communication tools
available to them is indeed naive. To expect new rhetorical formats (such as
sharper exchanges between the congressional and executive branches or cozy
town hall meetings via nationwide hookups) to change the fundamental
political conversation in the United States is unrealistic. To expect media

personnel to curtail their superb narrative instincts and become more spartan when telling the nation's political story is also impractical. The economics of the mass media being what they are, audience tastes alone will decide what politics will look like in the future.

And so audience tastes must be changed. But how? To imagine the American people being "instructed" back into the voting booth, their heads filled with GNP data, requires too much imagination. Besides, it is not what people know or do not know about politics that undoes them but what they *feel* about what they know. The American people need a new set of feelings. Better yet, they need an old set of feelings newly felt. I conclude by proposing a set.

Living With Television

Because of the lessons television teaches—that the human eye can be trusted, that selfhood is the child of media presence, that aesthetic and political values are the same thing—we must look beyond television, and even beyond politics, to cure what ails us. The solution I suggest is not simple but it is, I believe, suited to the feelings television inspires. My solution is reactionary. In a technocratic era, it looks to the past for guidance. In a functional age, it seeks a new kind of soul force in American politics. It acknowledges, but does not exalt, the economic and social remedies of the American Left, and it acknowledges, but does not exalt, the spiritual demands of the American Right. Above all, it looks to the heart and not to the head for political wisdom.

I suggest that only a New Puritanism can counteract civic laziness in the United States. Only a New Puritanism can turn viewers into voters once again. Only a New Puritanism can recommit them to the public sphere and turn them away from junk TV. Necessarily, I am thinking of a sectarian Puritanism here but a Puritanism nonetheless. I choose the Puritans as role models for several reasons:

1. *The Puritans were reformers.* They came on the scene during an "age of dislocation,"[15] an age not unlike our own in which new technologies and new social mores were beginning to threaten an older way of life. Still, they

displayed "the extraordinary tenacity" that people's "lives can be radically renewed."[16]

2. *The Puritans were essentialists.* They knew that any sort of lasting change must be internal to the individual, not external. They knew that "conversion is a conversion to a way of thinking, not [merely] a conversion to different social behavior."[17]

3. *The Puritans were synthesizers.* For them, the spiritual and material worlds were interlocked. They urged their people "to look with new eyes at the structure of government, at the role of the community, at the nature of the family; to have new attitudes toward work, toward leisure, toward witches and the wonders of the world."[18]

4. *The Puritans were individualists.* They preached personal rectitude and taking direct responsibility for one's own affairs: They "turned away from all forms of mediacy: historical, institutional, even scriptural—and dared to assert the direct apprehension by the believer of the divine."[19]

Puritanism probably seems a daft choice for imitation in the 21st century. Puritans were, were they not, a deeply prejudiced community that saw itself as "an elect people,"[20] a people who inflicted considerable treachery on two generations of Native Americans? They believed, also, that the "good wife earned the dignity of anonymity"[21] and on several occasions they burned women at the stake who threatened their way of life. The Puritan elder was tribal in the extreme, deeply suspicious of outsiders, one who rooted out heresy at every turn because he ostensibly "loves God with all his soul, but hates his neighbour with all his heart."[22] Zealots that they were, the Puritans could also be unconscionably cruel: "Other cultures exert acts of force against those who differ, but the Puritan legacy gives such acts a distinctive spirituality whereby the victimizer sees himself acting in a drama of beliefs rather than of flesh and sees the victim bleed opinions rather than blood."[23]

The list of sins goes on: The Puritans were, in many senses, anti-intellectual (even though they founded Harvard College), a people who believed that "learning did not mean new ideas; it meant the full exploration of existing ideas and the marshaling of them for the service of undeniable spiritual truths."[24] At the same time, they created a "bourgeois 'culture of discipline'"[25] in which ordinary human feelings were subordinated to the iron will of the church. "To be full of feeling, except for God," says one observer, "was associated with anxiety as well as with worldly lusts" by the Puritans. Even their poetry reflected the harsh New England winters of their souls, making them, according to historian Larzer Ziff, "uneasy poets of the summer."[26] H. L. Mencken said all of this more directly: "[Puritanism involves] the haunting fear that someone, somewhere, may be happy."[27]

Unquestionably, we contemporaries will find it difficult to re-embrace these more distant ancestors. A revived Puritanism, it will seem to many, may stifle the modern spirit just as its unmourned predecessor stifled the American colonists three centuries ago. But I am calling for a *New* Puritanism here, a Puritanism purged of its most regressive and monolithic features. I am calling for a more politically correct Puritanism, one that resists insularity and intolerance, a Puritanism that says its prayers to a more generous God.

But the New Puritanism I envision would acknowledge its historical roots as well. It would decry television's stock-in-trade—emotional excess and servile distraction. It would warn against unseemly hero-worship, against media personalities becoming too central in our lives. It would alert us to the dangers of graven images, of television's visual charms. It would make us sit straightbacked and purposeful, pulling back from the fleshy temptations of bedroom politics and campaign hijincks. It would urge us to rediscover the essence of politics and to shut our ears to the siren song of cultural cynicism.

A tall order. But let us imagine how a New Puritan might deal with modern life. Above all, he or she would resist vanity, a most grievous sin for the original Puritans. And yet resisting vanity would be difficult for today's television viewers who often seem so well informed about politics and so superior to it as well. Because television is "a manner of speech that calls attention to itself,"[28] it constantly tempts us with narcissism. In that sense, television is the modern counterpart to the Anglican church, that bastion of formalism that inspired the Puritans' "plain speech." "The true convert," said the Puritans, "begins with complete self-abasement before the Father"[29] and rejects all pretensions. Can a clever viewer adopt such a humble posture today?

Television is also the modern counterpart of Elizabethan theater, which allegedly treated the issues of its day "scoffingly, floutingly, and jibingly."[30] Can one find even a single moment of TV programming without a scoff or a flout or a jibe? Also, does not televised politics "bewitch idle ears with foolish vanities . . . making fooles laugh at sinne and wickednesse,"[31] as did the London stage? The theater threatened the Puritans philosophically (because it offered an alternative vision, a poetic vision), but it also threatened them psychologically. According to David Leverenz, "The theater, in its social and literary form, mirrored aspects of themselves that most threatened their identities as Puritans . . . [and that] mirrored everything the Puritan did not want to be: idle, lower class, spendthrift, disorderly, womanizing."[32]

Would New Puritanism become a new form of class prejudice that denounces all vulgar entertainments? Not at all. In fact, New Puritanism would reclaim civic consciousness for all persons regardless of their station in life. Television, I have argued, substitutes mass appeals, mass pleasures, for the political self and offers in its place a variety of skepticisms. In doing so, it deadens political consciousness, an especially illiberal crime for a medium consumed so heavily by the underclass in the United States. When political cynicism increases among those already inclined toward cynicism for economic reasons, a second awakening is sorely needed.

Such an awakening would, like its predecessor, place all visual reproductions and ceremonial objects under scrutiny. John Calvin, a kindred spirit to the Puritans, once complained that "the shape of the idol's bodily members makes and in a sense compels the mind dwelling in a body to suppose that the idol's body too has feeling, because it looks like its own body."[33] Television's instruments of motion and sound—and its resulting phenomenology of closeness—have increased such compulsions since Calvin's day. Because of television, we can now obtain "demonstrable" knowledge of political life whenever we wish. Whereas the Puritans thought of visual images as "dead matter,"[34] that is hard to do today because television brings all passions, all fears, to life.

But are all "sensual aids to piety"[35] invitations to idolatry? No. Television teaches us, often brilliantly. But the one lesson television seems unable to teach is a stunningly important one: personal obligation. Because television locates so much responsibility in (a) political personalities, and (b) institutional forums, it leaves precious little for the voter to do. In the words of the great Puritan preacher, John Cotton, television causes a viewer to "put out his owne eyes to see by another mans."[36] This stands in stark contrast to the daily spiritual routines of the devout Puritan who kept diaries "in which they checked the assets and liabilities of their souls in faith." "When they opened these books," says Edmund Morgan, "they set down the lapses of morality with appropriate expressions of repentance and balanced them against the evidences of faith."[37] Television makes such forms of self-reckoning seem quaint.

Whether old or new, then, Puritanism is a demanding conviction. But can a functioning polity be erected atop it? Does New Puritanism have positive inducements? In fact, it has several:

1. A New Puritan is a fundamentalist.

A French contemporary of the second generation Puritans, Rousseau said that recognition of political identity "makes of a stupid and unimaginative man an intelligent being and a man."[38] For Rousseau, a political identity was not a suit of clothes to be worn or discarded as one wished. It came with life itself and was forsaken only by those who wished to live an unlife. Television offers such an unlife—a world of fantasies, a world apart—and therefore can draw us away from the *polis*. Because of television, I argue, politics no longer seems a site for the essential work of citizenship but a place inhabited by specialists who manipulate symbols for a living. It is easy to become distanced from such a world, to think of politics as a game. The Puritans, in contrast, concentrated on fundamental truths: "The very word 'church' ceased to mean a building, which as only a 'meeting house' was spare and unadorned. A church was simply a body of the faithful."[39]

Shorn of its trappings, citizenship means (a) becoming informed, and (b) making choices. For many of the reasons laid out in this book, television makes it hard to think of ourselves as choosers. Choice depends on a sense of hierarchy, on the ability to keep two things in mind at once and to judge them relative to one another. Television, in contrast, is filled with equivalences. Television's world is flat, filled with individual images incapable of dominating our perceptions for very long. These images come at us quickly and then rush back into the vortex of electronic space. George Bush's dog just died. Bill Clinton now owns a cat. What, exactly, is the point?

In a postmodern world, it is impertinent to say that one thing is more important than another and so we have become intimidated by hierarchies. That stands in sharp contrast to the Puritans who believed that "life was all of a piece and lower values should properly be subordinated to higher ones."[40] A New Puritan is willing to risk such subordination, to risk judging. The ineluctably "plain" work of citizenship—voting, meeting, contributing, petitioning—becomes part of a sacred covenant for a New Puritan because he or she is "full of zeal, suspicious of pleasure, racked by guilt."[41]

Guilt? Today? Surely not. Surely television's story of politics—that it is inhabited by aliens, that cynicism runs in their veins—has relieved us of such ancient, sordid emotions. Surely the birth of the modern age has meant the death of sin itself. Surely the new technologies of politics have moved it from the moral to the scientific realm. Not for a New Puritan. He or she accepts that "there is no greater hindrance to . . . holy Meditation than froathy

Company and Companions, while a man is in the crowd amongst such wretches there is no possibility in reason that one should search his own heart."[42]

This talk of covenants, of personal responsibility and civic guilt, falls hard on modern ears, but we can easily twist free of such charges because television locates all political action outside of ourselves. As a result, we are politicians no longer. We are meta-politicians, shorn of moral language, refreshed for psychic play. In an age of television, we are also Anglicans, faithfully awaiting revelation and numb to the satisfactions of personal examination. Television, despite its workers' best intentions, constantly invites us to live our lives apart from citizenship. A New Puritan resists.

2. A New Puritan is a communalist.

Living in a Puritan community in the 17th century was suffocating by modern standards. And yet Puritanism "never taught withdrawal from the world. There were no Puritan monasteries. . . . Solitary living was forbidden. During the years 1669-1677 Massachusetts persecuted sixty people for living alone."[43] A harsh communalism, no doubt. Television, in contrast, produces electronic communities in which people know together but do not live together. Whereas Puritanism offered "a straightforward language of collective dependence,"[44] television offers a language of the self. Whereas the Puritan elegies diffused grief "within the communal framework, where tradition and history provide consolation,"[45] television makes living alone more bearable.

Community was not an abstract thing for the Puritans. For us it is. Modern life is lived out in domes of glass and steel, some mobile, some stationary. Given our geographic separations, our *sensus communis* (what Kant called a "common feeling for the world")[46] is less real than hyper-real. The Puritan notion of a "commonwealth" is also hard to sustain, even though the mass media broadcast our civic rituals regularly.[47] The mutual obligations commanded by the Puritan community have evaporated for the most part. As a result, one could videotape *Court TV* from morning until night and find nothing like the confession of one Tyral Pore who, upon being accused of fornication by the Middlesex County Court in 1656, proclaimed "by this my sinn I have not only donn what I can to Poull doune Jugmente from the lord on my selve but also apon the place where I live."[48]

Naturally, people today still cling to one another, but they do so for personal and social reasons, less often for ideological reasons. How different were the motivations of Puritans like Jonathan Edwards who worked to prove that "evil always resides in the private will" and that "grace transforms the sinner only as he becomes a member of a group, the elect."[49] Communitarian thought is not dead in our times but it is surely daunted. Despite some evidence to the contrary,[50] people rarely use "collective frames" to discuss their problems, in part because the mass media so often stress their differences. Few Americans, for example, have ever traveled to south central Los Angeles. After the disruptions of 1991 (re: the Rodney King case), even fewer will. Media spectacles like this, as well as "reality shows" like *Rescue 911* and "unreality shows" like *Life Styles of the Rich and Famous*, explain how different life is outside of our neighborhoods. As a result, broad communal mysteries become harder to sustain.

Despite all this, the New Puritan searches for community. Pluralism may still reign and the myths of the past (e.g., *e pluribus unum*) may now be unsustainable, but the New Puritan still sees people as people. This is a prayer, yes, but it is an important prayer for any enlightened society. Attending to local politics will help in this regard. Unlike the Anglicans, who claimed a (federalist) unity of church and state, the Puritans "constantly worked for local organization and local participation as the center of religious practice."[51] And so grassroots politics can be a useful antidote to the anonymity of modern life. Equally, it can be a defense against the abstractions and cynicisms of the mass media. Modern life is hard, but it becomes even harder when mind and body live apart. Civic activism neutralizes that.

3. A New Puritan is a futurist.

The Puritans believed in another world, in a world yet to be. The more important fact is that they believed at all. They were not cynics. They saw life as hard but not without purpose. They found people fallible but redeemable. Distrustful of the "secondary visual"—the graven image—[52] they were not caught up in surfaces that pass for realities and hence could trust their eyes. They shared "with the apostle Paul a concept of providential history interpreted as an extended pattern of foreshadowings and fulfillments."[53] History was not an endless tragedy but "a continuum of progressively clearer revelations of God's will, each new dispensation more brilliantly anticipating the day of judgment."[54] Their language of Canaan freed them from bondage and promised "a new world with boundless, untapped resources; and the millennial prospect of peace."[55]

The Puritans were entrapped by what the anarchist Ravachol called the "voluptuousness of the great idea."[56] One finds few such ideas today, even less entrapment. Today, belief comes hard. Americans distrust utopian thought, in part because they are pragmatists and in part because they have seen what it wrought in Hitler's Germany, in Khomeini's Iran and, yes, in John Cotton's Boston. Americans also prefer living in the short-term, which is why Ronald Reagan's rhetoric so appealed to them in 1980. Reagan spoke of the Puritans' shining city on a hill but he also promised to cut people's taxes. Immediately. Twelve years later, Ross Perot garnered 20% of the vote by declaring that 20 minutes of looking under the nation's hood would set matters straight. The American people have never been patient, except when they were Puritans.

Given the uncertainties of modern life (death in Somalia, riots in Bogotá), a New Puritan must work hard for hope. But the nation's vision is still there, in its traditions, and can once again become a comfort: freedom to trade as one wishes; taxation only with representation, universal suffrage and mass education, rallies and demonstrations with minimal police presence, public assistance for the needy. Television adds new chapters to this story each day, but it does much to dispirit us as well. That is why New Puritanism looks beyond television for its answers.

As mentioned in Chapter 1, many have volunteered to fix television. The Entertainers, The Debaters, and The Heralds all present useful ideas, but they ultimately reduce the physician to self-help. Television can take us to the moon and back but it cannot hand-deliver democracy to us. Television's sins come with its technologies. No matter how hard PBS works to provide substantive political coverage, it will always make people feel busier and more knowing and more important than they have a right to feel.

Besides, why should it be television's job, and not our own, to root cynicism out of the polity? Why should television have to remind us that although one U.S. senator may have harassed the women on his staff, 99 have not? Why do we wait for television's plan to increase voter turnout and not anoint ourselves for the job? Why should George Bush's "thousand points of light" be an empty slogan and not a lived reality?

In truth, New Puritanism is little more than seventh-grade civics. In an age of television, and partly as an antidote to television, the nation must go back to school. While there, its citizens must do the things that seventh-grader students do: relearn geography, focusing anew on the complexities of life in an urbanized nation; study arithmetic, running fresh calculations on what it costs a farmer or a machinist to make a living in a computer-based society; review English grammar, imagining what it is like to be a Cuban or a Laotian immigrant in a monolingual culture. Above all, they must read civics rather than just watch it, imitating the Puritans' "overwhelming commitment to the certainty of words over commitment to ambiguous images, to the dominance of the pulpit over the altar."[57] The Puritans "placed a burden on the verbal disproportionate to that placed on it by other cultures, European as well as primitive, and, as a consequence, excluded almost all ends other than the didactic."[58] New Puritans, in short, must read the newspaper.

New Puritanism needs to be taught in the home as well. That will be hard. Parents, after all, compete every afternoon with MTV's swirling uncertainties and are upstaged each evening by the wry antics of David Letterman. To preach civic virtue and community obligation in the face of such competition is difficult. It is far easier to become alienated and to seed further alienations among one's children. As mentioned previously, cynicism is a language. Like any language, it is learned and taught. Many parents make their bids for respect by trying to speak it. They fear sounding old because they know that, on television, everyone sounds young.

New Puritanism requires courage, then, for it surely courts embarrassment. It gets almost no social reinforcement in popular culture and often gets none in political culture either. Journalists hate politicians. Politicians hate one another, as well as journalists. Everyone hates government. When NASA builds a space platform, only a handful marvel. Many more speak of cost-overruns. When the Centers for Disease Control spot a new pestilence, critics decry their tardiness in spotting it. When George Bush and Bill Clinton switch jobs, bloodlessly, no hosannas are sung. And yet these are marvelous things, maybe even absurd things. They are the products of a vast democracy made up of myriad, frequently disturbing, civilian tempers. Ignoring such wonders makes it hard to feel good about being a citizen.

Naturally, good feeling cannot supersede good government so, like the Puritans, we must be hard on sin—our own as well as those of others. A New Puritan must be equally stern. Fortunately, a legion of watchdog groups already displays that attitude, ranging from those who scrutinize education, government, and the press to those who examine corporate America and the military. But depending on such groups will not do. New Puritans still have *personal* responsibility—they are the children of both the Old and New

Testaments, persons whose "deference to the workings of a traditional society and to an all-disposing God receded before the ascension of their identities as self-governing individuals."[59]

Unquestionably, New Puritanism makes politics less fun than does television. Still, we cannot entrust television alone with the nation's vision. Television will boldly serve, if asked, but ultimately it will become diverted by the cats and dogs in the presidential menagerie. New Puritanism's lessons are best taught in primary places—at home and in the school.[60] It is there that the "affections" of democracy can be "smitten and wrought upon," just as the Puritan preacher Thomas Shepard hectored his parishioners three centuries ago.[61] For too long we have allowed television to superintend our feelings. We must now reclaim that responsibility.

Conclusion

Political commentary in the United States is largely a male preserve. As such, it resists all talk of spirituality in politics. The favored image of the American voter is also masculine. The voter is hard-bitten and stingy, suspicious of words, attracted to dramatic solutions, steadfast but unforgiving, and volatile if enraged. When politicians err, they err in male ways: fail to follow through on their plans, lose their tempers in the heat of battle, are duped by the unscrupulous, lack the killer instinct, prove untrustworthy or, worse, impotent. If political things need fixing, new platforms are hammered out or old wiring updated. When the body politic is sick, it is sick in the gut.

I have sent in no Marines in this book. No Corps of Engineers either. Television is what television is. It will not change fundamentally, no matter how many books are written to critique it, because its phenomenology is too seductive and its technologies too entrenched. If change is to come, it must come from the commonwealth. Despite their celebrity, New Puritans like Robert Coles, Jesse Jackson, and Marian Wright Edelman know that political consciousness begins in quiet places—in the home, in the classroom, in the church, in the wardroom, in the union hall. It lies in people's determinations not to let politics be reduced to computerized models or slick professionalism.

New Puritanism is an alternative to cynicism. Its roots lie in a simple religion with straightforward truths to tell; a rural religion that sowed self-denial but that reaped common purpose; a backward religion whose adherents managed to build a new nation. Puritanism was repressive, indeed, but some of the things it repressed—self-indulgence, for example—still deserve a pinch or two of repression. Puritanism was community-based and that also is a useful heritage in an age where mutuality is too often found in people's mutual antipathies.

The Puritans believed that God held people responsible for the few choices allotted them. With television, we have far more choices. We also have far more beguiling opportunities to defer our political obligations. But Responsibility, that most dreaded of all Puritan notions, also has its demands. It says: "If ye can be motivated by nothing else, let ye at least be motivated by shame." Without doubt, there is much to be ashamed about in political life, and so we should trade in television's five feelings for more abiding stores. In its best moments Puritanism drew upon these stores—duty, community, hope. If politics is to be more humane, more enlightened, they must be tapped again. Television may already be serving the polity as best it can. The Puritans would ask: Are we?

Notes

1. C. Schorske, *Fin-de-Siècle Vienna* (New York: Vintage, 1981), 9.

2. A. Rooney, "Return to *60 Minutes*," March 4, 1990; CBS Television Network; New York.

3. This is my own extrapolation from Villa's remarks on narratives and meta-narratives. See "Postmodernism and the Public Sphere," *American Political Science Review*, 86 (1992), 718.

4. R. Neuman, M. Just, and A. Crigler, *Common Knowledge: News and the Construction of Political Meaning* (Chicago: University of Chicago Press, 1992), xiv.

5. T. Pangle, *The Ennobling of Democracy: The Challenge of the Postmodern Age* (Baltimore: Johns Hopkins University Press, 1992), 195.

6. W. Chaloupka, "Cynical Nature: Politics and Culture after the Demise of the Natural." Paper presented at the annual convention of the American Political Science Association, Chicago, Illinois, September, 1992, 9.

7. R. Grant, "Rousseau's Ideal of Integrity." Paper presented at the annual convention of the American Political Science Association, Chicago, Illinois, September, 1992, 26.

8. B. Parekh, *Hannah Arendt and the Search for a New Political Philosophy* (London: Macmillan, 1981), 94.

9. For an interesting essay on the blurred boundaries of the modern state (and on Aramco Oil Co.), see T. Mitchell, "The Limits of the State: Beyond Statist Approaches and their Critics," *American Political Science Review*, 85 (1991), 77-96.

10. See M. Foucault, *Discipline and Punish*, A. Sheridan (trans.) (New York: Pantheon, 1977).

11. Neuman et al., 77, 91-92, 96.

12. W. L. Bennett, *The Governing Crisis: Media, Money and Marketing in American Elections* (New York: St. Martin's, 1992), 204-218.

13. D. Swanson, "The Political-Media Complex," *Communication Monographs*, 39 (1992), 397.

14. R. Gozzi and W. L. Haynes, "Electric Media and Electric Epistemology: Empathy at a Distance," *Critical Studies in Mass Communication*, 9 (1992), 226.

15. D. Leverenz, *The Language of Puritan Feeling: An Exploration in Literature, Psychology, and Social History* (New Brunswick, NJ: Rutgers University Press, 1980), ix.

16. A. Delbanco, *The Puritan Ideal* (Cambridge: Harvard University Press, 1989), 251.

17. A. Kibbey, *The Interpretation of Material Shapes in Puritanism: A Study of Rhetoric, Prejudice and Violence* (London: Cambridge University Press, 1986), 36.

18. A. T. Vaughn, "Introduction," in A. Vaughn (ed.), *The Puritan Tradition in America: 1620-1730* (New York: Harper, 1972), xiii.

19. Delbanco, 243.

20. Kibbey, 119.

21. Delbanco, 138.

22. Delbanco, 66.

23. L. Ziff, *Puritans in America: New Culture in a New World* (New York: Viking, 1973), 145.

24. Ziff, 109.

25. Delbanco, 222.

26. Ziff, 123-4.

27. Quoted in Vaughn, xviii.

28. Kibbey, 20.

29. Leverenz, 131.

30. Leverenz, 28.

31. Leverenz, 27.

32. Leverenz, 24.

33. Quoted in Kibbey, 47. The Puritans' iconoclastic tendencies have been linked by Kibbey (p. 2) to their several intolerances: "The violent destruction of artistic images of people developed into a mandate for sacrosanct violence against human beings, especially against people whose material 'image,' whose physical characteristics, differed from the Puritan man's own."

34. Kibbey, 47.

35. L. Haims, "Puritan Iconography: The Art of Edward Taylor's *God's Determinations*," in P. White (ed.), *Puritan Poets and Poetics: Seventeenth-Century American Poetry in Theory and Practice* (University Park: Pennsylvania State University Press, 1985), 84.

36. Delbanco, 83.

37. E. Morgan, *The Puritan Family: Religious and Domestic Relations in Seventeenth-Century New England* (New York: Harper, 1966), 5.

38. Quoted in A. Norton, *Reflections on Political Identity* (Baltimore: Johns Hopkins University Press, 1988), 46.

39. Leverenz, 9.

40. J. Walker, "Anagrams and Acrostics: Puritan Poetic Wit," in P. White (ed.), *Puritan Poets and Poetics: Seventeenth-Century American Poetry in Theory and Practice* (University Park: Pennsylvania State University Press, 1985), 252.

41. This is Everett Emerson's description of the Puritan preacher and poet, Michael Wigglesworth, who was, in Emerson's view, "the popular caricature of the Puritan." See *Puritanism in America: 1620-1750* (Boston: Twayne, 1977), 126.

42. Delbanco, 181.

43. Emerson, 134.

44. Leverenz, 6.

45. W. Scheick, "Tombless Virtue and Hidden Text: New England Puritan Funeral Elegies," in P. White (ed.), *Puritan Poets and Poetics: Seventeenth-Century American Poetry in Theory and Practice* (University Park: Pennsylvania State University Press, 1985), 292.

46. Villa, 719.

47. For a useful analysis of ceremony and the mass media, see D. Dayan and E. Katz, *Media Events: The Live Broadcasting of History* (Cambridge: Harvard University Press, 1992).

48. Quoted in Morgan, 10.

49. Leverenz, 131.

50. See W. Gamson, *Talking Politics* (New York: Cambridge University Press, 1992), 108.

51. Leverenz, 44.

52. This is Michael Clark's term for the Puritans. See "The Honeyed Knot of Puritan Aesthetics," in P. White (ed.), *Puritan Poets and Poetics: Seventeenth-Century American Poetry in Theory and Practice* (University Park: Pennsylvania State University Press, 1985), 68.

53. K. Rowe, "Prophetic Visions: Typology and Colonial American Poetry," in P. White (ed.), *Puritan Poets and Poetics: Seventeenth-Century American Poetry in Theory and Practice* (University Park: Pennsylvania State University Press, 1985), 47.

54. Rowe, 52.

55. Rowe, 52.

56. Quoted in C. Schorske, *Fin-de-Siècle Vienna* (New York: Vintage, 1981), 161.

57. Ziff, 119.

58. Ziff, 165.

59. Delbanco, 224.

60. For their part, the mass media hold out little hope that such humble agencies can solve national problems. In one study, researchers found that organized religion received only 2.3% of the news coverage devoted to agencies for conflict reduction and that educational institutions garnered but 1.1% of the credit. Individual workers received only a bit more (3.0%). The mass media, in short, can see only big solutions to big problems and therefore consistently fail to empower localities. See A. Cohen, H. Adoni, and C. Bantz, *Social Conflict and Television News* (Newbury Park, CA: Sage, 1990), 116-118.

61. As quoted in Ziff, 56.

Box 7.1 Inquiries and Transitions

Most books describing the problems of television conclude either by proposing new legislation or with a list of demands for TV producers. It is easy to blame network executives and hard-bitten reporters for the sins of the world, but is it naive to look elsewhere for help as well? Is it still possible, at the turn of the century, to expect the American people to take greater responsibility for their viewing habits and, more important, for their viewing attitudes? Putting a V-chip in our television sets is one thing, but must we wait for a C-chip to remove TV's cynicisms? And if we have an order of New Puritans, who will be its leaders? Has television now turned us off to politics so thoroughly that even senior citizens (normally a community-minded group) will jump ship? Can hard-working middle-agers be expected to ensure that television's mean-spirited take on politics doesn't overwhelm their democratic commitments? Will the schools build new civics curricula capable of dealing realistically, but also idealistically, with politics, thereby propelling energetic young people into the public square? Perhaps all this is naive, but the Old Puritans were naive as well and yet they founded a nation. Can New Puritans do worse?

Postscript

Seducing America is premised on the heretical notion that the tissue between politics and popular culture has evaporated, that the White House and *Melrose Place* are now neighbors. Television has enforced this connection, making all politicians media-conscious. That is both good and bad. It is good in that a governor or president must never forget that they serve a democracy; with television, the audience, the people, always beckon. But media-consciousness can lead to media-obsession and that can be pathological, as when Ronald Reagan confused real life with movie life[1] or when the Bush campaign allowed Willie Horton ads to savage an entire American subculture.[2] But whether good or ill, television is with us forever. Political life will never again be the same because of that fact.

Mostly, television has ushered in an age of displacement, allowing us to sense we are somewhere else even when we are at home. Geographical displacement—being here and there at the same time—is a luxurious feeling, an expansive feeling, as if we had a window on the world itself. Becoming enlarged in these ways is exciting and surely educational, as we swoop across the globe gobbling up culture and fashion on the fly. And yet a nomadic people can become irresponsible in at least two ways: (1) they can begin to see the whole world—and its dire problems— as fictions ("it's only television, after all") and (2) they can become unmoored from their own geographies. It is one thing for the citizens of Austin, Texas, to follow the privations in Bosnia on television and thereby build bonds of identification with a tormented people; it is quite another for Austinites to allow half their mass transit system to fall into shambles and the other half to remain unbuilt because of inattention.

Politics is always local, as former House speaker Tip O'Neil used to say, but television can make whereness a mere hypothesis.

People can "do" things without doing things in an age of displacement, making them feel participatory without demanding that they participate. Television also gives them a sense of authority in matters about which they are ignorant, thus framing an unnerving question: Is it more dangerous to be uninformed about political affairs or to think oneself wise when one is not? With television, authority has been displaced, too, which means that anyone deemed aesthetically powerful by the media—basketball player Charles Barkley, for example, or former General Colin Powell—is automatically deemed eligible for political office. This means that "lineage candidates," people like former president George Bush, who worked his way to power through the legislatures and bureaucracies of his day, have become albatrosses. His own photogenic sons prove that, persons who worked fitfully in business for awhile before using their millions (and our television sets) to run for governor.

Television also displaces time. Karl Marx once explained that modernism is filled with anxiety (only the anxious buy) and that is our lot today. Television thrusts us insistently into the present, making it seem silly to look to the past. CNN-junkies watch the news all day, forcing CNN to make as much news as it can make. Politicians cooperate, responding to every question asked lest they lose their moment in the sun. A time-anxious people is a demanding people, quickly bored and often surly. Such people become impatient with intractable problems—poverty, for example, disease and environmental degradation, too—a manifestly unfortunate condition because only governance can solve such problems. And so politicians repair to the future when addressing such matters and that adds, reflexively, to the frustrations we feel.

Television also displaces knowledge, which is to say it makes *people* not ideas, our objects of study. The psychology of intimacy is a powerful psychology. It encourages faith in lone individuals by providing close-to-home knowledge about them—Bill Clinton's new dog Buddy, the Al Gore/*Love Story* connection. But in doing so, it ignores the structural realities that determine how people live their lives—the monetary cartels, the bureaucratic structures, the ideological alliances, the separations of power, the geopolitical antagonisms, and the hundreds of other nonpsychological forces that decide who lives in peace and who does not, who has a lavish lifestyle and who goes malnourished. Television's displacements make us forget these matters, a fate not afforded those burdened by such conditions.

The dangers of displacement notwithstanding, television's most toxic product is cynicism. The cynic, a person who believes in human frailty and institutional corruption and who harbors an overwhelming need to predict future unhappiness, takes to television instinctively. Television explains painfully, endlessly, how a football player can go from Heisman trophy winner to murderer in a mere 20 years, how Bill Clinton's undocumented lusts are heinous even though they are undocumented. Television tells these stories unrelentingly. It is not surprising, then, that those who watch television the most are woefully uninformed about civic affairs.[3] But they are not so uninformed that they cannot have "an attitude."

Having an attitude is now an obsession. In an age of television everyone wants to be young, clever . . . and lazy. Television obliges, and so deeply cynical shows like *Politically Incorrect* become the rage. Cynics place faith in observation, not in participation, and they see irony as the only stable source of pleasure. If cynicism is a science—a way of making sense of the world—it is a lazy science. It embraces term limits laws because they minimize a citizen's need to stay informed. It embraces third-party candidacies because television adores the new, the null hypothesis. It embraces talk radio because only opinions, not facts, are needed.

Cynicism is also bad science because of its deplorable mathematics. From among the approximately 3,000 different persons who served in the U.S. House of Representatives between 1954 and 1989, it seizes on former Speaker Jim Wright's shady book deals as exemplars of that institution. From among the roughly 52,000 Catholic priests in the United States, it features the one pedophile in New Mexico who failed to get treatment. From among the 1,500 charitable organizations in Cincinnati, Ohio, it selects the one scam operation for the evening news. Taking such exposés to heart requires complete ignorance of the normal curve.

Whereas cynicism is lazy science, skepticism is not. The skeptic believes in these things: (1) because one's sensory powers are limited, appearances can deceive; (2) because impulsiveness is dangerous, deep reflection about human affairs is best; (3) because people are social creatures, and hence imitative, conventional wisdom is rarely wise; (4) because people are fallible, one should never trust but one source of information; (5) because most data are mediated, primary (not secondary) sensation should be prized. With these as its tenets, skepticism becomes an important adjunct to enlightened political decision making. The skeptic has no need for the cynic's foundational myths (e.g., original sin) or the cynic's concepts of the future (e.g., perdition is near) because the world is constantly unfolding, reshaping itself all the while. Skeptics are buoyed up by the need to know.

Because life is complex, an enlightened politics requires a considerable amount of skepticism. But unlike the cynic, the skeptic has faith in human institutions because they were fashioned by group effort, not by lone individuals, and because the ravages of time could not vanquish them. Institutions are Darwinian to the core, constantly being reinvigorated, constantly requiring self-cleansing, and so it is not surprising that they have become the focal point of the modern state. This is not to say they are perfect. Slavery was something of an institution, after all, and sexism and ageism have found institutional shelter as well. Eliminating such deficiencies is the business of government.

Even a moment's reflection will reveal the institutional arrangements that have enriched our lives—taxation with representation, bi-partisan government, the Library of Congress, permissive voter registration laws, Yellowstone National Park, the Social Security Administration, a peacetime army, meat and poultry inspection, the National Centers for Disease Control, the space shuttle. All these bureaus and processes, all these gray ghosts of government have emanated from the collective will of the American people, have stood the test of time, have served the commonweal. It is possible to critique them endlessly but it is boring to do so.

Boredom, on the other hand, is often the lot of the cynic. Reciting the tired mantras of New Hollywood Chic must become burdensome as one ages, especially since government does so much good, despite its occasional treacheries. 60 Minutes, 20/20, and Prime Time Live feature the treacheries but, even as they do, governmental action somewhere is ensuring that sick children are being cured, new immigrants educated, and pedestrians protected from oncoming large trucks. These are not grand mysteries, these actions, but they do make modern life possible.

As Jeremy Rabkin has observed,[4] someone needs to write a political counterpart to William Bennett's Book of Virtues.[5] In his book, Bennett lionizes a set of highly individualistic virtues: self-discipline, responsibility, work, courage, perseverance, honesty, loyalty, faith. Fine virtues, every one. Equally fine, but harder to achieve, are the following: cooperation, civility, generosity, negotiation, tolerance, regularity, compromise. These are quintessentially political virtues but television rarely dramatizes them.

A political people dare not let these virtues go unloved. A political people must find ways of making them central to the education of youth. Practicing such virtues is hard work, sometimes Sisyphian work, but that makes them no less important. Says Albert Camus: "The struggle itself toward the heights is enough to fill a man's heart. One must imagine Sisyphus happy." Television makes it hard to imagine such things. We must imagine them in its stead.

Notes

1. M. P. Rogin, *"Ronald Reagan," the Movie: And other Episodes in Political Demonology* (Berkeley: University of California Press, 1987).

2. For more on this matter, see K. Jamieson, *Dirty Politics: Deception, Distraction, and Democracy* (New York: Oxford University Press, 1992).

3. See M. Delli Carpini and S. Keeter, *What Americans Know About Politics and Why It Matters* (New Haven, CT: Yale University Press, 1996).

4. J. Rabkin, "Roundtable Remarks on Civic Virtue and the Future of American Politics," annual meeting of the American Political Science Association, September, 1995.

5. W. J. Bennett, *The Book of Virtues* (New York: Simon & Schuster, 1993).

Scholarly References

Abramson, J., Arterton, G., & Orren, G. (1988). *The electronic commonwealth: The impact of new media technologies on democratic politics*. New York: Basic Books.

Adelman, M. (1992). Sustaining passion: Eroticism and safe-sex talk. *Archives of Sexual Behavior, 21*, 1-14.

Alinsky, S. (1972). *Rules for radicals: A practical primer for realistic radicals*. New York: Vintage.

Allen, R., & Kuo, C. (1990, June). The impact of symbolic social reality on political orientations. Paper presented at the annual convention of the International Communication Association, Dublin, Ireland.

Allen, W. (1982). Hannah Arendt: Existential phenomenology and political freedom. *Philosophy and Social Criticism, 9*, 171-90.

Almond, G., & Verba, S. (1963). *The civic culture*. Princeton, NJ: Princeton University Press.

Ansolabehere, S., Behr, R., & Iyengar, S. (1993). *The media game: American politics in the television age*. New York: Macmillan.

Arendt, H. (1958). *The human condition*. Chicago: University of Chicago Press.

Arendt, H. (1971). Thinking and moral considerations: A lecture. *Social Research, 38*, 417-446.

Arendt, H. (1972). *Crises of the republic*. New York: Harvest-Harcourt.

Armstrong, G. B., & Neuendorf, K. (1992). TV entertainment, news, and racial stereotypes of college students. *Journal of Communication, 42*, 153-176.

Austin, J. L. (1962). *How to do things with words*. Oxford: Oxford University Press.

Bakhtin, M. (1981). *The dialogic imagination*. M. Holquist (Ed.), C. Emerson & M. Holquist (Trans.). Austin: University of Texas Press.

Barber, J. D. (1972). *The presidential character: Predicting performance in the White House*. Englewood Cliffs, NJ: Prentice Hall.

Barber, J. D. (1989). The candidates' analysts. In W. D. Pederson (Ed.), *The 'Barberian' Presidency* (pp. 57-69). New York: Peter Lang.

Barber, J. D. (1990). The promise of political psychology. In *Political Psychology, 11*, 173-183.

Bartley, R. (1979). Business and the new class. In B. Bruce-Briggs (Ed.), *The new class?* (pp. 57-66). New Brunswick, NJ: Transaction.

Baudrillard, J. (1983). The ecstacy of communication. In H. Foster (Ed.), *The anti-aesthetic: Essays on postmodern culture* (pp. 126-134). Port Townsend, WA: Bay Press.

Baudrillard, J. (1988). *Jean Baudrillard: Selected writings*. M. Poster (Ed.). Stanford: Stanford University Press.

Bellah, R. (1985, Fall). Populism and individualism. *Social Policy*, 30-33.

Benjamin, W. (1969). The work of art in the age of mechanical reproduction. In H. Arendt (Ed.), *Illuminations* (pp. 217-251). New York: Schocken.

Bennett, S. E. (1988). 'Know-nothings' revisited: The meaning of political ignorance today. *Social Science Quarterly*, 69, 476-490.

Bennett, S. E.(1989). Trends in Americans' political information, 1967-1987. *American Politics Quarterly*, 17, 422-435.

Bennett, W. L. (1983). *News: The politics of illusion*. New York: Longman.

Bennett, W. L. (1989). Marginalizing the majority: Conditioning public opinion to accept managerial democracy. In M. Margolis & G. Mauser (Eds.), *Manipulating public opinion: Essays on public opinion as a dependent variable* (pp. 321-361). Pacific Grove, CA: Brooks/Cole.

Bennett, W. L. (1992). *The governing crisis: Media, money and marketing in American elections*. New York: St. Martin's.

Bennett, W. L. (1993). *The book of virtues*. New York: Simon & Schuster.

Berger, P. (1987). Different gospels: The social sources of apostasy. *This World*, 17, 6-17.

Berger, P., Berger, B., & Kellner, H. (1973). *The homeless mind*. New York: Random House.

Best, S., & Kellner, D. (1991). *Postmodern theory: Critical interrogations*. New York: Guilford.

Boggs, C. (1986). *Social movements and political power: Emerging forms of radicalism in the West*. Philadelphia: Temple University Press.

Bosso, C. (1989). Setting the agenda: Mass media and the discovery of famine in Ethiopia. In M. Margolis & G. Mauser (Eds.), *Manipulating public opinion: Essays on public opinion as a dependent variable* (pp. 153-174). Pacific Grove, CA: Brooks/Cole.

Brenkman, J. (1979). Mass media: From collective experience to the culture of privatization. *Social Text*, 1, 94-109.

Brody, R. (1991). *Assessing the president: The media, elite opinion, and public support*. Stanford: Stanford University Press.

Brown, P. (1981). *The cult of the saints: Its rise and function in Latin Christianity*. Chicago: University of Chicago Press.

Bruce-Briggs, B. (1979). An introduction to the idea of the new class. In B. Bruce-Briggs (Ed.), *The new class?* (pp. 1-18). New Brunswick, NJ: Transaction.

Brummett, B., & Duncan, M. C. (1990). Theorizing and totalizing: Specularity and televised spots. *Quarterly Journal of Speech*, 76, 227-246.

Buchanan, B. (1987). *The citizen's presidency*. Washington, DC: Congressional Quarterly Press.

Buchanan, B. (1990, August). Media coverage of Campaign '88: A content analysis. Paper presented at the annual convention of the American Political Science Association, San Francisco, California.

Campbell, R., & Reeves, J. (1994). *Cracked coverage: Television news, the anti-cocaine crusade, and the Reagan legacy*. Durham: Duke University Press.

Cappella, J., & Jamieson, K. H. (1997). *Spiral of cynicism: The press and the public good*. New York: Oxford University Press.

Carey, J. (1987). The dark continent of American journalism. In R. Manoff & M. Schudson (Eds.), *Reading the news* (pp. 146-196). New York: Pantheon.

Chaffee, S., Nass, C., & Yang, S-M. (1990). The bridging role of television in immigrant political socialization. *Human Communication Research*, 17, 266-288.

Chaloupka, W. (1992, September). *Cynical nature: Politics and culture after the demise of the natural*. Paper presented at the annual convention of the American Political Science Association, Chicago, Illinois.

Citrin, J. (1981). The changing American electorate. In A. J. Meltsner (Ed.), *Politics and the Oval Office: Towards presidential governance* (pp. 31-62). San Francisco: Institute for Contemporary Studies.

Clark, M. (1985). The honeyed knot of Puritan aesthetics. In P. White (Ed.), *Puritan poets and poetics: Seventeenth-century American poetry in theory and practice* (pp. 67-83). University Park: Pennsylvania State University Press.

Clarke, P., & Fredin, E. (1978). Newspapers, television, and political reasoning. *Public Opinion Quarterly, 42*, 143-160.

Cline, R. (1985). The Cronkite-Ford interview at the 1980 Republican National Convention: A therapeutic analogue. *Central States Speech Journal, 36*, 92-104.

Cloud, D. (1998). *Control and consolation in American culture and politics: The rhetoric of therapy.* Thousand Oaks, CA: Sage.

Cmiel, K. (1990). *Democratic eloquence: The fight over popular speech in nineteenth-century America.* New York: Morrow.

Cohen, A., Adoni, H., & Bantz, C. (1990). *Social conflict and television news.* Newbury Park, CA: Sage.

Conway, M., Stevens, A. J., & Smith, R. (1975). The relationship between media use and children's civic awareness. *Journalism Quarterly, 52*, 531-538.

Cook, T. (1990, August). *Thinking of the news media as political institutions.* Paper presented at the annual convention of the American Political Science Association, San Francisco, California.

Cook, T. (1991, September). *Domesticating a crisis: Washington newsbeats, human interest stories, and international news in the Persian Gulf war.* A paper delivered at the Social Science Research Council Workshop on Media and Foreign Policy, Seattle, Washington.

Cook, T. (1998). *Governing with the news: The news media as a political institution.* Chicago: University of Chicago Press.

Cormier, F. (1977). *LBJ the way he was.* New York: Doubleday.

Davis, D. K. (1990). News and politics." In D. Swanson & D. Nimmo (Eds.), *New directions in political communication: A resource book* (pp. 147-184). Newbury Park, CA: Sage.

Davis, O., Hinich, M., & Ordeshook, P. (1970). An expository development of a mathematical model of the electoral process. *American Political Science Review, 64*, 426-448.

Dayan, D., & Katz, E. (1992). *Media events: The live broadcasting of history.* Cambridge: Harvard University Press.

Debord, G. (1982). *Society of the spectacle.* Detroit: Red and Black.

deCerteau, M. (1984). *The practice of everyday life.* Berkeley: University of California Press.

Delbanco, A. (1989). *The Puritan ideal.* Cambridge: Harvard University Press.

Delli Carpini, M., & Keeter, S. (1996). *What Americans know about politics and why it matters.* New Haven: Yale University Press.

Delli Carpini, M., & Williams, B. (1990, June). *Is Dan Rather more real than E.T.? "Fictional" and "non-fictional" television celebrates Earth Day.* Paper presented at the annual convention of the International Communication Association, Dublin, Ireland.

Demaitre, L. (1985). Insanity, treatment of. In J. R. Strayer (Ed.), *Dictionary of the Middle Ages,* Vol. 6 (pp. 489-493). New York: Scribner's.

Dennis, E., et al. (1992). *Covering the presidential primaries.* New York: The Freedom Forum Studies Center.

Dewey, J. (1946). *The public and its problems.* Chicago: Gateway.

Dionne, E. J. (1991). *Why Americans hate politics.* New York: Simon & Schuster.

Donsbach, W., Brosius, H-B., & Mattenklott, A. (1993). How unique is the perspective of television: A field experiment on the perception of a campaign event by participants and television viewers. *Political Communication, 10*, 37-53.

Dossa, S. (1989). *The public realm and the public self: The political theory of Hannah Arendt.* Waterloo, Canada: Wilfrid Laurier University Press.

Eagleton, T. (1985, July/August). Capitalism, Modernism and postmodernism. *New Left Review, 152*, 60-73.

Edelman, M. (1977). *Political language: Words that succeed and policies that fail.* New York: Academic Press.

Edelman, M. (1988). *Constructing the political spectacle.* Chicago: University of Chicago Press.

Ehrenhaus, P. (1990, June). *On doing violence to "the past."* Paper delivered at the annual convention of the International Communication Association, Dublin, Ireland.

Elliott, D. (1988). Family ties: A case study of coverage of families and friends during the hijacking of TWA Flight 847. *Political Communication and Persuasion, 5,* 67-75.

Ellul, J. (1967). *The political illusion.* New York: Vintage.

Elsthain, J. B. (1981). *Public man, private woman: Women in social and political thought.* Princeton, NJ: Princeton University Press.

Emerson, E. (1977). *Puritanism in America: 1620-1750.* Boston: Twayne.

Entman, R., & Rojecki, A. (1991, May). *Limiting democracy by containing public opinion: Media and elite politics from Watergate to the nuclear freeze.* Paper presented at the annual convention of the International Communication Association, Chicago, Illinois.

Featherstone, M. (1991). *Consumer culture and postmodernism.* London: Sage.

Fishkin, J. (1991). *Democracy and deliberation: New directions for democratic reform.* New York: Yale University Press.

Fishkin, J. (1995). *The voice of the people: Public opinion and democracy.* New Haven: Yale University Press.

Fiske, J. (1987). *Television culture.* London: Methuen.

Fokkema, D. (1984). *Literary history, modernism and postmodernism.* Amsterdam: John Benjamins.

Foote, J., & Davis, D. (1987, June). *Network visibility of congressional leaders: 1969-1985.* Paper presented at the annual convention of the International Communication Association, Montreal, Canada.

Foucault, M. (1972). *The archaeology of knowledge.* New York: Pantheon.

Foucault, M. (1977). *Discipline and punish.* (A. Sheridan, Trans.). New York: Pantheon.

Foucault, M. (1980). *Power/knowledge.* New York: Pantheon.

Frank, R. (1988). *Passion within reason: The strategic role of the emotions.* New York: Norton.

Gallup, G. (1989). *The Gallup Poll: Public opinion, 1989.* Wilmington, DE: Scholarly Resources.

Gamson, J. (1992). The assembly line of greatness: Celebrity in twentieth-century America. *Critical Studies in Mass Communication, 9,* 1-24.

Gamson, W. (1992). *Talking politics.* New York: Cambridge University Press.

Geertz, C. (1983). *Local knowledge: Further essays in interpretive anthropology.* New York: Basic Books.

Genovese, E. (1976). *Roll Jordan roll: The world the slaves made.* New York: Vintage.

George, A. (1974). Assessing presidential character. *World Politics, 27,* 234-282.

Ginsberg, B. (1986). *The captive public: How mass opinion promotes state power.* New York: Basic Books.

Giroux, H. (1988). *Schooling and the struggle for public life: Critical pedagogy in the modern age.* Minneapolis: University of Minnesota Press.

Gitlin, T. (1980). *The whole world is watching: Mass media in the making and unmaking of the New Left.* Berkeley: University of California Press.

Gitlin, T. (1990). Who communicates what to whom, in what voice and why, about the study of mass communication. *Critical Studies in Mass Communication, 7,* 185-196.

Glasser, T. L. (1991). Communication and the cultivation of citizenship. *Communication, 12,* 235-248.

Goldfarb, J. C. (1991). *The cynical society: The culture of politics and the politics of culture.* Chicago: University of Chicago Press.

Goldman, E. (1963, June 16). Can public men have private lives? *New York Times Magazine, 13*, 60-61.

Goodin, R. (1980). *Manipulatory politics.* New Haven, CT: Yale University Press.

Gozzi, R., & Haynes, W. L. (1992). Electric media and electric epistemology: Empathy at a distance. *Critical Studies in Mass Communication, 9*, 217-228.

Graber, D. (1988). *Processing the news: How people tame the information tide.* New York: Longman.

Graber, D. (1990). Seeing is remembering: How visuals contribute to learning from television news. *Journal of Communication, 40*(3), 134-155.

Grant, R. (1992, September). *Rousseau's ideal of integrity.* Paper presented at the annual convention of the American Political Science Association, Chicago, Illinois.

Gray, H. (1989). Television, black Americans, and the American dream. *Critical Studies in Mass Communication, 6*, 376-386.

Greenstein, F. (1965). Popular images of the president. *American Journal of Psychiatry, 122*, 523-529.

Groombridge, B. (1972). *Television and the people: A programme for democratic participation.* Harmondsworth, England: Penguin.

Gusfield, J. (1981). *The culture of public problems: Drinking-driving and the symbolic order.* Chicago: University of Chicago Press.

Habermas, J. (1989). The public sphere: An encyclopedia article. In S. Bronner & D. Kellner (Eds.), *Critical theory and society: A reader* (pp. 136-142). New York: Routledge.

Haims, L. (1985). Puritan iconography: The art of Edward Taylor's *God's determinations.* In P. White (Ed.), *Puritan poets and poetics: Seventeenth-century American poetry in theory and practice* (pp. 84-98). University Park: Pennsylvania State University Press.

Hallin, D. (1985). The American news media: A critical theory perspective. In J. Forester (Ed.), *Critical theory and public life* (pp. 121-146). Cambridge: M.I.T. Press.

Hallin, D. (1992). Sound bite news: Television coverage of elections, 1968-1988. *Journal of Communication, 42*, 5-24.

Hallin, D., Manoff, R., & Weedle, J. (1990, August). *Sourcing patterns of national security reporters.* Paper presented at the annual convention of the American Political Science Association, San Francisco, California.

Hargrove, E. (1973). Presidential popularity and revisionist views of the presidency. *American Journal of Political Science, 17*, 819-835.

Hart, R. (1977). *The political pulpit.* West Lafayette, IN: Purdue University Press.

Hart, R. (1982). A commentary on popular assumptions about political communication. *Human Communication Research, 4*, 366-379.

Hart, R. (1984). *Verbal style and the presidency: A computer-based analysis.* New York: Academic Press.

Hart, R. (1987). *The sound of leadership: Presidential communication in the modern age.* Chicago: University of Chicago Press.

Hart, R., Jerome, P., & McCombs, K. (1984). Rhetorical features of newscasts about the president. *Critical Studies in Mass Communication, 1*, 260-286.

Hart, R., Smith-Howell, D., & Llewellyn, J. (1991). The mindscape of the presidency: *Time* magazine, 1945-1985. *Journal of Communication, 41*, 6-25.

Hassan, I. (1987). *The post-modern turn: Essays in post-modern theory and culture.* Columbus: Ohio State University.

Hinchman, L., & Hichman, S. (1984). In Heidegger's shadow: Hannah Arendt's phenomenological humanism. *The Review of Politics, 46*, 183-211.

Hinckley, B. (1990). *The symbolic presidency: How presidents portray themselves.* New York: Routledge.

Hirsch, A. (1991). *Talking heads: Political talk shows and their star pundits.* New York: St. Martin's.

Hitchens, C. (1992, April). Voting in the passive voice: What polling has done to American democracy. *Harpers*, pp. 45-52.

Horton, D., & Wohl, R. (1986). Mass communication and para-social interaction: Observation on intimacy at a distance. In G. Gumpert & R. Cathcart (Eds.), *Inter/media: Interpersonal communication in a media world*, (3rd ed.; pp. 185-206). New York: Oxford University Press.

Hurwitz, J. (1989). Presidential leadership and public followership. In M. Margolis & G. Mauser (Eds.), *Manipulating public opinion* (pp. 222-249). Pacific Grove, CA: Brooks/Cole.

Huspek, M., & Kendall, K. (1991). On withholding political voice: An analysis of the political vocabulary of a "nonpolitical" speech community. *Quarterly Journal of Speech, 77*, 1-19.

Illouz, E. (1997). *Consuming the romantic Utopia: Love and the cultural contradictions of capitalism.* Berkeley: University of California Press.

Iyengar, S., & Kinder, D. (1987). *News that matters: Television and American public opinion.* Chicago: University of Chicago Press.

Jacoby, R. (1987). *The last intellectuals: American culture in the age of academe.* New York: Basic Books.

Jameson, F. (1984, July/August). Postmodernism, or the cultural logic of late capitalism. *The New Left Review, 146*, 53-92.

Jamieson, K. (1988). *Eloquence in an electronic age: The transformation of political speechmaking.* New York: Oxford.

Jamieson. K. (1992). *Dirty politics: Deception, distraction, and democracy.* New York: Oxford University Press.

Jennings, M. K. (1991). Thinking about social injustice. *Political Psychology, 12*, 187-204.

Jensen, J. (1990). *Redeeming modernity: Contradictions in media criticism.* Newbury Park, CA: Sage.

Joslyn, R. (1990). Election campaigns as occasions for civic education. In D. Swanson & D. Nimmo (Eds.), *New directions in political communication: A resource book* (pp. 86-119). Newbury Park, CA: Sage.

Jung, H. Y. (1972). Introduction. In H. Y. Jung (Ed.), *Existential phenomenology and political theory: A reader* (pp. xvil-lv). Chicago: Henry Regnery.

Just, M., & Crigler, A. (1989). Learning from the news: Experiments in media, modality, and reporting after Star Wars. *Political Communication and Persuasion, 6*, 109-127.

Just, M., et al. (1996). *Crosstalk: Citizens, candidates, and the media in a presidential campaign.* Chicago: University of Chicago Press.

Kanter, D., & Mirvis, R. (1989). *The cynical Americans: Living and working in an age of discontent and disillusion.* San Francisco: Jossey-Bass.

Keeter, S. (1987). The illusion of intimacy: Television and the role of candidate personal qualities in voter choice. *Public Opinion Quarterly, 51*, 344-358.

Keith, B. E., et al. (1992). *The myth of the independent voter.* Berkeley: University of California Press.

Kellner, D. (1989). *Jean Baudrillard: From Marxism to postmodernism and beyond.* Cambridge: Polity Press.

Kern, M. (1989). *Thirty-second politics: Political advertising in the eighties.* New York: Praeger.

Kernell, S. (1997). *Going public: New strategies of presidential leadership* (3rd ed.). Washington, DC: Congressional Quarterly Press.

Kibbey, A. (1986). *The interpretation of material shapes in Puritanism: A study of rhetoric, prejudice and violence.* London: Cambridge University Press.

Kirkpatrick, J. (1979). Politics and the new class. In B. Bruce-Briggs (Ed.), *The new class?* (pp. 33-48). New Brunswick, NJ: Transaction.

Klinkowitz, J. (1988). *Rosenberg, Barthes, Hassan: The postmodern habit of thought.* Athens: University of Georgia Press.

Korda, M. (1981, October 25). Politicians on television: Is what you see what you get? *Family Weekly*, pp. 4-8.

Krauthammer, C. (1990, May 21). In praise of low voter turnout. *Time*, p. 88.

Kroker, A. (1985). Baudrillard's Marx. *Theory, Culture and Society, 3*, 69-83.

Kubey, R., & Csikszentmihalyi, M. (1990). *Television and the quality of life: How viewing shapes everyday experience*. Hillsdale, NJ: Lawrence Erlbaum.

Lane, R. (1962). *Political ideology: Why the American common man believes what he does*. New York: Free Press.

Langer, J. (1981). Television's "personality system." *Media, Culture and Society, 4*, 351-365.

Lapham, L. (1980, August). Political discourse. *Harper's*, pp. 8-9.

Lazarsfeld, P., & Merton, R. (1948). Mass communication, popular taste, and organized social action. In W. Schramm (Ed.), *Mass communications* (pp. 492-503). Urbana: University of Illinois Press.

Lea, F. J. (1982). *Political consciousness and American democracy*. Jackson: University of Mississippi Press.

Leverenz, D. (1980). *The language of Puritan feeling: An exploration in literature, psychology, and social history*. New Brunswick, NJ: Rutgers University Press.

Lichter, S. R., Amundson, D., & Noyes, R. (1988). *The video campaign: Network coverage of the 1988 primaries*. Washington, DC: A.E.I. Institute.

Lippmann, W. (1925). *The phantom public*. New York: Harcourt.

Livingston, C. D. (1986). The televised presidency. *Presidential Studies Quarterly, 16*, 22-30.

Llewellyn, J. (1990). *The rhetoric of corporate legitimation: Public relations and philanthropy as social responsibility*. Unpublished doctoral dissertation, University of Texas at Austin.

Lord, A. (1981). The master's tools will never dismantle the master's house. In C. Moraga, G. Anzaluda, & T. Bambara (Eds.), *This bridge called my back: Writings by radical women of color* (pp. 98-101). Watertown, MA: Persephone.

Lowi, T. (1985). *The personal president*. Ithaca, NY: Cornell University Press.

Luke, T. (1978). Culture and politics in the age of artificial negativity. *Telos, 35*, 55-72.

Luke, T. (1989). *Screens of power: Ideology, domination, and resistance in informational society*. Urbana: University of Illinois Press.

Lyotard, J-F. (1984). *The postmodern condition: A report on knowledge*. G. Bennington & B. Massumi (Trans.). Minneapolis: University of Minnesota Press.

Maier, C. (1987). Introduction. In C. S. Maier (Ed.), *Changing boundaries of the political: Essays on the evolving balance between the state and society, public and private* (pp. 1-26). Cambridge: Cambridge University Press.

Major, A., & Atwood, L. E. (1990, June). *The U.S. press covers two presidential elections*. Paper delivered at the annual convention of the International Communication Association, Dublin, Ireland.

Masters, R., Frey, S., & Bente, G. (1991). Dominance and attention: Images of leaders in German, French, and American TV news. *Polity, 25*, 373-394.

Masters, R., & Sullivan, D. (1993). Nonverbal behavior and leadership: Emotion and cognition in political attitudes. In S. Iyengar & W. McGuire (Eds.), *Explorations in political psychology*. Durham, NC: Duke University Press.

Melucci, A. (1985). The symbolic challenge of contemporary movements. *Social Research, 52*, 789-816.

Merelman, R. (1984). *Making something of ourselves: On culture and politics in the United States*. Berkeley: University of California Press.

Merelman, R. (1990). The promise of political psychology: A critique and an alternative. *Political Psychology, 11*, 419-433.

Mickelson, S. (1989). *From whistle stop to sound bite: Four decades of politics and television.* New York: Praeger.

Milburn, M., Cistuli, B., & Garr, M. (1990, July). *Survey and experimental studies of the effect of television news on individuals' attributions about terrorism.* Paper presented at the annual convention of the International Society of Political Psychology, Washington, DC.

Miller, A., Goldenberg, E., & Ebring, L. (1979). Type-set politics: Impact of newspapers on public confidence. *American Political Science Review, 73,* 67-84.

Miller, M. (1973). *Plain speaking: An oral biography of Harry S Truman.* New York: Berkley Medallion.

Miller, N., & Stiles, W. (1986). Verbal familiarity in American presidential nomination acceptance speeches and inaugural addresses, 1920-1981. *Social Psychology Quarterly, 49,* 72-81.

Miller, W. (1989). *American national election studies data sourcebook: 1958-1988.* Cambridge: Harvard University Press.

Mitchell, T. (1991). The limits of the state: Beyond statist approaches and their critics. *American Political Science Review, 85,* 77-96.

Morgan, E. (1966). *The Puritan family: Religious and domestic relations in seventeenth-century New England.* New York: Harper.

Morgan, M. (1989). Television and democracy. In I. Angus & S. Jhally (Eds.), *Cultural politics in contemporary America* (pp. 240-253). New York: Routledge.

Morse, M. (1990). An ontology of everyday distraction: The freeway, the mall and television. In P. Mellencamp (Ed.), *Logics of television: Essays on cultural criticism.* (pp. 193-221). Bloomington: Indiana University Press.

Mumby, D., & Spitzack, C. (1983). Ideology and television news: A metaphoric analysis of political stories. *Central States Speech Journal, 34,* 162-171.

Murphy, J. (1989). *Postmodern social analysis and criticism.* New York: Greenwood.

Naisbitt, J. (1982). *Megatrends: Ten new directions transforming our lives.* New York: Warner.

Nesbit, D. (1988). *Videostyle in senate campaigns.* Knoxville: University of Tennessee Press.

Neuman, W. R. (1986). *The paradox of mass politics: Knowledge and opinion in the American electorate.* Cambridge: Harvard University Press.

Neuman, W. R., Just, M., & Crigler, A. (1992). *Common knowledge: News and the construction of political meaning.* Chicago: University of Chicago Press.

Norton, A. (1988). *Reflections on political identity.* Baltimore: Johns Hopkins University Press.

Offe, C. (1985). New social movements: Challenging the boundaries of institutional politics. *Social Research, 52,* 817-868.

Offe, C. (1987). Challenging the boundaries of institutional politics: Social movements since the 1960s. In C. S. Maier (Ed.), *Changing boundaries of the political: Essays on the evolving balance between the state and society, public and private* (pp. 63-105). Cambridge: Cambridge University Press.

O'Neil, J. (1991). *Plato's cave: Desire, power, and the specular functions of the media.* Northwood, NJ: Ablex.

Ong, W. (1982). *Orality and literacy.* London: Methuen.

Pangle, T. (1992). *The ennobling of democracy: The challenge of the postmodern age.* Baltimore: Johns Hopkins University Press.

Parekh, B. (1981). *Hannah Arendt and the search for a new political philosophy.* London: Macmillan.

Patterson, T. (1991). More style than substance: Television news in U.S. national elections. *Political Communication and Persuasion, 8,* 145-161.

Patterson, T. (1993). *Out of order.* New York: Knopf.

Pekonen, K. (1989). Symbols and politics as culture in the modern situation: The problems and prospects of the "new." In J. R. Gibbins (Ed.), *Contemporary political culture: Politics in a postmodern age* (pp. 127-143). London: Sage.

Peterson, S. (1990). *Political behavior: Patterns in everyday life.* Newbury Park, CA: Sage.

Pfau, M., & Kang, J. G. (1991). The impact of relational messages on candidate influence in televised political debates. *Communication Studies, 42,* 114-128.

Pfeil, F. (1988). Postmodernism as a "structure of feeling." In C. Nelson & L. Grossberg (Eds.), *Marxism and the interpretation of culture* (pp. 381-404). Urbana: University of Illinois Press.

Pitkin, H. (1990, August). *Conformism, housekeeping, and the attack of the blob: Hannah Arendt's concept of the social.* Paper presented at the annual convention of the American Political Science Association, San Francisco, California.

Piven, F. F., & Cloward, R. A. (1988). *Why Americans don't vote.* New York: Pantheon.

Pollock, M. (1991, May). *The social and the political on TV: Implications of Hannah Arendt's political philosophy for analyzing televised politics.* Paper presented at the annual convention of the International Communication Association, Chicago, Illinois.

Postman, N. (1985). *Amusing ourselves to death: Public discourse in the age of show business.* New York: Penguin Books.

Rabkin, J. (1995, September). *Roundtable remarks on civic virtue and the future of American politics.* Annual meeting of the American Political Science Association.

Ragsdale, L. (1987). Presidential speechmaking and the public audience: Individual presidents and group attitudes. *Journal of Politics, 49,* 704-736.

Ranney, A. (1983). *Channels of power, the impact of television on American politics.* New York: Basic Books.

Rapping, E. (1987). *The looking glass world of nonfiction TV.* Boston: South End Press.

Rawlence, C. (1979). Political theatre and the working class. In C. Gardner (Ed.), *Media, politics and culture: A socialist view* (pp. 61-70). London: Macmillan.

Real, M. (1986). Demythologizing media: Recent writings in critical and institutional theory. *Critical Studies in Mass Communication, 3,* 458-496.

Reese, S., & Danielian, L. (1992, May). *The structure of news sources on television: A network analysis of CBS News, Nightline, MacNeil-Lehrer, and This Week with David Brinkley* (pp. 15-16). Paper presented at the annual convention of the International Communication Association, Miami, Florida.

Reid, H., & Yanarella, E. (1974). Toward a post-modern theory of American political science and culture: Perspectives from critical marxism and phenomenology. *Cultural Hermeneutics, 2,* 91-166.

Rieff, P. (1968). *The triumph of the therapeutic: Uses of faith after Freud.* New York: Harper.

Robinson, J. (1990, September). I love my TV. *American Demographics,* 24-27.

Robinson, J. P., & Davis, D. (1990). Television news and the informed public: An information-processing approach. *Journal of Communication, 40*(3), 106-119.

Robinson, M. (1975). American political legitimacy in an era of electronic journalism: Reflections on the evening news. In D. Cater & R. Adler (Eds.), *Television as a social force: New approaches to TV criticism* (pp. 97-139). New York: Praeger.

Robinson, M. (1976). Public affairs television and the growth of political malaise: The case of "The Selling of the Pentagon." *American Political Science Review, 70,* 409-432.

Robinson, M., & Kohut, A. (1988). Believability and the press. *Public Opinion Quarterly, 51,* 174-189.

Robinson, M., & Sheehan, M. (1983). *Over the wire and on TV: CBS and UPI in Campaign '80.* New York: Russell Sage.

Rogin, M. P. (1987). *Ronald Reagan, the movie: And other episodes in political demonology.* Berkeley: University of California Press.

Rosenblatt, R. (1982, March 8). The staff ate my homework. *Time,* p. 95.

Rowe, K. (1985). Prophetic visions: Typology and colonial American poetry. In P. White (Ed.), *Puritan poets and poetics: Seventeenth-century American poetry in theory and practice* (pp. 47-66). University Park: Pennsylvania State University Press.

Sabato, L. (1991). *Feeding frenzy: How attack journalism has transformed American politics.* New York: Free Press.

Scheick, W. (1985). Tombless virtue and hidden text: New England Puritan funeral elegies. In P. White (Ed.), *Puritan poets and poetics: Seventeenth-century American poetry in theory and practice* (pp. 286-302). University Park: Pennsylvania State University Press.

Schmitt, C. (1976). *The concept of the political.* G. Schwab (Trans.). New Brunswick, NJ: Rutgers University Press.

Schmuhl, R. (1990). *Statecraft and stagecraft: American political life in the age of personality.* South Bend, IN: Notre Dame University Press.

Schorske, C. (1981). *Fin-de-siècle Vienna.* New York: Vintage.

Schram, S. (1991). The post-modern presidency and the grammar of electronic engineering. *Critical Studies in Mass Communication, 8,* 210-216.

Schudson, M. (1982). The politics of narrative form: The emergence of news conventions in print and television. *Daedalus, 111,* 97-112.

Schudson, M. (1992). *Watergate in American memory: How we remember, forget, and reconstruct the past.* New York: Basic Books.

Schulte-Sasse, J. (1987). Electronic media and cultural politics in the Reagan era: The attack on Libya and Hands Across America as Postmodern events. *Cultural Critique, 8,* 123-152.

Sennett, R. (1977). *The fall of public man.* New York: Knopf.

Shaw, D., & McCombs, M. (1977). *The emergence of American political issues: The agenda-setting function of the press.* St. Paul, MN: West.

Sigelman, L., & Yanarella, E. (1986). Public information on public issues: A multivariate analysis. *Social Science Quarterly, 67,* 402-410.

Silverstone, R. (1986). The agonistic narratives of television science. In J. Corner (Ed.), *Documentary and the mass media* (pp. 81-106). London: Edwin Arnold.

Simons, H. (1994). Going meta: Definition and political applications. *Quarterly Journal of Speech, 80,* 468-481.

Skirrow, G. (1979). Education and television: Theory and practice. In C. Gardner (Ed.), *Media, politics and culture: A socialist view* (pp. 25-39). London: Macmillan.

Sloterdijk, P. (1984). Cynicism—the twilight of false consciousness. *New German Critique, 33,* 190-206.

Sloterdijk, P. (1987). *Critique of cynical reason.* (M. Eldred, Trans.). Minneapolis: University of Minnesota Press.

Smith-Howell, D. (1993). *Using the past in the present: The rhetorical construction of the presidency.* Unpublished doctoral dissertation, University of Texas at Austin.

Smoller, F. (1988). Presidents and their critics: The structure of television news coverage. *Congress and the Presidency, 1,* 75-89.

Spencer, H. (1970). Politics and rhetorics. *Social Research, 37,* 567-623.

Spurling, L. (1977). *Phenomenology and the social world: The philosophy of Merleau-Ponty and its relations to the social sciences.* London: Routledge.

Stam, R. (1983). Television news and its spectator. In E. A. Kaplan (Ed.), *Regarding television: Critical approaches—an anthology* (pp. 23-43). Frederick, MD: American Film Institute.

Stanfield, R. (1990, March 10). The golden rolodex. *National Journal,* 552-557.

Stark, R., & Bainbridge, W. (1985). *The future of religion: Secularization, revival and cult formation.* Berkeley: University of California Press.

Stewart, D., & Mickunas, A. (1974). *Exploring phenomenology: A guide to the field and its literature.* Chicago: American Library Asssociation.

Streitmatter, R. (1985). The impact of presidential personality on news coverage in major newspapers. *Journalism Quarterly, 62,* 66-73.

Swanson, D. (1992). The political-media complex. *Communication Monographs, 39,* 397-400.

Tatalovich, R., & Byron, W. D. (1984). *Presidential power in the United States.* Monterey, CA: Brooks/Cole.

Teixeira, R. (1987). *Why Americans don't vote: Turnout decline in the United States.* New York: Greenwood.

Thiele, L. P. (1990). The agony of politics: The Nietzchean roots of Foucault's thought. *American Political Science Review, 84,* 907-925.

Touraine, A. (1988). *Return of the actor: Social theory in postindustrial society.* (M. Godzick, Trans.). Minneapolis: University of Minnesota Press.

van Dijk, T. (1989). Mediating racism: The role of the media in the reproduction of racism. In R. Wodak (Ed.), *Language, power and ideology* (pp. 199-226). Amsterdam: John Benjamins.

Vaughn, A. T. (1972). Introduction. In A. Vaughn (Ed.), *The Puritan tradition in America: 1620-1730* (pp. xi-xxviii). New York: Harper.

Villa, D. (1992). Postmodernism and the public sphere. *American Political Science Review, 86,* 712-721.

Walker, J. (1985). Anagrams and acrostics: Puritan poetic wit. In P. White (Ed.), *Puritan poets and poetics: Seventeenth-century American poetry in theory and practice* (pp. 247-257). University Park: Pennsylvania State University Press.

Weber, M. (1978). The nature of charismatic domination. In W. G. Runciman (Ed.), *Weber: Selections in translation* (pp. 226-250). Cambridge: Cambridge University Press.

Whalen, S. (1989). The institutionalization of relations of power through practices of speech: A theoretical inquiry. Unpublished doctoral dissertation, Pennsylvania State University.

Wilkins, L., & Patterson, P. (1988, May). Media coverage of disasters and hazards: The political amplification of risk. Paper presented at the annual convention of the International Communication Association, New Orleans, Louisiana.

Williams, R. (1977). *Marxism and literature.* New York: Oxford University Press.

Wolin, S. (1985). Postmodern politics and the absence of myth. *Social Research, 52,* 217-239.

Wolin, S. (1990). Democracy in the discourse of postmodernism. *Social Research, 57,* 5-30.

Wood, M., & Zurcher, L. (1988). *The development of a postmodern self: A computer-assisted analysis of personal documents.* New York: Greenwood.

Young, I. (1990). *Justice and the politics of difference.* Princeton, NJ: Princeton University Press.

Ziff, L. (1973). *Puritans in America: New culture in a new world.* New York: Viking.

Zullow, H., et al. (1988). Pessimistic explanatory style in the historical record: CAVing LBJ, presidential candidates, and East versus West Berlin. *American Psychologist, 43,* 673-682.

Index